D0360057

Managing for the future

Other Books by Peter F. Drucker

MANAGEMENT

Managing the Non-profit Organization
The Frontiers of Management
Innovation and Entrepreneurship
The Changing World of the Executive
Managing in Turbulent Times
Management: Tasks, Responsibilities, Practices
The New Markets and Other Essays
The Effective Executive
Managing for Results
The Practice of Management
Concept of the Corporation

ECONOMICS, POLITICS, SOCIETY

The New Realities
Toward the Next Economics
The Unseen Revolution
Men, Ideas and Politics
The Age of Discontinuity
The Landmarks of Tomorrow
America's Next Twenty Years
The New Society
The Future of Industrial Man
The End of Economic Man

FICTION

The Temptation to Do Good
The Last of All Possible Worlds

AUTOBIOGRAPHY

Adventures of a Bystander

MANAGING
FOR THE FUTURE

Peter F. Drucker

Butterworth-Heinemann Ltd
Linacre House, Jordan Hill, Oxford OX2 8DP

 PART OF REED INTERNATIONAL BOOKS

OXFORD   LONDON   BOSTON
MUNICH   NEW DELHI   SINGAPORE   SYDNEY
TOKYO   TORONTO   WELLINGTON

First published in Great Britain 1992
Reprinted 1992, 1993
First published as a paperback edition 1993

British Library Cataloguing in Publication Data
A catalogue record for this book is
available from the British Library

ISBN 0 7506 0492 1 (Hardback)
ISBN 0 7506 0909 5 (Paperback)

Photoset by Deltatype Ltd, Ellesmere Port, Cheshire
Printed in England by Clays Ltd, St Ives plc

Contents

Preface

About a year after my 1985 book, *The Frontiers of Management,*
had come out, I received the following letter: "I am the CEO of a
still fairly small but fast-growing specialty-chemicals company. I
try to read five or six of your chapters every weekend, and ask my
senior associates to do likewise. When I finish one of the chapters I
then ask myself in writing: 'What does this chapter mean for me as a
senior business executive? What does it mean for my colleagues on
the management team? What does it mean for the company? What
action does it imply – for me, the management team, the company?
What opportunities does it identify for us? What changes in goals,
strategies, policies, structure, might it point to?' We then discuss our
respective answers at one of our management meetings. And six
months later we discuss the same answers again to see what actions
we have actually taken and how they have worked out, but also what
actions we should have taken and might still undertake. Of course, a
good many of your chapters do not directly apply to us; they lead to
understanding rather than to action. But a good many, again and
again, stimulate us to do something or to stop doing something. And
the most valuable ones are the chapters that make me say: 'Of course,
I have known this all along. Why haven't I acted on it?' "

The chapters in this book cover a wide range of topics, and they were written over a five-year period. The individual chapters were not "planned" to fill a spot on an outline sketched out five years ago. But each was most definitely designed from the beginning to address one of the dimensions of the executive's world: the economy and economics; people; management; organization – both outside and inside the executive's particular enterprise.

In addition, each chapter was planned from the beginning to achieve two purposes. One: to explain to executives immersed in the demands of their own tasks and their own enterprise to understand the rapidly changing world in which they work and produce results. The other was to stimulate them to action and to provide tools for effective action.

The executive's world has been turbulent for as long as I can remember – I started work two years before the 1929 crash! It surely has always been turbulent, but never as much as in these past few years – or in the years immediately ahead. Only a few short years ago, for instance, we worried about inflation and about the ascendancy of all kinds of new financial superpowers: global banks, transnational brokerage houses, junk-bond kings, takeover tycoons, and the like. Inflation is, of course, still a danger – and will remain one as long as governments pile up huge deficits. But executives in the '90s are more likely to be worried by financial stringencies and credit crunches – that is, by the typical deflation symptoms. The monetary giants of yesterday are everywhere in full retreat and mired in scandal. The international economy of 1992 also bears almost no resemblance to that of 1980 or 1981 (when Japan still ran a trade deficit, the European Economic Community was still pie in the sky, and lending billions to Brazilian generals still seemed to be the truly conservative thing to do). So, every chapter in this book tries to create understanding of what changes are ahead and what they mean for the economy, people, markets, the management, the organization. Every one of the chapters tries to create the understanding the executive needs to manage for tomorrow rather than for yesterday.

But every chapter was also designed from the beginning to stimulate action – to identify new opportunities; to point out areas where changes – in process and product, policies, markets, and structure – might be needed; where and what to do and where and what to stop doing.

The five years during which the chapters of this book were being written were years of unprecedented political upheaval. The earliest chapter in this book was written in August 1986; in the same week I wrote the first draft of what was published – in early winter of 1989 – as Chapter 4 in my book *The New Realities* under the title 'When the Russian Empire Is Gone' – an essay in which I predicted the inevitable failure of Mr. Gorbachev's economic policies, the equally inevitable collapse of communism, and the disintegration of the Soviet Union. But the chapter I wrote that week for *this* book – it is Chapter 22 – bears the title 'How to Manage the Boss.' The most recently written chapter in this book, (Chapter 24), was done almost exactly five years later, in August 1991 in the week after the Communist hardliners putsch against Mr. Gorbachev had failed. Its title however is 'The New Japanese Business Strategies.' This book, in other words, focuses on executives, in their organizations and in their work. 'The show must go on' is its motto – and management's 'show' is effective action for results. To help executives act and to produce results, to help them *perform* – in a turbulent, dangerous, fast-changing economy, society, and technology – that is the purpose and mission of this book.

Peter F. Drucker
Claremont, California
December 1991

Acknowledgments

All the material in this book – balanced equally between nine long and thirty-three short chapters – has already been published. The first of the long chapters – the opening interview – first appeared in *New Perspective Quarterly*. The concluding Afterword – the longest chapter – was first published as a London *Economist* 'Management Briefing'. Four other long chapters (chapter 13, 28, 31, 40) first appeared in the *Harvard Business Review*. Of the remaining long chapters, Chapter 1 first appeared in the London *Economist*, Chapter 21 in *Industry Week*, and Chapter 29 in *Non Profit Management & Leadership*. Of the short chapters, Chapter 2 first appeared in *New Management*, Chapter 10 in *The New York Times*, and thirty-one chapters (chapters, 3–9, 11–12, 14–20, 22–27, 30, 32–39) in *The Wall Street Journal*.

In preparing the chapters for publication in this volume I have changed some titles and corrected typographical errors. Otherwise I have left them as they first appeared. But I have added at the end of each chapter the year of its first publication. This should enable readers to know what year is meant when the chapter talks of 'this year' or 'last year'. It should above all enable readers to decide for themselves whether the author's conclusions and predictions have stood the test of time.

Interview: Notes on the Post-Business Society

Q: You have written that there is a profound sense of unreality about both politics and economics today. What do you mean?

A: Most of what we assume axiomatically no longer fits our reality, lending a surreal air to our work and lives. The world seems to have dissolved into a series of media events that appear either bigger than reality or totally formless. This is especially true in political life, where we have entered *terra incognita*.

The reason for the present confusion is that, at some point between 1965 and 1973, we passed a 'great divide' into the next century, leaving behind the creeds, commitments and alignments that had shaped politics for a century or two. At the most profound level, the Enlightenment faith in progress through collective action – 'salvation by society', which had been the dominant force of politics since the eighteenth century – was thoroughly dashed. American Democrats of Great Society lineage are no longer true believers, and, neither the nominally socialist François Mitterrand, nor even Mikhail Gorbachev, espouse the faith any longer. In the rise of Western ideas, especially Marxism, to world dominance, the West's superiority in machines, money, and guns was probably less important than the promise of salvation by society. Now that is gone.

Yet, the only effective nonideological counterforce of political integration – interest bloc politics – is also finally spent. Witness the demise of Jim Wright, the factional crisis and collapse of the Liberal Democratic Party in Japan, and the precarious political coalitions of Europe's economic anchor, Germany.

The last such divide was crossed a century earlier, in 1873. That Liberal century, in which the dominant political creed was *laissez-faire*, began in 1776 with Adam Smith's *The Wealth of Nations* and ended with the nonevent of the Vienna stock market crash and the short-lived panics in Paris, London, Frankfurt, and New York in 1873. Although the economy of the Western world had recovered 18 months later, politics – which would now seek security and protection from the upheavals associated with the Industrial Revolution – was changed forever.

Within 10 years of the Vienna crash, German Chancellor Otto Von Bismarck had invented national health insurance and compulsory old-age insurance. Within 20 years, Marxist socialists had become the largest political party in every major country of continental Europe. In the U.S., the 1880s brought a shift away from the unrestricted market to the Interstate Commerce Commission for regulation of the railroads, the antitrust laws and the first state laws regulating securities. The 1880s also brought about the first distinctly 'antibusiness' movement in the U.S., the populists, and their successful 'socialization' of the local power company in Lincoln, Nebraska – only the second city in the Western world to do so, after Vienna.

Following these early events, the 'progressive' cause of government control of the economy and direction of society became widespread. The great political debate of the last century was not over the 'welfare state'. Instead, the debate was over unrestricted government power, as we saw in the case of Hitler, Stalin, Mussolini, and Mao, versus democratic and legal constraints on the power of the state as we saw in the U.S., Japan and postwar Europe.

The period 1968–73 is a divide fully comparable to 1873. Whereas 1873 marked the end of *laissez-faire*, 1973 marked the end of the era in which government was the 'progressive' cause, the instrument embodying the principles of the Enlightenment. The 'oil shock', the floated dollar, and the student rebellions across the West set us adrift from the century in which we had lived.

To be sure, the slogans of the welfare state persist, but they do not provide a guide for action or motive power. They are all that remain, like the smile on the Cheshire Cat, when all else is gone.

Q: After the turbulence of 'creative destruction' that accompanied the Industrial Revolution, a whole set of mechanisms – whereby the state absorbed social risk – were set in place. As government's role as insurer against social risk grew, it came to be seen as an impediment to the new wave of innovation, the 'entrepreneurial burst' associated with the bioengineering and Information Revolutions and the internationalization of the economy.

Here we just completed a long trend toward a culture of security that is now being cast off in favour of a culture of risk? Isn't that the common thread that runs through the post-1973 era of Reagan-Thatcher-Gorbachev?

A: First of all, let's be clear that government is still growing. Ronald Reagan increased the size of the federal budget more than any predecessor. And, while we have deregulated the airlines, we have also made drug testing mandatory. Drug testing is far more interventionist than airline regulation. The state is hardly withering away.

Risk and security are not in opposition, but parallel. After all, Social Security is an invention of the nineteenth century's industrial 'entrepreneurial burst'. It was created precisely because there was so much risk being generated. And, I am sure new forms of security will be created to cope with the risks of the current entrepreneurial period.

What might the new forms of security be? One response, resulting from the present economic upheaval, is to me the most significant development of the late twentieth century: the emergence of the job as a property right. These last years have seen a spate of court rulings sharply limiting the traditional right of the employer to terminate employees at will, even if they have no contract.

The risk of dislocation now means losing the security of the position a person has achieved after working 22 years at General Electric If this person was the managing engineer, he once knew that if he made steam turbines yesterday he would make them tomorrow. And he knew that when GE controlled 45 percent of the market he did not have to work too hard to stay where he was. There would always be a job for him and raises ahead. Now, that person knows GE may move out of steam turbines altogether, at any time. A young person he has never heard of could come up with a gadget tomorrow that would make GE's 45 percent control of the market obsolete.

That is an outrage to this vested employee. His illusion of security has been exploded. He had come to accept his job as a right, his position as a law of nature. So he sues to keep that job, seeking to redefine it as his 'property'.

In human history, nothing has had greater impact than the redefinition of property rights. That is fundamental to the transformation of social orders. In the transition from *laissez-faire* to the welfare state, the important property became the commercial wealth created by trading merchants; it was no longer land.

The redefinition of the job as property right is largely a reaction to today's great wave of entrepreneurialism.

Q: In the perpetually innovating 'knowledge society' characterized by economic instability, isn't education both the mechanism of mobility and security, a kind of *mobile security* that allows one to move between careers and different organizations?

A: The right kind of education is a new form of security. However, our schools have yet to accept the fact that in the 'knowledge society', the majority of people make their living as employees. They work in an organization in which they have to be effective. Yet, this is the exact opposite of what our educational system assumes.

The 'knowledge society' is a society of large organizations – government and business – that necessarily operate on the flow of information. In this sense, all the advanced societies of the West have become 'post-business'. Business is no longer the main avenue of advancement in society. Career opportunity increasingly requires a university diploma. The centre of gravity has shifted to the knowledge worker. Yet, no educational institution – not even the graduate school of management – tries to equip students with the elementary skills that would make them effective as members of an organization: the ability to present ideas orally and in writing; the ability to work with people; the ability to shape and direct one's own work, contribution and career. The 'educated person' ought to be the new archetype of the post-business society.

Q: What new economic realities have made our economic thinking outmoded?

A: There is a new configuration to economic life today which confounds all the old analytical categories.

For the first time, the raw material economy has become uncoupled from the industrial economy. For the non-Communist world, at least, the raw material economy has become marginal.

For almost a decade now, the raw material economy has been in a deep depression, yet the industrial economies are booming. In all past business cycles, a slump in food and raw materials has been followed within 18 months by a crisis in the industrial economy. Not this time.

I think there are a couple of related reasons for this uncoupling. There is a worldwide surplus of farm products, caused by the enormous expansion of agricultural production in the developing world. While that glut has caused farm income in the U.S., for example, to drop by two-thirds in some regions between 1984–87, it has had little effect on the overall spending power in the economy because the farm population is now insignificantly small.

As important, manufactured products contain far less raw materials than they used to. In the 1920s, for example, raw materials and energy comprised 60 percent of the cost of the key product at the time, the automobile. The key product of our time, the microchip, has a raw material and energy content of less than 2 percent. Japan increased its industrial production between 1965 and 1985 two and a half times, but it barely increased its raw material and energy consumption at all!

Manufacturing is also becoming uncoupled from labour. In 1988, the same volume of goods could be produced as in 1973 with only two-fifths the blue-collar man hours.

Investment used to follow trade. Now, investors put production facilities anywhere in the global market instead of producing at home and exporting. They can now just as easily produce abroad and then import back home. They do research where there are researchers and design where there are designers. The Pontiac Le Mans, for example, was designed in Germany and built with Japanese parts in Korea. Honda makes cars in America and exports them back to Japan.

The 'real' economy of goods and services has been uncoupled from the money economy. Every day, the London Interbank market turns over 15 times the amount of Eurodollars, Euroyen, and Euromarks needed to finance world trade. Ninety percent of the transnational economy's financial transactions serve no 'economic function' in terms of production. Yet, a substantial activity of every transnational firm must involve managing their inherently unstable foreign exchange exposure. The transnational money economy is no longer the 'veil of reality' as Marx once said. It *is* the reality to which goods and services are subservient.

Complementary and competitive trade have been replaced by adversarial trade. In Adam Smith's eighteenth century, trade was complementary: England sold wool to Portugal for wine it could not produce; Portugal sold the wine for wool it could not produce. In the mid-nineteenth century, trade became competitive: Germany and the U.S. competed to sell chemicals to each other and to the world.

Complementary trade sought a partnership. Competitive trade sought a customer. Adversarial trade aims to dominate entire industries. While competitive trade was fighting a battle, adversarial trade seeks to win the war by destroying the enemy's army and capacity to fight.

Protectionism is not an answer to adversarial trade. As far as I can see, only reciprocity – where each country enjoys the same access to the other country's market and no more – is the only trading relationship that will avoid degeneration into protectionism. And I suspect that reciprocity will function most effectively in regional units – the EEC, Japan-Far East, North America – so that the smaller economies will have a large enough market to generate enough production and sales to sustain themselves.

Q: Let's talk about economic theory. Why do we find it so difficult to conceptualize the workings of the economy these days?

A: For 60 years, mainstream economic policy in the West was based on the ideas of John Maynard Keynes. Now, the assumptions of his concepts are obsolete.

Keynes could not see the shape of the global economy, which would undercut his theories, until the end of his life in the late 1940s. Indeed, before he died, Keynes admitted his theory of the economy could no longer work. But it was too late, the Keynesians were already in full control.

Under the influence of those Keynesians, economic theory still assumes that the sovereign state is the predominant unit of economic life, and thus the only effective unit for economic policy.

In actuality, there are four economies, each, as the mathematicians would say, a 'partially dependent variable' – interdependent but not controlled by each other. First, there is the economy of the *nation*; increasingly, however, power is shifting to the *region* – North America, the European Economic Community, and the Far East region grouped around Japan; there is also an almost autonomous *world economy of money, credit, and investment flows*; finally, there is the economy of the *transnational enterprise*, which views the world as one market.

With OPEC and Nixon's floating of the dollar in the mid-1970s, the world economy changed from international to *transnational*. The transnational economy is shaped mainly by the dynamic of money flows rather than goods and services; sovereign nation-states react to, rather than initiate or control, events in the global capital markets. The traditional factors of production – land, labour and even money, because it is so mobile – no longer assure a particular nation competitive advantage. Rather, *management* has become the decisive factor of production. And the goal of management in a transnational enterprise that operates in one world market is *maximization of market share*, not the traditional short-term 'profit maximization' of the old-style corporation.

Q: So, Keynes was only viable as long as one force – the national economy – was a sovereign entity that had some control over its internal situation and could calculate its policy effect in the international economy. Now, that is gone.

A: As long as there was some reality to the nation-state, Keynes 'perfect gas' theory of the economy seemed to work. He felt that if the national government could control the temperature and pressure of the macroenvironment through money, credit and interest rates, individuals and firms – the micro-economy – would react predictably.

But this theory of how an economy works cannot explain any of the main economic events of the last 15 years.

In order to promote exports and create jobs in the mid-1970s, Jimmy Carter pushed down the value of the dollar, vis-à-vis the yen, from 250 to 180. Exports boomed but unemployment continued to rise, which should have caused deflation. Instead, inflation skyrocketed as high as 14 percent.

When Reagan came to office, he raised interest rates to halt inflation. He succeeded, but drove the dollar back up to 250 against the yen, damaging American exports and creating an unprecedented market in the U.S. for Japanese products. According to all available theory, that should have caused more unemployment; instead, unemployment rates under Reagan fell to the lowest level in decades, with acute labour shortages appearing in some areas by 1989.

When Reagan tried to adjust the dollar 'slightly' in the fall of 1985, it went unexpectedly into freefall down to 125. Instead of massive 'flight from the dollar', which available theory predicted, the main holders of the dollar – Japan, Taiwan, West Germany, and Canada – who had placed large amounts of their dollar reserves in U.S. debt obligations, actually *increased* their lending to the U.S.

To confound theory further, the price of raw materials, from Danish butter to Arab petroleum – which the Japanese pay for in dollars – plummeted. That further depressed worldwide commodity prices.

Additionally, the devaluation of the dollar should have raised the price of Japanese goods in the U.S. Instead, the Japanese firms did something unprecedented: they absorbed a 50 percent cut in profits to maintain their share of the U.S. market. To compensate for that cut in foreign profits, Japanese companies sharply raised prices at home. But instead of triggering a recession, Japan experienced the largest consumer binge in its history. Presumably, it was the maturing baby-boomers emulating their consumer counterparts elsewhere in the West that frustrated the expectation that higher prices would curb spending but raise savings.

What has happened? First of all, it turns out that the microeconomy – the decisions of the multitude of individuals and firms – has sabotaged the supposedly controlling macroeconomy of the sovereign nation. The servants are in control of the master.

For example, Keynes assumed that the 'velocity of the turnover of money' – how fast individuals spend their money – was a social habit that remained unchanged over long periods of time. But, every time this assumption has been put to the test it has been proven wrong.

Indeed, the individual's ability – not the government's ability – to control the rate of spending money explains Jimmy Carter's policy disaster. Consumers did not follow the textbook by spending and creating jobs; they hoarded instead. In a rapid reversal, American consumers then increased their spending during the Reagan years, which explains why his policies worked in expanding the economy even with a huge trade deficit.

Similarly, the Japanese firms frustrated attempts to balance trade because they sought 'market maximization' instead of 'short-term profit maximization', thus confounding what they were 'rationally' expected to do according to present economic theory. In the world economy, economic rationality means something different than it meant in the national economy. As the Japanese have understood, 'sales' in the world market are returns on long-term investment: What matters is the total return over the lifetime of the investment, and the return over time depends on monopolizing market share.

And, of course, there is no room in contemporary economic theory for technology and innovation. Yet, entrepreneurship, invention and innovation can profoundly alter the economy in a very short time.

So, both individuals and firms, especially transnational firms, sabotage the attempted macroeconomic policies of nation-states that are no longer sovereign. The new realities have turned Keynes on his head.

Keynes was the last great synthesizer of economic thought. Without a new synthesis that presents a model of how the 'four economies' interact to create economic reality, we may be at the end of economic theory. And without economic theory there can be no economic policy – no foundation for governmental action to manage the business cycle and economic conditions.

Any functioning economic theory of the future must integrate the macroeconomy of money, credit and interest rates, and the microeconomic decisions about how firms and individuals spend money. Such a theory must also account for the dynamic of entrepreneurship and innovation.

We may well conclude that the new reality means we can no longer control the economic 'weather' of recession and boom cycles, unemployment, savings and spending rates, but only the 'climate' – avoiding protectionism, or educating the working population to function in a knowledge society. In short, preventive medicine instead of blind attempts at short-term fixes.

[1989]

Part I

ECONOMICS

1

The Futures Already Around Us

In five important areas the 1990s will bring far-reaching changes in the social and economic environment, and in the strategies, structure and management of business.

For a start, the world economy will be quite different from what businessmen, politicians and economists still take for granted. The trend towards *reciprocity as a central principle of international economic integration* has by now become well-nigh irreversible, whether one likes it or not (and I don't).

Economic relations will increasingly be between trading blocks rather than between countries. Indeed an East Asian block loosely organized around Japan and paralleling the EC and North America may emerge during the decade. Relationships will therefore increasingly be conducted through bilateral and trilateral deals in respect both of investment and of trade.

Reciprocity can easily degenerate into protectionism of the worst kind (that's why I dislike it). But it could be fashioned into a powerful tool to expand trade and investment, if – but only if – governments and businessmen act with imagination and courage. In any event, it was probably inevitable. It is the response to the first emergence as a major economic power of a non-western society, Japan.

In the past, whenever a new major economic power appeared, new forms of economic integration soon followed (e.g., the multinational company, which was invented in the middle of the nineteenth century – in defiance of everything Adam Smith and David Ricardo had taught – when the United States and Germany first emerged as major economic powers. By 1913, multinationals had come to control as much of the world's industrial output, (maybe more), as they do now). Reciprocity is the way, for better or worse, to integrate a modern but proudly non-Western country such as Japan (and the smaller Asian 'tigers' that are now following it) into a West-dominated world economy.

The West will no longer tolerate Japan's adversarial trading methods of recent decades – a wall around the home market to protect social structures and traditions, plus a determined push beyond it for world dominance for selected Japanese industries. Yet the Western pattern of an autonomous, value-free economy in which economic rationality is the ultimate criterion, is alien to a Confucian society; is indeed seen by it as cultural imperialism. Reciprocity may make possible close economic relationships between culturally distinct societies.

Into Alliance

Second, *businesses will integrate themselves into the world economy through alliances:* minority participations, joint ventures, research and marketing consortia, partnerships in subsidiaries or in special projects, cross-licensing, and so on. The partners will be not only other businesses but also a host of nonbusinesses such as universities, health-care institutions, local governments. The traditional forms of economic integration – trade and the multinational company – will continue to grow, in all likelihood. But the dynamics are shifting rapidly to partnerships based neither on the commodity nexus of trade nor on the power nexus of ownership by multinationals.

There are several reasons for this rapidly accelerating trend:

- Many middle-sized and even small businesses will have to become active in the world economy. To maintain leadership in one developed market, a company increasingly has to have a strong presence in all such markets worldwide. But middle-sized and small companies rarely have the financial or managerial resources to build subsidiaries abroad or to acquire them.

● Financially, only the Japanese can still afford to go multinational. Their capital costs them around 5 percent or so. In contrast, European or American companies now pay up to 20 percent for money. Not many investments, whether in organic growth or in acquisitions, are likely to yield that high a return (except acquisitions by management experts such as Lord Hanson or Warren Buffet, who know how to find a healthy but undermanaged business and turn it around). This is especially true of multinational investment, whose risks are increased by currency variations and unfamiliarity with the foreign environment. Financially, it is hard to justify most of the recent acquisitions in America made by European companies. To say that they are 'cheap' because of the low dollar is nonsense: the companies acquired, after all, earn in these low dollars. Only a very big and cash-rich company can really still afford today to go the multinational route.

● The major driving forces, however, behind the trend towards alliances are technology and markets. In the past, technologies overlapped little. Electronics people did not need to know much about electrical engineering or about materials. Papermakers needed to know mainly about paper mechanics and paper chemistry. Telecommunications was self-contained. So was investment banking. Today there is hardly any field in which this is still the case. Not even a big company can any longer get from its own research laboratories all, or even most, of the technology it needs. Conversely, a good lab now produces results in many more areas than can interest even a big and diversified company. So pharmaceutical companies have to ally themselves with geneticists; commercial bankers with underwriters; hardware-makers like IBM with software boutiques. The need for such alliances is the greater the faster a technology grows.

Markets, similarly, are rapidly changing, merging, crisscrossing and overlapping each other. They too are no longer separate and distinct.

Alliances, while needed, are anything but easy. They require extreme – and totally unaccustomed – clarity in respect of objectives, strategies, policies, relationships, and people. They also require advance agreement on when and how the alliance is to be brought to an end. For alliances become the more problematic the more successful they are. The best text on them is not to be found in a management book; it is in Winston Churchill's biography of his ancestor the first duke of Marlborough.

Reshaping Companies

Third, *businesses will undergo more and more radical restructuring* in the 1990s than at any time since the modern corporate organization first evolved in the 1920s. Only five years ago it was treated as sensational news when I pointed out that the information-based organization needs far fewer levels of management than the traditional command-and-control model. By now a great many – maybe most – large American companies have cut management levels by one-third or more. But the restructuring of corporations – middle-sized ones as well as large ones, and, eventually, even smaller ones – has barely begun.

Businesses tomorrow will follow two new rules. One: to move work to where the people are, rather than people to where the work is. Two: to farm out activities that do not offer opportunities for advancement into fairly senior management and professional positions (e.g., clerical work, maintenance, the 'back office' in the brokerage house, the drafting room in the large architectural firm, the medical lab in the hospital) to an outside contractor. The corporation, in stock market jargon, will be unbundled.

One reason is that this century has acquired the ability to move ideas and information fast and cheaply. At the same time the great nineteenth-century achievement, the ability to move people, has outlived its usefulness; witness the horrors of daily commuting in most big cities and the smog that hovers over the increasingly clogged traffic arteries. Moving work out to where the people are is already in full train. Few large American banks or insurance companies still process their paperwork in the downtown office. It has been moved out to a satellite in the suburbs (or farther afield – one insurance company ships its claims by air to Ireland every night). Few airlines still locate their reservations computer at the main office or even at the airport.

It may take another 'energy crunch' for this trend to become a shock wave. But most work that requires neither decision making nor face-to-face customer contact (and that means all clerical work) will have been moved out by the end of the decade, at least in Western countries; Tokyo and Osaka will take a little longer, I suspect.

(What, by the way, does this mean for the large cities, the children of the nineteenth century's transport revolution? Most of them – London, Paris, New York, Tokyo, Frankfurt – successfully made in this century the transition from manufacturing centre to office centre. Can they make the next transition – and what will it be? And is the worldwide urban real-estate boom that began in eighteenth-century London at last nearing its end?)

The trend toward 'farming out' is also well under way, even in Japan. Most large Japanese hospitals are today cleaned by the local affiliate of the same maintenance contractor that services most American hospitals. Underlying this trend is the growing need for productivity in service work done largely by people without much education or skill. This almost requires that the work be lodged in a separate, outside organization with its own career ladders. Otherwise, it will be given neither enough attention nor importance to ensure the hard work that is needed not just on quality and training, but on work-study, work-flow, and tools.

Finally, corporate size will by the end of the coming decade have become a strategic decision. Neither 'big is better' nor 'small is beautiful' makes much sense. Neither elephant nor mouse nor butterfly is, in itself, 'better' or 'more beautiful'. Size follows function, as a great Scots biologist, D'Arcy Wentworth Thompson, showed in his 1917 classic *On Growth and Form*.

A transnational automobile company such as Ford has to be very large. But the automobile industry also has room for a small niche player like Rolls-Royce. Marks & Spencer, for decades the world's most successful retailer, was run as a fair-sized rather than as a large business. So is Tokyo-based Ito-Yokado, arguably the most successful retailer of the past decade. Successful high-engineering companies are, as a rule, middle-sized. But in other industries the middle size does not work well: successful pharmaceutical companies, for instance, tend to be either quite large or quite small. Whatever advantages bigness by itself used to confer on a business have largely been cancelled by the universal availability of management and information. Whatever advantages smallness by itself conferred have largely been offset by the need to think, if not to act, globally. Management will increasingly have to decide on the right size for a business, the size that fits its technology, its strategy and its markets. This is both a difficult and a risky decision – and the right answer is rarely the size that best fits a management's ego.

The Challenge to Management

Fourth, the governance of companies themselves is in question. The greatest mistake a trend-spotter can make – and one, alas, almost impossible to prevent or correct – is to be prematurely right. A prime example is my 1976 book *The Unseen Revolution*. In it I argued that the shift of ownership in the large, publicly held corporation to representatives of the employee class – i.e., pension funds and unit trusts – constitutes a fundamental change in the locus and character of ownership. It is therefore bound to have profound impact, especially on the governance of companies: above all, to *challenge the doctrine*, developed since World War II, *of the self-perpetuating and professional management* in the big company; and to raise new questions regarding the *accountability and indeed legitimacy* of big-company management.

The Unseen Revolution may be the best book I ever wrote. But it was prematurely right, so no one paid attention to it. Five years later the hostile takeovers began. They work primarily because pension funds are 'investors' and not 'owners' in their legal obligations, their interests, and their mentality. And the hostile takeovers do indeed challenge management's function, its role and its very legitimacy.

The raiders are surely right to assert that a company must be run for performance rather than for the benefit of its management. They are, however, surely wrong in defining 'performance' as nothing but immediate, short-term gains for shareholders. This subordinates all other constituencies – above all, managerial and professional employees – to the immediate gratification of people whose only interest in the business is short-term payoffs.

No society will tolerate this for very long. And indeed in the United States a correction is beginning to be worked out by the courts, which increasingly give such employees a 'property right' in their jobs. At the same time the large American pension funds (especially the largest, the funds of government employees) are beginning to think through their obligation to a business as a going concern; that is, their obligation as owners.

But the raiders are wrong also because immediate stockholder gains do not, as has now been amply proven, optimize the creation of wealth. That requires a balance between the short term and the long term, which is precisely what management is supposed to provide, and should get paid for. And we know how to establish and maintain this balance.

The governance of business has so far become an issue mainly in the English-speaking countries. But it will soon become an issue also in Japan and West Germany. So far in those two countries the needed balance between the short term and the long has been enforced by the large banks' control of other companies. But in both countries big companies are slipping the banks' leash. And in Japan pension funds will soon own as high a proportion of the nation's large companies as American ones do in the United States; and they are just as interested in short-term stock market profits. The governance of business, in other words, is likely to become an issue throughout the developed world.

Again, we may be further advanced towards an answer than most of us realize. In a noteworthy recent article in the *Harvard Business Review*, Professor Michael C. Jensen, of the Harvard Business School, has pointed out that large businesses, especially in the United States, are rapidly 'going private'. They are putting themselves under the control of small number of large holders; and in such a way that their holders' self-interest lies in building long-term value rather than in reaping immediate stock market gains. Indeed, only in Japan, with its sky-high price/earnings ratios, is a public issue of equity still the best way for a large company to finance itself.

Unbundling too should go a long way toward building flexibility into a company's cost structure, and should thus enable it to maintain both short-term earnings and investments in the future. Again the Japanese show the way. The large Japanese manufacturing companies maintain short-term earnings (and employment security for their workers) and long-term investments in the future, by 'out-sourcing'. They buy from outside contractors a far larger proportion of their parts than Western manufacturers usually do. Thus they are able to cut their costs fast and sharply, when they need to, by shifting the burden of short-term fluctuations to the outside supplier.

The basic decisions about the function, accountability and legitimacy of management, whether they are to be made by business, by the market, by lawyers and courts, or by legislators –

and all four will enter the lists – are still ahead of us. They are needed not because corporate capitalism has failed but because it has succeeded. But that makes them all the more controversial.

The Primacy of Politics

Fifth, rapid changes in *international politics and policies*, rather than domestic economics, are likely to dominate the 1990s. The lodestar by which the free world has navigated since the late 1940s, the containment of Russia and of communism, is becoming obsolescent, because of that policy's very success. And the other basic policy of these decades, restoration of a worldwide, market-based economy, has also been singularly successful. But we have no policies yet for the problems these successes have spawned: the all-but-irreversible breakup of the Soviet empire, and the decline of China to the point where it will feature in world affairs mainly because of its weakness and fragility.

Besides, new challenges have arisen that are quite different: the environment; terrorism; third-world integration into the world economy; control or elimination of nuclear, chemical, and biological weapons; and control of the worldwide pollution of the arms race altogether. They all require concerted, common, trans-national action, for which there are few precedents (suppressing the slave trade, outlawing piracy, the Red Cross are the successful ones that come to mind).

The past 40 years, despite tensions and crises, were years of political continuity. The next ten will be years of political discontinuity. Save for such aberrations as the Vietnam era in the United States, political life since 1945 has been dominated by domestic economic concerns such as unemployment, inflation or nationalization/privatization. These issues will not go away. But increasingly international and transnational political issues will tend to upstage them.

So?

The trends that I have described above are not forecasts (for which I have little use and scant respect); they are, if you will, conclusions. Everything discussed here has already happened; it is only the full impacts that are still to come. I expect most readers to nod and to say, 'Of course.' But few, I suspect, have yet asked themselves: 'What do these futures mean for my own work and my own organization?'

[1989]

2

The Poverty of Economic Theory

What creates wealth? For the last 450 years, economists have either neglected the question, sought easy answers, or dismissed previous assessments. Nonetheless, we have something to learn from every interpretation.

The first generation of economists, the mercantilists, said, 'Wealth is purchasing power.' Their goal was to increase monetary wealth with an accumulation of bullion and a favourable trade balance. Another theory stated that wealth is not created by man, but by nature – that land creates wealth.

Yet another group of theorists related wealth to man. 'Wealth,' they said, 'is created by human labour.' This tenet signalled the beginning of economics as a discipline because it related wealth to something that man creates. And yet it was totally unsatisfactory. It could not be made to predict or analyse anything.

A little more than 100 years ago the field of economics split in two. The mainstream simply gave up the search for any creation of wealth, became purely analytical, and stopped relating economics to the behaviour of people. Economics was a discipline that governed the behaviour of commodities. Ironically, analysis is a great strength of contemporary economics, but it also explains why the public at large is bored stiff by the field. It has nothing to say to them because it lacks a foundation in value.

Another Wrong Answer

Karl Marx understood this shortfall when he stuck to the labour theory of value. 'Marxist economics' is a contradiction in terms – it has no analytical or predictive power – but it has a tremendous appeal precisely because it is grounded in a value. It defines the creators of wealth – human beings, labour. And yet, we know it's the wrong answer, too.

For the last 100 years, therefore, we have had a choice between an economics that has great analytical power but no foundation in value and an economics that wasn't economics at all, but a manifesto based on the human being. Today we've finally reached a point where that dilemma can be bridged, where we can begin to understand the right approach, if not the right answer. We now know that the source of wealth is something specifically human: knowledge. If we apply knowledge to tasks we already know how to do, we call it 'productivity'. If we apply knowledge to tasks that are new and different, we call it 'innovation'. Only knowledge allows us to achieve those two goals.

Tradition of Labour

This wasn't always true. Two hundred years ago when Adam Smith wrote about 'the tradition of labour', his examples were people in what is now central Germany, who, because of the heavy winters with lots of snow, learned to be woodworkers and make clocks and violins. It takes 200 years to build such a tradition, Smith said, except for rare cases when refugees or immigrants bring their skills to a community.

Such was certainly the case when the U.S. won its independence. Every American consul had an unlimited slush fund (which probably meant $180) to bribe an English craftsman and supply him with false papers to come to this country and teach us how to build textile machinery and dye cotton. That's how New England became an industrial power around 1810.

During the nineteenth century, however, apprenticeship (a German invention) telescoped the 200 years into 5, and during the twentieth century, training (an American invention) telescoped 5 years into 6 months or even ninety days. We invented training during World War I because we had no tradition of labour. After World War II, our invention spread worldwide, which is one reason why nations can no longer compete solely on the basis of a labour tradition.

Learning and Knowledge

Indeed, until recently, the quickest way for a person living in a developed country to make a decent living was to become a semiskilled machine operator. After six weeks, he probably was better paid than associate professors, not to mention assistant deans. But that's over. Today he can make a middle-class living only through learning and knowledge.

(Consider that 30 years ago, there wasn't a person in Korea who had any tradition of skill or craft, if only because Japan didn't allow its neighbours to acquire any for 50 years. Today, Korea can do almost anything any advanced industrial nation does, thanks to training.)

Of course, the realization that knowledge is the source of wealth has major implications for economics, which today is at a dead end. Economics used to be an enjoyable discipline because it was so humble. When someone asked an economist of 1925 a question, his answer was, 'I don't know,' which in many ways is a respectable answer. (At least it's a modest one.) And then he said, 'We don't know and therefore the intelligent thing to do is as little as possible and pray. Keep taxes low, expenditures low, and pray.'

New Philosophy

But my generation of economists became arrogant, largely as a result of an incredible performance during World War I. In military terms, World War I is the all-time low of performance, but the civilian accomplishment was incredible. Every country was bankrupt by December 1914, and according to the traditional rules of the game, should have had to stop fighting. But they kept on killing each other for four more years because the civilian administrators were so incredibly competent. And that competency corrupted and gave us delusions of grandeur.

When 1929 came along, suddenly there was a curious belief that government should be able to do something about the economy.

That was totally unheard of in earlier days, but it became a popular demand, similar to the question, 'If you can put a man on the moon, why can't you do something about AIDS?' And thus we saw the development of economics that knew the answers.

Keynes knew the answer: Whatever ails you, just create more purchasing power. Milton Friedman, who may be the last surviving member of the great generation, refined it and said, 'You don't even have to do that. All you have to do is just make sure the money supply grows.' For the supply-siders it was even easier: just cut taxes. What could appear nicer and more pleasant?

End of Euphoria

In the nineteenth century economics was known as the 'dismal science', because it always forced us to make choices, and we always had to forgo something. Suddenly it became the euphoric science. For 50 years, it's been an euphoric science, but believe me, that's over.

Economics hasn't worked. Whatever we tried, it failed. What's more, the basic assumptions of modern economic theories are unreasonable and invalid. All of them assume that the sovereign state is alone in this world and can control its destiny. If the five or six leading industrial nations would simply agree to hand over their economic policy to a czar, a commissioner, or a common organ, economic theory would work. But chances are it won't happen; by comparison, winning a million dollars at a Las Vegas slot machine is a cinch.

Most economists have assumed, too, that the velocity of the turnover of money is a social habit and a constant – against all evidence. When the U.S. tested the theory for the first time in 1935 and pumped a lot of purchasing power into American pockets, we did not spend, we hoarded. The economy collapsed the following year, and it was much worse than in 1930 or 1931 because the American public sabotaged the economic policy. The same thing happened under Mr Carter and Mr Reagan. The velocity of turnover of money is about as mercurial as teenage fashions and even less predictable.

Invalid Theory

In essence, macroeconomic theory is no longer a basis for economic policy because no one knows *what* is going to happen. Mr Reagan came to power promising to cut the budget, but government expenses have never grown faster in the history of any country. He didn't betray his trust; politically, he had no choice. Political leaders have no economic theory they can trust, a fact which escapes many businessmen.

The economics of tomorrow must do what economists have not been able to do: integrate the realms of the domestic and the world. (Note the use of the word *world* rather than *international*. *International* implies economies outside the domestic realm; *world* economies are 'inside'.)

Tomorrow's economics must also answer the question: how do we relate the way we run a business to results? What *are* results? The traditional answer – the bottom line – is treacherous. Under a bottom-line philosophy, we cannot relate the short term to the long term, and yet the balance between the two is a crucial test of management.

Two Guideposts

The beacons of productivity and innovation must be our guideposts. If we achieve profits at the cost of downgrading productivity or not innovating, they aren't profits. We're destroying capital. On the other hand, if we continue to improve productivity of all key resources and our innovative standing, we are going to be profitable. Not today, but tomorrow. In looking at knowledge applied to human work as the source of wealth, we also see the function of the economic organization.

For the first time we have an approach that makes economics a human discipline and relates it to human values, a theory that gives a businessman a yardstick to measure whether he's still moving in the right direction and whether his results are real or delusions. We are on the threshold of post-economic theory, grounded in what we now know and understand about the generation of wealth.

[1987]

3

The Transnational Economy

To maintain a leadership position in any one developed country, a business – whether large or small – increasingly has to attain and hold leadership positions in all developed markets worldwide. It has to be able to do research, to design, to develop, to engineer and to manufacture in any part of the developed world, and to export from any developed country to any other. It has to go transnational.

This new need largely explains the worldwide boom in transnational direct investments. The front-runners are the British. Since 1983, British companies have spent at least $25 billion on acquiring American businesses – the most massive British thrust into the world economy since Victorian times. The West Germans may not be far behind. Unlike the British they concentrate, however, on smaller, closely held companies. And, contrary to popular belief, many of the U.S. multinationals are advancing rather than entrenching in Western Europe and in Japan.

There is also a transnational push of small and medium-sized businesses. The vehicle often is not an acquisition or a financial transaction but what the Germans call 'a community of interest': a joint-venture, research-pooling, joint-marketing, or cross-licensing agreement.

A small speciality producer in the American Midwest with world leadership in one component of single-cylinder gasoline engines had facilities only in the U.S. seven years ago. Now it owns three plants in Japan that directly supply Japanese motorcycle manufacturers. But the firm also has entered into a joint venture in the Midwest with a similarly small Japanese speciality producer of another component of single-cylinder engines. The Japanese supply capital and technology and the Americans supply management and marketing.

Banding Together

Four small, closely held firms, an American, a Dutch, a German and a Japanese – each a leader in one narrow line of chemical solvents – have merged their separate research labs with the lab of an American university with expertise in the solvents field. Only by banding together do they have the $200 million in sales needed to support a decent research budget in a rapidly changing technology.

And then there is the Belgian producer of processed meats – the largest producer in its speciality lines within the Common Market but still with sales of only about $60 million a year. Early this year, the firm and an even smaller Spanish meat processor formed a partnership. The firms stay independent. But the Spaniards will do all the labour-intensive manufacturing for both firms and the Belgians the research, the product development and the marketing.

Such communities of interest are by no means confined to small and medium-sized businesses. Two of the world's largest companies – GM and Toyota – are in such a partnership. The big plant in Fremont, Calif., is a GM plant. But it is managed by Toyota. And it produces cars under both the Toyota and the GM marques.

The world's largest heavy-engineering company with $15 billion in annual sales will start operations next January. It is being formed by merging the electrical-apparatus businesses of Sweden's ASEA and Switzerland's Brown Boveri. Each of these big, old companies has leadership in important European markets. But only by combining their electrical-apparatus businesses in a joint venture can they hope to become a factor in North America and the Far East.

Going transnational is not confined to manufacturing firms. It is becoming imperative for any business that aims at a leadership position any place in the developed world. The only exceptions are businesses that by the nature of their activity are confined to a locality or region – hospitals, schools, cemeteries, electric-power suppliers – and governmental monopolies.

Banking and finance have, of course, become increasingly transnational ever since the major New York banks went world-wide in the '60s. Now major insurance companies, foremost among them Germany's Allianz, are aggressively expanding across national and continental boundaries. British, German and Dutch book publishers have bought major U.S. publishing houses – but U.S. publishers have similarly moved aggressively into British book publishing.

Again, a good deal of the development is not 'big-company stuff' and is based on a community of interest. A highly specialized, medium-sized American asset-management firm has, for instance, recently formed a partnership with an equally specialized, medium-sized Japanese asset-manager and a somewhat larger financial house in London. Each firm remains independent, but the American firm manages all U.S. investments for the three partners; the Tokyo firm, all Japanese investments; and the British firm, all investments in Europe.

One reason leadership in any one developed market in-creasingly requires leadership in all is that the developed world has become one in terms of technology. All developed countries are equally capable of doing everything, doing it equally well and doing it equally fast. All developed countries also share instant information. Companies can therefore compete just about every-where the moment economic conditions give them a substantial price advantage. In an age of sharp and violent currency fluctua-tion, this means a leader must be able to innovate, to produce and to market in every area of the developed world – or else be defenceless against competition should foreign-exchange rates sharply shift.

What triggered the present transnational rush was the over-valued dollar of the early '80s. It demonstrated that currency fluctuations can be life-threatening even to the strongest business. But it also showed that there is an effective defence: a trans-national leadership position across the faultlines of currency earthquakes.

U.S. exports dropped like a stone in the years of the overvalued dollar and imports soared: not one major American industry could maintain its exports in the face of a currency fluctuation of almost 50 percent. Yet only in steel, automobiles, consumer electronics, machine tools, and a few semiconductor lines did the world share of American products go down at all.

Overall, the world-market share of manufactured goods produced by U.S.-based companies stayed at the 20 percent to 22 percent level it has held since the '60s. But this actually masks a substantial increase in the standing of American-based goods in the developed economies, since the slump in raw-material prices during the same period almost knocked out purchases by some of the U.S.'s best customers, the developing countries of Latin America. By contrast, American manufacturers with Western European ventures substantially increased their market penetration in computers and computer software, in pharmaceuticals, speciality chemicals, telecommunications equipment, and financial services. In Japan a good many U.S. companies bought out their joint-venture partners.

This remarkable, unprecedented performance may explain in large measure why the overvalued dollar, despite its disastrous impact on American exports and the American balance of trade, did not push the U.S. into depression. And because the world-market share of products made by U.S.-based companies remained steady, the American businesses with foreign affiliates and units also maintained earnings and cash flow and could thus maintain research, product development and their capacity to innovate and to grow.

For while the overvalued dollar made American exports noncompetitive, it was a boon for the foreign affiliates and units of American companies. Their parent companies' dollars bought, during that period almost 50 percent more – in new plants and machinery, in research, in product development, in marketing, promotion, and service, and in cash flow and earnings. The prices the Americans paid for the buyouts gave their former Japanese partners a handsome profit in yen, but in dollars they were a bargain for the Americans.

These benefits required, however, a transnational base. They did not accrue to the American machine-tool industry, for instance. Ten years ago it had world leadership. But it operated almost entirely in, and out of, the U.S. Hence the overvalued dollar sapped the industry's ability to export and made it defenceless against imports, depriving it of the cash flow and the profits to maintain research and to develop new products.

Ford vs. GM

The automobile industry offers a similar lesson. No company was hit harder in the early '80s by the tide of Japanese imports into the U.S. than Ford. What saved it was its leadership position in the European market. It gave Ford the profits and the cash flow that pulled it through the dismal years. And because the dollar bought so much in Europe in those years, Ford could develop there the new models for the American market that now have made Ford highly profitable again in the U.S. and a serious contender for the domestic leadership it held 60 years ago. GM, though twice Ford's size, is essentially a one-country company – and is still floundering.

A transnational strategy is probably not compatible with diversification. Instead, it requires a concentration of efforts. An example is GE's recent move to divest itself of its large consumer-electronics businesses in which it could not hope to attain world-wide leadership, in exchange for a substantial position in the European market for medical electronics, an area in which GE has a reasonable chance to be a world leader.

Transnational strategy, in other words, is not an easy strategy. But except for believers in miracles – and that is unfortunately what a belief in an early return to stable exchange rates amounts to – going transnational may be the only rational strategy for any business aiming at a leadership position anywhere in the developed world, whether in a mass market or in a market niche.

[1987]

4

From World Trade to World Investment

International trade has been steadily slowing down for most of the past decade. But international investment is booming as never before. It has now become the dominant factor in the world economy. Most of it is investment in securities, of course. But the growing portion – by now, a third or more – is permanent investment in manufacturing and financial services.

Traditionally investment has followed trade. But trade is increasingly becoming dependent on investment.

U.S. exports in the years of the overvalued dollar would have been even lower had the European subsidiaries of American companies and American joint ventures in Japan not continued to buy machinery, chemicals, and parts from the U.S. Similarly, the foreign subsidiaries of America's financial institutions, such as the major banks, accounted for something like one-half of U.S. service income during those dismal years. And now, in turn, the Japanese are investing heavily in manufacturing subsidiaries in the Americas and in Western Europe so as to defend their export business. Even the South Koreans are investing in manufacturing subsidiaries in North America – especially in plants on the Mexican side of the U.S.-Mexico border – to create dependable customers for their exports to North America.

Multinational Competition

By now, about one-fifth of the total capital invested in U.S. manufacturing firms is in facilities outside the U.S. In addition, a similar proportion of the output of U.S. manufacturing industries is being produced offshore. Three-quarters of this output is for sale abroad and one-quarter is for export back to the U.S. to be sold in, or incorporated into goods for, the American market. Major American commercial banks and major brokerage firms have a similar proportion of their assets invested abroad and derive an even larger proportion of their total business through their foreign branches.

No other major country yet outdoes America as a 'multinational' – although West Germany is probably coming closer every day. But within a few years, every single major trading country will proportionately produce as much outside its boundaries as does the U.S., if not more. In 1983, Japanese manufacturers produced only 2 percent of their output outside of Japan. By 1986, this had grown to 5 percent of a much larger output. By 1992 or so, only five years hence, Japanese offshore output is likely to match America's one-fifth, with most of the growth concentrated in North America and in Spain (for sale in the European market).

At least one-third of the world trade in manufactured goods may now be intracompany trade – e.g., from the Mexican border plant of Sony to Sony's final assembly plant across the border in San Diego, or from a Ford Motor Co. engine plant in the U.S. to a Ford plant in Europe or in Brazil.

Protectionism, or the fear thereof, is a minor factor in world investment. The multinational expansion of the Americans into Europe began 30 or more years ago, long before there was any fear of protectionism. It was most vigorous in the two countries where there was the least danger of protectionism: Britain and West Germany. Similarly, the multinational investment of the Japanese in manufacturing plants in the U.S. began long before there was any threat of protectionism. Far more important are marketing pressures.

It is simply not possible to maintain substantial market standing in an important area unless one has a physical presence as a producer. Otherwise, one will soon lose the 'feel' of the market. The most recent example of this truism is the experience of Volkswagen in America.

Just over 20 years ago, in 1969–70, Volkswagen had 10 percent of the American automobile market. Then the German labour unions vetoed the company's plan to establish a manufacturing plant in the U.S.: they were not going to allow 'the exportation of German jobs'. When the American car market changed a few years later, after the first oil crisis, Volkswagen had lost its 'feel' for the market – and the 10 percent of the market that Volkswagen had is now held by the Japanese.

Wage differentials also are not a major cause of world investment. To be sure, the *maquiladoras*, the plants along the Mexican border, which supply labour-intensive parts and products to the American market, or the electronic-assembly plants in Taiwan and Singapore owe their existence to wage differentials. But blue-collar labour rates are less and less important as factors in manufacturing production. There are few industries in which they account these days for more than 8 percent or so. And even in these industries – textiles, cars, electronic assembly, steel–labour costs as a factor in production are decreasing so fast that 'out-sourcing' abroad to obtain wage-cost advantages can be considered a phenomenon unlikely to survive this century.

The major force behind world investment is, however, human resources. Exporting goods primarily creates employment for blue-collar workers. Investing abroad in a multinational affiliate primarily generates employment for educated people in the home country – for engineers and chemists, for accountants, managers, and quality-control staffs, and so on. And as one developed country after another shifts its supply of new workers from semiskilled or unskilled machine operators to people with long years of education, investment abroad is the way in which it can both optimize its human resources and create the jobs a developed country needs.

We can thus expect that, barring world depression or world war, world investment will continue to grow – and probably faster than world trade. And yet we have almost no figures on it. We also, which may be more serious, have no theory for an international economy that is fuelled by world investment rather than by world trade. As a result, we do not understand the world economy and cannot predict its behaviour or anticipate its trends.

We also have no law for this new world economy. No country permits totally unrestricted foreign investment. But no country has thought through the rules. Recently, for instance, the U.S. – the country that by and large has the fewest restrictions on investment by foreigners – frowned on the transfer of ownership of a major semiconductor producer, Fairchild, from one foreigner, a French company, to another foreigner, a Japanese company (even though Fairchild, one of America's largest semiconductor manufacturers may not be able to survive under its present ownership or by itself). Other countries are equally arbitrary and equally inconsistent.

One of the great achievements of the period after World War II was the codification of the rules for international trade in GATT, the General Agreement on Tariffs and Trade. Even though it is honoured as much in the breach as in the observance, it still serves as the norm. And to its great credit, the U.S. is now seeking the extension of GATT to cover international trade in services and in data. But no one, so far, is talking about an international agreement to set the norms for world investment. All we have so far are some feeble attempts to specify compensation to be paid when expropriating a foreign investment. But what should the conditions be for permitting it in the first place?

War-Recovery Plans

Equally urgent is the development of international law for the position of world investment in case of war. By now, we should all have learned that the protection of foreign investment in case of war is in the self-interest of every single Free World country. Even after the most destructive and most bitter war, the survivors will have to live together on this small, crowded planet. And then their chances for recovery depend on the speediest possible restoration of the bonds of economic interdependence. The nineteenth century knew that even the most ferocious war eventually ends. This has been forgotten in this century. As a result, there are no legal rules at all for foreign investment in case of war.

Increasingly, world investment rather than world trade will be driving the international economy. Exchange rates, taxes, and legal rules will become more important than wage rates and tariffs. This is one of the major changes in the world economy and one to which neither government nor economists nor businessmen have given adequate attention.

[1987]

5

The Lessons of the U.S. Export Boom

The most important event in the world economy during the 1980s was surely the boom in U.S. manufacturing exports. In just five years, from 1986 to 1991, these exports almost doubled, with the biggest increases in sales to our major competitors, Japan and West Germany.

This came as a surprise to businessmen, economists, and government forecasters. When the overvaluation of the dollar, especially against the yen, was corrected in the fall of 1985, everyone was absolutely certain that imports into the U.S. would fall sharply. Instead they have risen steadily, thanks mainly to our unquenchable thirst for oil and to the continuing decline of the American automobile industry. But exports? No one then thought seriously that they could do more than hold their own at best.

The U.S. export boom was also unprecedented, in U.S. history, and in economic history altogether. Never before have the manufactured-goods exports of a fully developed country risen so fast; and the U.S. was of course already the world's number-one exporter. This performance is all the more impressive as most of Latin America – traditionally the best U.S. manufactured-goods customer – is still deeply depressed; only Mexico – and then only during the last two years – has come to life again as a big buyer. The export boom fuelled the continuing U.S. economic expansion during the second Reagan term. It kept the recent recession from turning into full-blown depression with double-digit unemployment. And U.S. manufactured-good exports are likely to continue to do well unless the world economy slumps. But their explosive growth has slowed down sharply. The export boom has clearly peaked. What then are its lessons for U.S. business and for world business altogether?

At first glance there seems to be no pattern. The list of goods whose exports jumped contains high-tech stuff such as jet engines, heart valves, and sophisticated software to program paper machines and engineering work stations. It also includes goods normally not considered 'tech' at all: movies and rock recording, running shoes, blue jeans, and office furniture – and everything in between. The star performers among companies came in all sizes: giants such as Boeing selling aeroplanes and GE selling body scanners and aircraft engines; any number of middle-sized companies; and, amazingly, many small and even tiny firms such as the machine shop with 35 employees making a specialized control instrument for the pharmaceutical industry or the equally small shop making hospital paging systems. Among the star performers are firms that have been active in the world economy for a long time, including many who for decades have big plants abroad, e.g., 3M. The list also includes quite a few firms that never before had filled a foreign order.

Yet, for all their diversity, the winning products and their makers have some features in common. And it is these that explain their success. Indeed, these features may altogether be the keys to success in today's world economy.

All the successful export products have clear product differentiation. They are distinct. Not one is a 'commodity'. They are priced competitively; but not one is sold primarily on price. The successful export products are all high 'value added' goods. And what adds high value to them is knowledge, or, at least ingenuity, as in the case of 3M's 'Post-its'.

Most of the export successes also have clearly defined markets, having, indeed, clearly known customers. 'I never before shipped anything overseas,' says the maker of the control instrument for the pharmaceutical industry. 'But I've known every one of my overseas customers for any number of years from trade shows and industry conventions. As customers they were new, but as people they weren't "foreigners" but "old friends". Boeing knows every single airline in the world and Hollywood equally knows every single major movie distributor anywhere. The Japanese engineers buying U.S.-made word processors or the East German teenagers queuing up for U.S.-made rock tapes are not, of course, known personally to the U.S. producers. But they too are not 'foreigners'. They have the same tastes, the same values, the same buying habits as American engineers or American teenagers. 'I do not sell on the world market,' says the heart-valve manufacturer. 'I sell to cardiac surgeons.'

This then is probably the most important lesson of the export boom: the world market is a 'foreign' market only in terms of trade statistics. As to doing business in it, it is a congeries of 'familiar' markets, at least for knowledge-intensive products. And these are the products that increasingly dominate world trade in manufactured goods.

Another important lesson: bigness is not an advantage, let alone a prerequisite to world-market success (as we believed 30 years ago and as the Japanese still seem to believe). The 'winners' in the U.S. export boom have been middle-sized companies with high expertise in a given field, whether in making movies or in designing heart valves. And all successful companies in the export boom have been high concentrated. They are all single-product or single-technology businesses. Boeing is very big, but all it makes are aeroplanes. General Electric is engaged in a multitude of different businesses. But its medical-electronics division makes and sells only medical electronics, its jet-engine division only aircraft engines. The world market does not pay for what is still fashionable among financial people and still taught in the business schools: running a company as a 'portfolio' of businesses; 'balancing' businesses with different cyclical characteristics; or keeping old products as 'milch cows' to offset the cash demands of new technologies and new products.

One more lesson: there is one additional skill needed to be a successful exporter in today's world market – to manage foreign exchange exposure and thus to avoid foreign-exchange losses. During the Carter and early Reagan years U.S. exporters took huge foreign-exchange losses. European and Japanese exporters still do. But for American firms such losses are now quite rare even though the last five years saw extreme currency fluctuations. Compared to the Europeans – especially the Germans – the Americans are still babes in the woods when it comes to taxes. Small exporters rarely know that they can get substantial tax savings under American law (though as a rule only with professional help). But even the small American exporter now knows how to minimize foreign-currency exposure. This newly acquired skill has become a major competitive advantage for U.S. business in today's world markets.

Exporting and manufacturing abroad, the U.S. export boom shows, complement each other. Once an exporter of a knowledge-intensive product holds a substantial share of a foreign market, he has to produce there. Otherwise he simply creates market opportunity for a domestic competitor. This holds true even for the small exporter. When he had gained 35 percent of the market in Western Europe and Japan, the maker of hospital-pagers had to start operations there; 'local imitators were beginning to sell around us,' the owner reports. 'We began with assembly operations. Within two years we had to put in small but fully equipped machine shops.' But far from 'exporting American jobs', manufacturing overseas for overseas markets creates U.S. jobs. Within two years the hospital-pager firm had to hire an additional 15 Americans to supply parts and machinery to its new overseas operations.

Finally, the export boom of the last five years provides strong support for the contention of Harvard economist Robert Reich (in his recent book *The World of Nations*) that knowledge rather than national boundaries defines today's developed markets. But it also supports the opposite thesis of the importance of a national economy and of the structure of the home market – the thesis recently put forth by another Harvard professor, Michael Porter (in his book, *The Competitive Advantage of Nations*): America's manufacturing industry responded so fast and so successfully to the export opportunities opened by the dollar-devaluation of 1985 because the structure of the U.S. home market, with its vigorous competition, makes it opportunity-driven and market-driven. And, as would follow from Porter's thesis, the major US industry that not only failed to benefit from the opportunity but heavily lost ground in the last five years – the automobile industry – has all along been an oligopoly of three firms operating as much in 'coexistence' as in competition, and forced into conformity by a labour-union monopoly.

[1991]

6

Low Wages: No Longer a Competitive Edge

Wage levels for blue-collar workers are becoming increasingly irrelevant in world competition. Productivity still matters – indeed it matters increasingly more. Quality, design, service, innovation, marketing, all are becoming more important. But blue-collar wages as a direct cost are rapidly becoming a minor factor.

The reason is, blue-collar labour no longer accounts for enough of total costs to give low wages much competitive advantage. A well-tested rule says offshore production must be at least 5 percent, and probably 7½ percent, cheaper than production nearby to compensate for the considerable costs of distance: transportation, communications, travel, insurance, finance. And if wage costs fall below 15 percent of total cost, it takes a 50 percent wage differential – at the same labour productivity – to offset the costs of distance. That is practically unheard of, certainly in developed countries.

Blue-collar costs in U.S. manufacturing account for 18 percent of total costs. But they are down from 23 percent only a few years ago. And they are dropping fast as productivity is rising at a good clip. An industry or company that today operates at a blue-collar cost of more than 15 percent is already way behind. GM still has blue-collar costs of nearly 30 percent – in part because of the restrictive work rules in its union contracts. But Toyota and Honda in their U.S. plants, paying the same wage rates, operate at labour costs of less than 20 percent and expect to reduce this to 15 percent within a decade, as does Ford.

Competing Neck-to-Neck

Integrated steel mills still have blue-collar costs of 25 percent. But the 'minimills' operate at blue-collar costs of 10 percent or less – and they now produce a fifth of all steel made in the U.S. and are likely to produce well over half in another 10 years. The textile industry says it's been killed by imports from low-wage countries. But about half the industry actually operates at costs fully competitive with the lowest-wage producer anywhere – Malaysia, for instance, or Indonesia. These companies – mostly the large ones – have brought their labour costs down to 10 per cent or 12 percent of the total – and not only in making commodity products, such as sheeting, but in many cases for finished goods as well, e.g., blue jeans and housedresses.

In this restructuring in which blue-collar wages cease to be the dominant factor in competitive strength – and almost cease to be a factor altogether – American and Japanese industry are neck-to-neck. The Japanese are ahead in reducing labour-cost content in traditional industries, e.g., autos and tyres; what helps them, of course, is that they are largely unhampered by union restrictions. In the new, fast-growing industries – pharmaceuticals, speciality chemicals, biotechnology, communications, computers – and in some old industries such as paper or turbines, the U.S. is ahead. Europe, by and large, has barely begun; but it is waking up.

One result of this is that American manufacturers are slowly beginning to bring back to the U.S. operations they had moved offshore – precisely because they do not have to restore the blue-collar jobs they abolished when they moved offshore 10 years ago. Another result – a paradoxical one – is that manufacturing employment has not gone down in the U.S., contrary to union claims. Because unit labour costs have been falling steadily, U.S. manufacturing has been able to expand total production fast enough to maintain blue-collar employment in absolute figures. This is in glaring contrast to Western Europe, where blue-collar manufacturing employment is about five million lower than 10 years ago, and a little better than the Japanese record. What has been happening is a shift from industries with yesterday's wage costs, e.g., autos and steel, to those with tomorrow's labour costs, e.g., telecommunications and pharmaceuticals.

The shrinking importance of blue-collar costs as a decisive competitive factor also underlies the rapid movement of manufacturers to their markets all over the developed world. American industry made this shift in the 1960s and '70s – in part through the multinationals buying European companies or building in Europe, in part through joint ventures in Japan. Even so, U.S. manufacturers, despite the dollar's greatly reduced purchasing power abroad, are now increasing their direct investments abroad – and contrary to what almost everybody believes, at about the same rate at which foreigners are increasing their direct invest-ments in the U.S.

Now it is Europe and Japan that are moving production offshore into developed countries where their markets are – the Europeans mainly into the U.S., the Japanese into the U.S. and Western Europe. The official Japanese reason, especially for building or buying plants in the U.S., is 'fear of protectionism'. But that is mainly PR for domestic Japanese consumption. The real reason is blue-collar wages are becoming relatively insignificant as a com-petitive factor, so that costs of the distance to the market are becoming more onerous.

These trends spell greatly increased competition among manu-facturers in developed countries. It will not be competition based on wage differentials but on managerial competence – productivity of knowledge work and of money, process technology, manage-ment of foreign-exchange risks, quality, design, innovation, service, marketing. Increasingly, concentration rather than con-glomeration or diversification will be needed, with growing emphasis on knowing one's technology, market, and customers.

In the developed countries these trends will mostly intensify the integration that has been going on for quite some time – at least since American business started 'multinationalization' 30 years ago. But for the developing countries the trend threatens to close the broadest avenue toward rapid economic development: export-led development based on low-wage but productive labour.

Some of the development of the postwar period, notably Brazil's, has been based on the classical nineteenth-century recipe: export-led development based on selling foodstuffs and raw materials to the developed countries – exemplified by the U.S. during the nineteenth century with its exports to Europe of pork bellies, lard, beef, cotton, corn, tobacco, and copper.

But the far more spectacular development of the postwar period was that of Japan, followed by the 'four tigers' of Southeast Asia: South Korea, Taiwan, Hong Kong, and Singapore (about to be joined by a fifth tiger, Thailand). What these countries did was quite new. They took an American invention of World War II – it was called 'training' and it enabled the U.S. during the war years to change pre-industrial, unskilled people into efficient, high-productivity workers – and turned these unskilled and low-wage people rapidly into highly productive but still low-wage workers whose output could then compete in the developed markets.

Neither development route is likely to be open in the future. There are few food importers left. Among developed countries, only Japan still has a food deficit; all the other developed non-Communist countries have food surpluses. Industrial production is rapidly becoming less raw-material intensive. The typical product of the 1920s, the auto, has a raw-material content of almost 50 percent; the typical product of the 1980s, the semiconductor, has one of 1 percent. The raw-material and energy content of a glass-fibre cable is about 12 percent; the copper cable that it replaces has a raw-material and energy content of nearly 50 percent, and so on.

The Last Nineteenth-Century Model?

Brazil may thus have been the last country to finance its development the nineteenth-century way, by paying for capital imports with food and raw-material exports. And today's crisis of the Brazilian economy is largely the result of the collapse of world-market prices for raw materials and foods brought about by the shift from food shortages to food surpluses and from raw-material-intensity in manufacturing to knowledge-intensity.

But the access to economic development through exports based on the productivity of low-cost labour may become blocked, too, when wages are no longer a major factor in total costs. The managerial contributions that then count are precisely in the areas in which a poor, developing country finds it hardest to compete. For manufacturers in developed countries the shift means heightened demands in areas in which they should excel anyhow. The Third World may, however, have to find new development strategies based probably on the domestic market, that is on freedom and market incentives for farmers and for small, local (and tax-aversive) entrepreneurs. Northern Italy and India, rather than Japan, may become tomorrow's development models.

[1988]

7

Europe in the 1990s: Strategies for Survival

For European businessmen the question is no longer: Will there be a true European Common Market? It is: What do we do today to prosper in the Europe of 1993?

The Common Market governments have pledged themselves to abolish the barriers to the intra-European flow of people, money, goods and services by the end of 1992. If they live up to these commitments, Europe will have fewer internal barriers than there are in the U.S., considering all our state and city regulations.

But do the European governments really mean it? Is it pure coincidence, for instance, that the French discovered drug smuggling from Spain just when France had to open its markets to Spanish fruits and vegetables? No drugs have been found so far, but Spanish produce trucks must wait for hours at the border, while the vegetables wilt. West Germany has introduced a bill that would make it expensive for middle-size, family-owned businesses to sell out or merge across frontiers. And, though London's bankers and brokers would clearly benefit, Prime Minister Margaret Thatcher staunchly resists the trend toward a common European currency or European central bank.

Businesses Are Off and Running

Yet what governments do or not do may no longer matter much. Businesses of all sizes have the bit between their teeth and are off and running. 'We all know,' says the chief executive officer of a middle-sized speciality-chemicals firm, 'that we have to act today as if 1993 were already here.'

Unilever, the foods, soap, and detergent multinational, called its European managers to Hamburg recently to put into effect a new organization and new strategies for a truly unified Europe. Another multinational, Philips, has reorganized its consumer-electronics business on the assumption that 1993 is already here. It replaced its 60-year-old structure of autonomous national companies – a Dutch Philips, a German Philips, etc. – with Europe-wide product-based businesses, a television-receiver company, for example.

Recently, five medium-sized, family owned food brokers – German, French, Spanish, Italian, and Danish – formed a 'community of interest'. Each family holds 51 percent of its domestic company and 9.8 percent of each of the others. The five will act as one company in representing manufacturers and serving supermarket chains across national boundaries. 'Knowing politicians, I expect all the present governmental barriers still to be here four years hence,' says the Italian most responsible for the deal. 'But they will have become nuisances and additional costs rather than the dominant market reality they have always been, and this is the only possible basis I can see for picking a business strategy in Europe today.'

But it is also a shaky basis. It means committing one's business to highly risky assumptions.

What, for instance, should a financial business assume regarding the future of Europe's stock markets? London is, of course, by far Europe's leading exchange. But its position is quite different from that of the New York Stock Exchange in the U.S. For the majority of European businesses, their own local exchange is the only one that matters – the only one that trades the shares of national companies and on which they can float their equity.

This national monopoly of the local exchange is highly profitable for the domestic banks. Small wonder then that the Continentals are committed to its perpetuation. But can it survive? Institutions, especially the pension funds, are rapidly becoming the dominant investors in Europe as they did in the U.S. 10 or 15 years ago. The local markets do not have the liquidity they need. And they are chafing under the high costs of the present monopolistic system. Perhaps the local exchanges will survive as the places where prices are officially registered, with the actual trading done off-market by transnational brokerage forms, especially for institutional customers.

Something like this is clearly what, judging by their recent actions, the Japanese, e.g., Nomura, are positioning themselves for. The large American and probably the major Swiss firms are acting on an even more radical assumption: the existing stock exchanges in Europe will become irrelevant, especially for large institutional investors, and will be replaced, in effect, by a trans-European over-the-counter discount market.

The future structure of commercial banking in Europe is another major area of uncertainty. Traditionally, competition among European banks was confined to one's own country. But a few years ago the three big Swiss banks shocked everyone by moving into Frankfurt in an open bid for domestic German business. Deutsche Bank, Europe's biggest, then moved aggressively into the domestic banking business in Italy. Is this going to be the trend of the future? Europe, after all – unlike the U.S. – has a long tradition of multibranch, nationwide banks with multiple headquarters. Or is the future prefigured by the recent Spanish development in which the country's four largest banks merged into two even larger but purely domestic banks? And what future role is there for that peculiarly European institution: the bank that is a giant in its own small country where it controls the bulk of industry, but which is at best 'supporting cast' on the world financial scene? Can banks like this survive in a unified common market? Will they have to ally themselves with a major-country bank, or perhaps even with a major U.S. or Japanese bank? Or will they themselves join in a transnational European 'middle-class' banking league?

Even more critical – and perhaps a good deal more risky – are the decisions facing middle-sized, privately held firms. Quantitatively, such firms are neither more numerous nor more important in Europe than they are in the U.S. But sociologically, psychologically, and politically they loom much larger almost everywhere. Few of them, most observers agree, are likely to survive unchanged the shift to a truly integrated Common Market.

But which of three possible strategies should a given firm

choose? The speciality-chemicals maker mentioned earlier is moving aggressively into Europe, marketing its products all over Europe, and even producing in several countries. But for this to be the right course, a firm needs distinctive products or distinctive technology and considerable marketing expertise. It also needs access to finance – and, in contrast to the U.S., that's limited for middle-sized European companies. Above all it needs managerial resources that the European family-owned firm still finds hard to attract and hold.

Another strategy is the one chosen by the five food brokers mentioned above: to create a European company by transnational merger or affiliation. But a large number of European privately held companies seem to opt for what is least likely to work: merger or affiliation of their own non-European, national firm with other non-European, national firms in their own country, thus creating national miniconglomerates. Others are giving up and trying to sell their businesses to large publicly held companies in their own countries.

What makes decisions doubly difficult and highly emotional is that they get entangled in the 'generation gap' in the European privately held firms. The people who built the businesses after World War II are reaching retirement and their whole experience has been within one domestic economy. The generation about to take over has, however, grown up as 'European'. Where the other people see European economic integration as a threat, the younger ones see it as an opportunity.

Altogether the most important decision a European company has to make – but also an American multinational operating in Europe – is whether the Common Market will be primarily a market of competing national economies or of competing European businesses.

To explain: Deutsche Bank sees the European financial market as a common market for competing individual banks. Indeed, Deutsche Bank has announced that it intends to become a factor in all major European countries. But industrial companies with which Deutsche Bank itself is most closely affiliated have made it equally clear that they foresee a different Europe in which very large but purely national enterprises compete against one another.

'Europe of Fatherlands'

French official policy similarly pushes French business toward what General de Gaulle once called a 'Europe of Fatherlands', that is, toward strictly French supercompanies. For the existing 'European companies' – the subsidiaries of the American multi-nationals first and foremost, but also the large European companies headquartered in small countries, such as Philips and Unilever in Holland, the Swiss pharmaceuticals giants, Sweden's Ericsson and Electrolux – a unified European economy transcend-ing national boundaries is the only thing that makes any sense at all; the only thing that can possibly work. And this is also how the newcomers, the Japanese and Koreans, see it. But while economically rational, it may not work politically – or only against tremendous opposition.

Almost certainly, the Europe of tomorrow will be both an economy of competing national economies and an economy of competing European businesses – in that respect it will look quite different from the 'common market' of the U.S. But which industry and which market will go which way? Of the two leading telecommunications manufacturers of Europe, one, the Germany company Siemens, expects European telephone markets to remain national; the other, Ericsson in Sweden, is equally convinced that such major buyers as the Bundespost in Germany and PTT in France will tomorrow buy 'European'. Can both be right? And will a large national retailer – Marks & Spencer in the U.K., for instance – buy 'European' tomorrow or will it continue to buy 'British'?

In a meeting of senior European executives I attended in London recently, the participants split 50–50 on this question. But they all agreed that any European business – and not only the big one – will have to make up its mind within a year or two to which of these two assumptions it entrusts its future.

[1988]

8

U.S.–Japan Trade
Needs a Reality Check

Trade negotiations with Japan are high on the agenda of the incoming administration. But they will produce only frustration unless the U.S. faces up to some unpopular realities.

(1) *The trade concessions the U.S. needs from Japan are not where most people seek them, including a good many people in the administration and Congress.* They are not in manufactured and agricultural products. Dismantling barriers to the entry of manufactured goods is unlikely to produce substantial sales. And if it did, the impact on U.S. employment and the balance of trade might even be negative, because Japan is by far the largest foreign buyer of American-brand products.

American goods have a share of the Japanese market that is about twice as much per capita than goods made by Japanese companies have of the American market. Japanese brands have leadership in the U.S. market in cars, consumer electronics, and cameras; U.S.-brand goods have leadership in Japan in computers and software, soft drinks, candy, analytical and clinical instruments, and pharmaceuticals.

However, most U.S.-brand goods sold in Japan are manufactured there rather than imported. They are made by subsidiaries of

U.S. companies – increasingly wholly owned rather than joint ventures – that tend to buy their machinery and tools from the U.S., thus creating high-value exports and well-paying American jobs. Displacing these Japanese-made U.S. brands – IBM computers, for instance, or Mars bars or Merck antibiotics – with exports from the U.S. is about the most that could be accomplished by the dismantling of barriers to entry of American products. It would mean neither more American jobs nor a lower trade deficit.

(2) *The major concern of American made policy vis-à-vis Japan must be the preservation of our farm exports.* Japan is by far the largest buyer of U.S. farm products and the only large buyer that pays full price and in cash. Yet there is not one American-grown product that Japan could not get elsewhere at the same, or lower, price. So far, it has been buying from the U.S. in order to protect its exports to America. But in the next few years Japan will be sorely tempted to use the bait of farm purchases in bargaining with the European Community – and the EC is desperate to find markets for its growing farm surpluses and more than willing to subsidize farm exports.

It makes sense for the U.S. to try to beat down Japanese barriers against American beef and feed – commodities in which the U.S. leads and for which there is substantial Japanese demand. But it is counterproductive to waste bargaining power on minor products, pineapples, for instance, or citrus fruit, and downright asinine to press for the entry of American rice. In fact, maintenance of Japan's ban on foreign rice and high domestic rice price is very much in America's interest. Japanese tastebuds much prefer rice to any other cereal. It is only the high rice price that induces the housewives in Tokyo to buy American wheat instead. Also, there is a surplus of domestic rice in Japan – the high price is the result of government monopoly.

(3) *But it does make sense to press Japan for concessions in services.* Japanese barriers to foreign entry are extremely high, whereas there are few barriers in the U.S. to Japanese entry into services (e.g., banking). Wherever Americans have been permitted to operate services in Japan, in foreign-exchange trading, fast food, bond underwriting, insurance, large-scale building-maintenance, or supplying temporary help – they have done well while substantially improving standards and quality. And there are large – but largely closed – opportunities in information, construction and transportation. However, services are rarely given much

attention in public opinion or in the press, and as a result are not given high priority by the government.

(4) *The method as well as the content of our trade policy vis-à-vis Japan needs refocusing.* The Japanese do not lead from strength, but from political weakness. The most highly protected areas of Japan's economy – retail distribution, farms, financial services – are antiquated, high-cost, and splintered, as protected industries always are. However, these sectors have even more political clout than their American counterparts – e.g., tobacco farmers and the handful of beet-sugar growers in Colorado. They supply the money for the increasingly greedy political parties – outsiders are getting a glimpse of this in the current Japanese stock scandal. Japanese civil servants have no love for foreigners – if only because they cannot easily control them.

However, they need outside pressure to force change on their own politically powerful interest groups. But they cannot 'negotiate', they must be 'coerced'; they must be able to plead 'We were raped'. And they cannot give in often – once, at most twice, a year.

The U.S. must think through its strategy rather than react to every complaint by an American industry. What is the *one* major economic concession we really want to attain from Japan this year? And what demands are we going to make for the sole purpose of abandoning them gracefully? How do we say 'no' to domestic American claimants whose demands can only weaken the U.S. bargaining position? And how do we prevent being used by the Japanese for their own purposes as they are now using the demand for access to the rice market both to whip up support for more government control and politically to justify cuts in their exorbitant rice subsidies (without the slightest intention, of course, of letting in American rice)?

(5) *Finally, the central problem for American trade policy the next few years is not going to be Japan; it will be the European Community.* We must prevent it from becoming a 'Fortress Europe'. Yet that is precisely what many European politicians and businessmen have in mind. They see in European economic unification the road to General de Gaulle's old objective of a Europe without the Americans.

There is pervasive fear of the Japanese in Europe; if allowed free entry, Japanese cars and Japanese consumer electronics would indeed have a larger share of the European market than they have of the American. But there is a danger that this fear will be manipulated to keep out American goods, services and investments. In fact, the way our trade relations with the European Economic Committee are settled in these next several years is bound to determine what our economic relations with Japan will be; for the new principles for international economic relations will evolve out of negotiations between the U.S. and Europe rather than out of negotiations between the U.S. and Japan.

Under 'reciprocity' – the current buzz-word in Europe – the U.S. would be in a strong position; our markets – for goods, services, investment – are on the whole quite a bit more open than those of many European countries. And if 'reciprocity' were established as the principle we also would have the strongest possible position for our relationship with Japan and the one most favourable to American economic interests and American economic beliefs.

[1989]

9

Japan's Great Postwar Weapon

'What makes Japan succeed?' is the hottest discussion topic today. But what few mention is Japan's cost of capital.

American and other Western companies pay between 10 percent and 15 percent for money, whether short-term borrowings, fixed debt, or equity. The large Japanese firm has been paying 5 percent at most. And a capital-cost advantage of 200 percent or 300 percent is almost unbeatable. Neither 'culture' nor 'structure' – the factors most often invoked to explain Japan's success – underlie Japan's low cost of capital. The American Occupation gave it to Japan, 40 years ago.

It's common knowledge that the Japanese savings rate is twice as high as the American, and is, indeed, the developed world's highest. But only a few historians note that before World War II Japan had one of the lowest savings rates among major countries. After Japan's defeat, this rate plunged even further and in fact became a dissavings rate, with inflation and violent labour strife rapidly eating up whatever savings had survived confiscatory taxation and destruction during the war.

With cities and factories largely reduced to rubble, the country needed massive capital investment – and there was no possibility to borrow abroad and no Marshall Plan. In this crisis the Americans brought in a Detroit banker, Joseph Dodge, as the Occupation's economic adviser. He decided that only a radical shift to an investment-driven economy could stave off disaster. He proposed a very sharp increase in income-tax rates even on fairly low incomes; to this day tax rates, especially marginal rates on large incomes, are a good bit higher in Japan than in the U.S. But he also proposed exempting from all taxes the interest earned on Postal Savings Bank deposits of up to three million yen per person.

The Experts Howled

In 1950, three million yen was equal to only a little more than $8,000. Yet in 1950 Japan that was an astronomical sum – 25 times the annual income of the average Japanese, and more than any but the top 2 percent of the population earned in a year.

All the experts howled: the Japanese because of the horrendous loss of tax revenue to an already deficit-wracked treasury; the Americans (especially Washington's 'liberal' economists and politicians) because of the horrendous giveaway to the rich. But Dodge succeeded in persuading a new, young Japanese Minister of Finance, Hayato Ikeda (10 years later to become prime minister) of the merits of his plan. Ikeda pushed it through a sceptical cabinet and an openly hostile Diet.

Inflation disappeared within weeks. Six months later the savings rate turned up and kept on climbing. But tax revenues also began to rise almost immediately. And when the tax-exempt accounts, having done their work, were finally scrapped in 1988, practically every Japanese – poor, middle-income, or affluent – had one. (Some had as many as 20; the limit of one account per person was ignored.) And the highest concentration of tax-exempt accounts was among fairly low-income earners.

These savings financed the explosive growth of the Japanese economy and the export drive. They explain why – almost unprecedented in economic history – a rapidly growing Japan has not had to borrow abroad. And, of course, these tax-free savings explain Japan's low-cost capital and the tremendous competitive edge it provided.

But that an investment-driven economy worked in Japan is not nearly as important as that America's and Britain's alternative – the consumption-driven economy – has not delivered what it promised: investment and low capital costs. Yet the consumption-driven economy still dominates economic theory and economic policy in both the U.S. and the U.K.

Despite their differences, Keynesians, monetarists, and supply-siders all accept a few basic Keynesian postulates: 'Over-saving' is an ever-present danger, causing underconsumption and depression. Saving should therefore not be encouraged and might even be penalized safely. If consumption drives the economy, the necessary and productive investment will take care of itself. Rising consumption will create demand for new and profitable production and productive capacity. It will act as the 'multiplier' for investment. Fostering and promoting consumption will thus automatically generate both rising incomes and high capital formation.

That there are serious flaws in these postulates was immediately noted by such eminent mid-1930s economists as Lionel Robbins at the London School of Economics and Joseph Schumpeter at Harvard.

No oversaving, they showed, had ever been documented. Nor is there the slightest evidence that, as John Maynard Keynes asserted, oversaving had caused the Great Depression. Worse, Keynes's own theory rules out the multiplier on which his consumption-driven economy depends. For at the heart of all of Keynes is the postulate that businessmen will invest only if they have 'confidence', which in Keynesian theory is a function of low interest rates and low costs of capital. To play down saving, let alone to discourage it, must drive up interest rates and thus undermine confidence.

The consumption-driven economy triumphed – though mainly in English-speaking countries – because it perfectly fitted the political mood of the postwar period. To penalize saving 'soaks the rich'. And to promote consumption 'spreads the wealth'. Politic-ally, Keynes himself was pretty much what we now call a 'neo-conservative' (then called a 'Liberal' with a capital L). He had nothing but biting contempt for Progressives and 'bleeding hearts'. Yet, in superb irony, the Progressives accepted his theories and gave them dominance. These theories bestowed legitimacy on their political agenda.

By now we know, however, that to promote saving does not favour the rich. Any country that has given a tax exemption or tax deferment to saving has had the same experience as Japan:

middle-and lower-income earners take the most advantage of these opportunities. This has, for instance, been the experience with whatever meagre tax deferments have been offered for saving in the U.S. (e.g., in individual retirement accounts or in Keogh plans).

We also know that a consumption-driven economy does not 'spread the wealth'. There is far more equality of income in investment-driven Japan than in consumption-driven America or Britain. In addition, though the Internal Revenue Service still refuses to accept this, tax revenues are higher within a few years when saving is favoured.

We have learned in the 40 years since Joseph Dodge that nothing works as well in a developed country as legalized tax-avoidance. His tax-exempt accounts in Japan paid laughably low interest – never more than 2 percent a year. Yet the Japanese could not get enough of them. The money savings in America's IRAs and in its Keogh Plans for the self-employed are often more nominal than real. Yet they are always highly popular. And as attorneys and accountants will attest, people rush into the most dubious 'tax shelters' just because they want to beat the tax collector.

The 'Incidence' of Taxation

We know, in other words, how to jack up America's dismal savings rate and how to bring down America's prohibitively high cost of capital. It is less a matter of the level than of the 'incidence' of taxation – which is economists' double-talk for a chance legally to avoid taxes. And we also know that Keynes was right when he said that high costs of capital destroy 'confidence' and inhibit invest-ment. Few investments will earn enough to repay capital cost of 15 percent – but many can easily turn 5 percent, which is what the Japanese pay.

There are indeed profound differences between Japan's society and the West, especially the U.S. But there is little or nothing that the U.S. and the West as a whole can do about whatever Japanese differences there are. We can, however, do quite a bit to get rid of, or at least to assuage, the enormous competitive disadvantage we suffer vis-à-vis the Japanese through our prohibitive cost of capital. It is not 'structural'; it is the result of an inadequate savings rate caused in the main by our clinging to the belief in the consumption-driven economy against our own experience and against all the evidence.

[1990]

10

Misinterpreting Japan and the Japanese

For 40 years I've been trying to explain to my American friends that they misinterpret Japan. I haven't made much progress. The first challenge is explaining what any Japanese civil servant understands perfectly well: despite the country's economic miracle since World War II, Japan has not had an economic policy; it has had a *social* policy.

When I first started to work with the Japanese government and Japanese businesses in the early 1950s, Japan was not only a war-ravaged country, but an incredibly fragile society. Half the people lived on the land, and there was an exceedingly high number of small shopkeepers and small factories with a few dozen employees and pre-World War I machinery.

The policy Japan adopted at that time was to avoid taking any social risks – to protect domestic society, especially domestic employment, and at the same time to push a few carefully groomed industries into export opportunities. Nobody then believed that Japanese exports would ever earn enough foreign currency to pay for the imported food and raw materials on which the island country depends.

Japan today remains the world's largest importer of food and commodities. But the basic social, demographic, and economic foundations of the past 40 years are quickly shifting. Today, of the tens of thousands of small shops in Japan, many are franchisees of large chains such as 7-Eleven and Kentucky Fried Chicken. Only about 5 percent of the population now makes its living as farmers.

The new largest single group, though not the majority yet, is people who did not even exist in 1954: educated, middle-class, salaried employees. They are up for grabs politically. In the last election they still voted for the Liberal Democrats, not because they have any use for them, but because the opposition is even less credible. For the next 10 to 20 years, the big political and economic challenge in Japan will be to find the new consensus. The need for policies to protect Japanese society is gone, and in fact those policies are becoming increasingly unpopular among consumers, as the new dominant groups do not feel any need to be protected. What is now needed is a truly *economic* policy.

Without understanding the fundamental changes that are re-shaping Japan, Americans cannot hope to make sense of the United States' much lamented trade deficit with that country – or know whether the Japanese indeed pose the economic threat to the United States that some people in Washington would have us believe.

For all the headlines about Japan's trade surplus, I do not know a single Japanese in a responsible government or academic position who believes in it. The export surplus is a mirage. It exists on paper, but nowhere else.

To be sure, a good many of our industries are lagging behind the Japanese. But the United States' trade deficit with Japan has almost nothing to do with manufacturing, great though Japan's own industrial prowess may be. The Japanese trade surplus is largely the result of low prices in the raw materials and food that Japan imports.

There has been a glut of petroleum for nearly a decade, to the delight of Japan, which imports all of its oil. In the developed nations, farm productivity has increased dramatically in the last 40 years. At the same time, food consumption is not going up. As people become affluent, they do not eat more; in fact, they buy magazines that tell them how to eat less.

The Japanese have also benefited because food and commodities, with their low prices, are traded in dollars. And since 1985 the dollar has been devalued – at times by as much as half – against the yen. As a result of these various factors, the Japanese pay little more than one-third of what might be considered the 'normal' value of the food and raw materials they import.

Yet from the Japanese point of view, if prices ever go up, Japan will have difficulty earning enough through foreign exchange to pay for these imports. And there is a very good chance that in the next few years – not forever, but for a while – world food prices will skyrocket. Where is the food going to come from to feed Eastern Europe, where the food shortage is already great and growing day by day?

As we feed the declining Soviet empire, the food surpluses of the free world will diminish over the next five years. And the Japanese, quite rightly, see the need for a policy that is based on maintaining their present export surplus. Maybe food prices will stay low. Maybe petroleum will stay affordable. But what if not? That is Japan's nagging fear.

At the risk of sounding totally absurd, I've always considered Japanese-American trade negotiations Punch-and-Judy shows. Anyone who thinks the Japanese do not buy foreign goods need only go into any Tokyo shop. You will see nothing but foreign brand names – they just happen to be made in Japan. Does anyone seriously think that I.B.M. is going to ship computers to Japan when I.B.M. Japan controls 40 percent of the Japanese market and is one of the most profitable parts of I.B.M.? Or that Coca-Cola is going to ship anything to Japan?

And so I've never seen that mythical great, untapped Japanese market. When I sit down with my sharp pencil and try to figure out how much more Japan is likely to buy – with its American trade surplus of $50 billion a year – I come up with a maximum of $5 billion.

We are so hypnotized by the trade surplus that we do not understand how dependent upon the United States Japan has become. In economic history, the point at which a nation's dependence on one market becomes economically and politically dangerous is somewhere around 25 percent. Japan has surpassed that point with the United States, which buys more than 40 percent of Japanese exports.

Now, if you have a $50 billion trade surplus, you may be able to take a small portion home in goods. But what do you do with the rest of the money – dump it in the ocean? You must invest.

Since the Japanese know that there is tremendous political risk in buying American real assets – movie companies, Manhattan landmarks and so on – United States Treasury bills are almost the only thing they can buy. And here, we have them over a barrel. Were they to pull out their money, as so many people seem to fear, there would be a run on the market and the dollar might go down to 100 to the yen, which penalizes only the Japanese.

We might not feel the effects at all, but the Japanese would lose a lot of dough. As the old saw goes, if you owe your bank $10,000, the bank owns you. If you owe the bank $1 million, you own the bank. In this sense, the United States owns Japan; or, at least, the Japanese are much more dependent upon this country than they would like to be.

Last year Sony's chairman, Akio Morita, and a former cabinet minister and nationalist politician, Shintaro Ishihara, irritated many Americans with a book published in Japan, *The Japan That Can Say No*. The premise was that Japan's supposed technological superiority has made the United States dependent on the Japanese.

One of the most publicized examples was that if Japan stopped shipping one particular microchip to this country, we would have to stop making a major missile. In fact, most of the microchips for this missile are made here, and it would take us about six weeks to get the rest, if the Japanese cut us off. We know how to make chips. It is a matter of price, not of technical capability.

The same politician, Shintaro Ishihara, recognized the danger of single-market dependence during the 1960s and said, in effect, that Japan needed an outrigger on the left side, to balance its canoe on the right. He is the man who began to beat the drum for Japanese investment in China, and it has been a total disaster – not for political, but for economic reasons.

Some of us tried to tell him that no underdeveloped country has ever been a satisfactory market for the goods of a developed one. The first country to learn this was Great Britain in respect to India in the nineteenth century. Ishihara did not want to hear it, but it has turned out to be true. Toyota, for example, shipped 6,032 vehicles to China last year; the company shipped more than twice that number each *week* to the United States.

In looking to Europe as another possible outlet, the Japanese see major obstacles. The industries in which the Japanese are strongest are the ones in which Europe has the most overcapacity and incredible overemployment. Not counting Eastern Europe, there are still almost a million people too many in the European steel industry. The automobile and consumer electronics industry also have far more capacity than demand for products. And so, in a period when the European market is rapidly integrating, the Japanese are viewed as a tremendous external threat.

How are the Japanese to integrate themselves into the world economy in which – because of domestic political changes and external forces – they can no longer pursue the strategies of the past 40 years? The need to protect society in Japan is gone, and is in fact meeting stiff resistance from Japanese importers. Pushing more exports to the West is no longer a viable option.

Is it necessary to try to form an East Asian bloc? And how does one do this with countries of such incredibly uneven social and economic development as, let's say, Japan and Thailand? And can it be done without the coastal cities of China? And is Southeast Asia likely to allow itself to become dependent on Japan, considering the chilling memories of the 1930s that are still very much alive in China, Korea, Indonesia and Thailand?

If China breaks up again into regions controlled by economic warlords, which cannot be ruled out, then we could see an East Asian bloc organized around Japan. It wouldn't be easy, in view of the tension between those two cultures and two peoples, but I think Ishihara's China card might nevertheless finally come into play. So long as there remains a unified Communist China, however, Japan must look westward.

A very drastic course would be for Japan to shift 180 degrees and become the leader of 'freer' trade – do not call it free trade; no such thing exists except in textbooks – and enlist the United States in trying to prevent European-imposed protectionism. Japanese society could adjust to that.

It would basically require Japan to forget 40 years in which the fundamental policy was to never take a social risk or expose protected industries to the risk of competition. If you are one of the major corporations such as Sony or Toshiba or Toyota that has proved its ability to compete in the world market, you may be willing to take such a risk; it may be the only way you can maintain access to the American market and gain access to Europe.

One thing you can count on with Japan: behind the policy of

'take it easy, one step at a time', there is furious, hard thinking going on. Nobody in the world is as good at making decisions as the Japanese.

[1990]

11

Help Latin America and Help Ourselves

Who needs Latin America? 'We don't,' most American business-men would say. But it is the wrong answer. Latin America, rather than Japan, holds the key to the U.S. trade deficit.

Whatever may be wrong with American industry – and many things are surely wrong – it is not 'lack of international competi-tiveness'. Since the overvaluation of the dollar was corrected nearly five years ago, U.S. industry has turned in a stellar performance, especially in exporting to Western Europe and Japan. A host of industrial exporters – South Korea, Brazil, Taiwan, Singapore – became bigger players in world trade. Yet the U.S. has regained the share of the world's manufactured-goods exports it held before the overvaluation – as large a share as the U.S. ever held except in the immediate post-World War II period.

Nor can the U.S. trade deficit be blamed on 'excessive imports'. Manufactured-goods imports account for a smaller share of America's GNP – 9 percent – than they do in any other developed country except Japan. And the Japanese are now 'out-sourcing' at such a furious rate that the import share of manufactured goods in Japan's GNP is likely to match the U.S. figure within four or five years.

What then explains the massive American trade deficit? Its main cause is the collapse of the world's food and raw materials economy in the past decade.

World's Largest Producer

The U.S. is the world's largest producer and exporter of agricultural and forest products, and about one-third of the trade deficit is directly traceable to this collapse in prices and demand. Another third or so is owing to the impact of the raw-materials depression on what traditionally was one of U.S. manufacturers' best foreign customers – Latin America. Indeed in most Latin American countries U.S. imports traditionally accounted for half or more of all manufactured-goods imports. (By the way, most of Japan's trade surplus is far less a result of industrial prowess than of the raw-materials depression; Japan – the world's largest raw-materials importer – is the main beneficiary.)

The trade deficit will not be eliminated by increasing exports of manufactured-goods to Western Europe and Japan. Indeed if Japan removed *all* restrictions to U.S. imports, U.S. exports would at most grow by $5 billion – as against a trade deficit with Japan of $50 billion. And the U.S. will be hard pressed to maintain current export volume with the developed world in the years ahead, when world manufacturing competition is bound to intensify.

We also cannot realistically expect food exports to bounce back. For a few short years ahead there may be sharply increased demand to assuage almost certain famine in the Soviet Bloc, but food relief on a massive scale can be maintained only for a few short years. Yet the U.S. trade deficit cannot continue indefinitely, and perhaps not even for many more years.

The interest payments on the debt due our suppliers already greatly exceed our capacity to earn foreign exchange to service them. While the foreign creditors can convert their dollar claims into U.S. assets – that is, buy American businesses and real estate – and most economists consider this to be harmless and perhaps beneficial, 'buying America' clearly will not be tolerated long politically.

There are, in effect, only two ways to cut the trade deficit. In the wrong but traditional way, a very sharp recession cuts domestic consumption by 10 percent or so. The alternative: a revival of Latin America as a customer for U.S. manufactured goods.

It would be a great deal easier to turn around Latin America than to turn around Eastern Europe, the region on which most attention is focused now. Latin America is home to 300 million people – almost as many as in the Soviet bloc. In sharp contrast to the Soviet bloc, Latin America comfortably feeds itself and has a substantial surplus of both food and industrial raw materials. In the larger countries there is an excellent supply of well-trained engineers, entrepreneurs, accountants, economists and lawyers. And they did not have to become moral eunuchs to get an education or to get and hold a decent job.

Nor do the educated people of Latin America have to be 'reeducated' to function in a free economy. Until the raw-materials depression hit, Latin Americans worked effectively in a market economy and participated in rapid economic growth. And there is enormous pent-up demand for goods of all kinds.

Finally, Latin America, unlike the Soviet Bloc, has an adequate supply of capital. Indeed, Latin America probably has three times as much capital – or more – than it has foreign debt. There is only one thing wrong with it: It is not in Latin America. It has been driven out systematically – and often purposefully – by government policy.

But if the money that is now in Miami and New York, Zurich and Geneva – but also in the mattresses of virtually all but the poorest families in Latin America – could be enticed into productive investment at home, every Latin American nation, save perhaps the smallest and poorest, would have all the capital it needed for rapid economic growth. And the holders of Latin America's capital are willing, and indeed eager, to invest their money at home if only their governments were to stop expropriating savings and investment through inflation and punitive taxation, and were to stop discouraging productive investment through the granting of monopolies to military and governmental enterprise. As a result of these policies, even the shoeshine boys in Buenos Aires and Sao Paulo demand to be paid in dollars.

What needs to be done is clear enough: Stop inflation by turning off the spigot of government spending; dismantle the grossly overstaffed and unproductive monopolies owned by the government or the military (especially in Brazil and Argentina) or by the government's political cronies and the ministers' relatives (especially in Mexico); cut excessive nominal tax rates that discourage honest enterprise, and decrease actual tax collection.

That these things can be done, and without political catastrophe, has been shown by two of the smaller countries: Chile under Augusto Pinochet's dictatorship, and (reasonably) democratic Bolivia. And there is now widespread demand throughout the region for a return to sanity.

Mexico has taken some fairly big steps in the right direction, especially in dismantling protection for governmental monopoly industries; the immediate results have been most impressive (including a more than two-fold increase in Mexico's purchases from the U.S.). The first priority of the new government inaugurated in Brazil last week is to sell more than a hundred unproductive, overstaffed and loss-making government enterprises. And the albatross of the foreign debt that the Latin American countries incurred when the raw-materials economy collapsed has largely been removed – it has been written down in all but legal fiction.

Latin America's turnaround is, in other words, no longer a matter of economics, but largely of the political will. It requires, above all, the backbone not to cave in – as did the governments of both Argentina and Brazil in both 1988 and 1989 – at the first protest by a powerful group such as the labour unions or the army. The things that need to be done will at first be painful and unpopular. But within a year they will begin to produce results and to enjoy wide popular support.

But the U.S., too, has a crucial role to play: to stop the well-meaning but destructive policies it has pursued for almost 40 years. Maybe Latin America needs fairly small short-term loans to help assuage the pains of the transition. But the favourite 'aid' policies of the past four decades – government-to-government aid; military aid; World Bank loans – must not be continued. They are largely to blame for the current crisis of the continent.

Antientrepreneur Bias

These policies encouraged government spending. They paid for bloated government bureaucracies and for military establishments that are, in many countries, four or five times as large proportionately as that of the U.S. – and without any foreign threat. They diverted capital from productive investment into 'prestige projects' – steel mills, for instance – without domestic markets that, in their own way, were not too different from the monstrosities of

Stalinist planning. Above all, these policies all had a strong antibusiness and antientrepreneur bias. To continue them would be like pushing drink on an alcoholic.

What Latin America needs from the U.S. is trade, not aid. It needs political support for policies that reward enterprise and discourage monopolies and protectionism, policies that stress savings rather than spending, and economic growth rather than growth of the bureaucracy.

And these policies also are needed precisely because the U.S. needs Latin America.

[1990]

12

Mexico's Ace in the Hole: The Maquiladora

Few U.S. businessmen would name Mexico if asked who America's main trading partners are. Yet last year it ranked number three, behind Canada and Japan. Every day the Mexican economy is becoming more closely integrated with that of the U.S. And the Mexican government, with strong popular support, has decided to speed up this process and to make it irreversible. It has proposed a U.S.-Mexico free-trade agreement that would create a North American Economic Community of Canada, the U.S. and Mexico – more populous than the European Economic Community and not too far behind the EEC in output and gross national product.

This is as startling a policy reversal as anything that has occurred in the Soviet Union and in Eastern Europe. For 130 years, Mexico had one overriding political objective – to put the greatest possible distance between itself and those big, restless, pushy gringos up north. 'If only,' an old Mexican saying goes, 'the Rio Grande were as wide and as deep as the Atlantic Ocean.' Benito Juarez, the president who first created a unified Mexico, tried, at the time of the U.S.Civil War, to keep out the gringos by building a nation of self-contained Indian peasant-farmers. His successor, Porfirio

Diaz, hoped to accomplish the same objective by bringing in European bankers and industrialists as a countervailing force.

Failed Policies

Following Diaz's ouster, and after 20 years of bloody civil wars, the PRI (Institutional Revolutionary Party) came to power in the early 1930s – it is still ruling. It immediately set to work to create an economically isolated Mexico of self-sustained industries – government-controlled if not government-owned – that were meant to produce for a tightly protected domestic market alone.

Each of these policies ended in failure. Each made Mexico poorer and even more dependent on the U.S. – in food, money and banking, machinery, technology. So even the PRI finally had to accept that if you can't lick 'em you join 'em.

But this 180-degree turn would not have been possible but for Mexico's one economic success: the *maquiladoras*, or industrial parks, that, started only 25 years ago, now crowd the border with the U.S., from Tijuana on the Pacific to Reynosa and Matamoros where the Rio Grande flows into the Gulf of Mexico.

Mexico, until this year, banned or severely restricted ownership of Mexican industries by foreigners. But foreigners can own 100 per cent of a *maquila* – the plant in a maquiladora. Those importing industrial goods into Mexico pay exorbitant duties and face unremitting bureaucratic harassment. But parts and supplies for a maquila are waved through at the border and enter Mexico duty-free. In turn, the maquila's products when exported to the U.S. are subject to American duty only on the value added in Mexico.

Practically all new jobs in Mexico created in the past decade are in maquiladoras; they now employ almost 500,000. Maquiladoras account for four-fifths of the country's manufactured exports and for two-fifths of its total exports to its biggest customer, the U.S. They provide the bulk of Mexico's foreign-exchange earnings.

Where at first maquilas mostly turned out simple parts, they increasingly turn out finished products. The maquilas in Ciudad Juarez, for instance – across the river from El Paso, Texas – will assemble nine million TV sets this year. The maquiladoras' workers are now the most highly skilled labour in Mexico. And the maquiladoras have also trained large numbers of Mexican technicians, engineers, accountants and middle managers. The maquiladoras are the main – perhaps the only – reason Mexico, alone among Latin American countries, has experienced massive recovery after the collapse of its currency, trade and economy nine years ago.

They have also greatly benefited the U.S. Without them many small and medium-sized U.S. firms would have been driven out of business by foreign low-wage competition. Having their unskilled jobs done just across the border enabled these companies to preserve in the U.S. the jobs of their skilled and knowledgeable workers. And but for the maquiladoras, the 500,000 Mexicans they pay – and the 2.5 million to three million directly dependent on these pay cheques – might all be north of the border as illegal immigrants.

Yet the maquiladora has been treated as Mexico's ugly duckling rather than its swan. That it is unpopular in Mexico City is understandable. It flagrantly contradicts everything the Mexican intellectual holds sacred: his belief in statism and his deeply ingrained suspicion of the *yanqui*. But what is surprising is that the maquiladora has gone almost unnoticed in the U.S. And no one in the U.S. and Mexico seems ever to have wondered what explains the maquiladora's startling success.

Industrial parks were by no means new when the Mexicans first changed their laws to permit them. They go back 200 years, and so do the laws under which they operate everywhere including Mexico. In fact, industrial parks can be found all over the globe. But none save the Mexican maquiladora has been nearly as successful or as important to its country's economy.

This is because the maquiladora represents a seemingly small but crucial management innovation. It does what all industrial parks do: build the plant to the client's specifications and build and maintain physical facilities, such as roads, sewers, and power lines. But the maquiladora is a comanager too. It recruits, trains, and pays all the Mexicans in the work force – including supervisors, engineers, accountants, and, often, middle managers. It manages the maquila's relationships with the local community, with local governments, with the tax collector and so on. In the maquiladora the management job is split in two. The foreigner runs the business part: design, process, technology, quality, pricing, and marketing. The maquiladora runs the social tasks.

The big multinational may not need the maquiladora, though some very large ones use it to supply the U.S. market – GE, Sony,

Matsushita, and Hitachi, for example. But for a small or medium-sized firm from abroad the maquiladora may be the only way in which it can do business in a different culture.

And the maquiladora promises to give Mexico the advantage of foreign investment, foreign technology, access to foreign markets, and competitive prices at home, while cushioning Mexican culture from foreign values and ways. (Indeed the traditional policy of keeping out the gringo was based far more on fear of being overwhelmed by U.S. culture than on fear of U.S. economic domination.) In a world in which economic growth depends increasingly on the ability to transfer modern technology and modern management to countries of different traditions and cultures, the maquiladora's management innovation may be crucial.

It's not going to be all roses, of course. In fact, its very success is already making the traditional maquiladora obsolete. The border cities have become badly overcrowded and are outgrowing their supply of clean air and water, schools and hospitals, roads and sewers. Maquiladoras can no longer expand much along the border. But the Mexican government has already changed the laws so that maquiladoras can now be established in the country's interior. The biggest plant operating under maquiladora rules is now located some 175 miles south of the border, in Hermosillo: a brand-new Ford Motor Co. plant making the Escort model.

Maquilas had been allowed to produce only for the U.S. market. But Mexico is too big to rely entirely on export-led growth; it needs to develop its home market. The law has now been changed – despite strenuous opposition from the government-controlled companies that used to enjoy a domestic monopoly – to allow maquilas to sell everywhere, including the home market.

Of course, Mexico cannot grow if *totally* dependent on the foreign investment that the maquilas represent. It has to be able to bring back the millions of dollars in Mexican capital that have fled the country during the decades of misgovernment.

The present Mexican administration has moved further than any other Latin American government toward restoring investor confidence – by privatizing, by freeing markets, by removing the most restrictive controls on foreign exchange. And opening the country through a free-trade agreement with the U.S. might make Mexico the fastest-growing economy in the Western Hemisphere and one of the fastest-growing anywhere. But it will take a good

deal of convincing before Mexicans in large numbers will bring
their money back from Switzerland and Miami.

Unresolved Cleavage

The most serious problems for Mexico are, however, not economic
but political and social. While there is a great deal of support for
the government policy now, there may be growing resistance in the
future – from an entrenched bureaucracy, from dictatorial and
corrupt labour unions, from traditional manufacturers, from the
long tradition of anti-Americanism among Mexico's intellectuals.
There is still the unresolved cleavage between the northern two-
thirds of Mexicans who, while poor, are increasingly a part of
'North America' and the one-third in the South who are 'Central
America', with a great many people – a full third in some parts –
not even knowing Spanish yet and still speaking their own Indian
languages.

And there is the huge problem of Mexico's political transition.
After 60 years, the PRI monopoly on power – combining secretive
and near-dictatorial one-party rule with almost unlimited individual and intellectual freedom – is crumbling fast. It no longer has
the support of its own children: the educated middle and professional classes. But the transition to a new political integration has
not even begun, and the present policy of freeing the Mexican
economy and of integrating it with North America would be the
first victim of a serious political upheaval.

But if the country makes it, a good deal of the credit will have to
be given to the ugly duckling that no one loves: the management
innovation of the maquiladora.

[1990]

Part II

PEOPLE

13

The New Productivity Challenge

I

The productivity of the newly dominant groups in the work force, knowledge workers and service workers, will be the biggest and toughest challenge facing managers in the developed countries for decades to come. And serious work on this daunting task has only begun.

Productivity in making and moving things – in manufacturing, farming, mining, construction, and transportation – has increased at an annual rate of 3 to 4 percent compound for the last 125 years – for a 45-fold expansion in overall productivity in the developed countries. On this productivity explosion rests all the increases in these countries in both the standard of living and the quality of life. It provided the vast increase in disposable incomes and purchasing power. But between a third and a half of its fruits were taken in the form of leisure – something known only to aristocrats or to the idle rich before 1914, when everybody else worked at least 3,000 hours a year. (Now even the Japanese work no more than 2,000 hours a year, Americans around 1,800, West Germans 1,650.) The productivity explosion also paid for the 10-fold expansion of education and for the even greater expansion of health care. Productivity has become 'the wealth of nations'.

Rising productivity was something so totally unprecedented that there was no term for it in any language. For Karl Marx – as for all nineteenth-century economists – it was axiomatic that worker output could be increased only by working harder or longer – all of Marx is based on this belief. But though Frederic Winslow Taylor (1856–1915) disproved the axiom by starting to work on productivity in the early 1880s – his first substantial results came in 1883, the very year Marx died – he himself never knew the term. It did not come into general use until World War II – and then at first only in the U.S. The 1950 edition of the most authoritative English dictionary, the *Concise Oxford*, did not yet list *productivity* in its present meaning. By now it is commonplace that productivity is the true competitive advantage.

The productivity explosion was arguably the most important social event of the past hundred years, and one that had no precedent in history. There have always been rich people and poor people. But as recently as 1850 the poor in China were not measurably worse off than those in the slums of London or Glasgow. And the average income in the richest country of 1910 was at most three times the average income of the then poorest countries – now it is twenty to forty times as large, even without counting leisure, education, or health care. Before the productivity explosion it took at least fifty years for a country to become 'developed'. South Korea – as late as 1955 one of the world's truly 'backward' countries – did it in twenty years. This radical reversal of what has been the norm since time immemorial is in its entirety the result of the productivity revolution that started in the U.S. around 1870 or 1880.

Productivity in making and moving things is still going up at the same annual rate. It is going up – contrary to popular belief – fully as much in the U.S. as in Japan or West Germany. Indeed, the current productivity increase in U.S. farming – 4½ to 5 percent a year – is far and away the biggest increase recorded anywhere at any time. And the U.S. productivity increase in manufacturing during the '80s – 3.9 percent a year – was in absolute terms actually larger than the corresponding annual increases in Japanese and German manufacturing, for the U.S. base is still quite a bit higher.

But in the developed countries the productivity revolution is over. There are simply not enough people employed making and moving things for their productivity to be decisive. They now account for no more than a fifth of the work force in a developed economy – only thirty years ago they were still a near-majority. And the productivity of the people who do make the difference – knowledge workers and service workers – is not going up. In some areas it is actually going down. Salespeople in the department stores of all developed countries now sell, adjusted for inflation, no more than two thirds of what they sold in 1929. And few people would argue, I submit, that the teacher of 1991 is more productive than the teacher of 1901.

Knowledge workers and service workers range from research scientist and cardiac surgeon through draughtsman and store manager to sixteen-year-olds who work as car hops in the fast-food drive-in for a few Saturday afternoon hours. They even include large numbers of people who actually work as machine operators – washing dishes in a restaurant, polishing floors in a hospital, pushing computer keys in a claims-settling department of an insurance company. Yet knowledge workers and service workers, for all their diversity, are remarkably alike in what *does not work* in raising productivity. But there are also important similarities in what *does work* for these workers, no matter how much they might otherwise differ in knowledge, skill responsibility, social status, and pay.

II

The first thing we have learned – and it came as a rude shock – is that capital cannot be substituted for labour (i.e., for people) in knowledge and service work. Nor does new technology by itself generate higher productivity in such work. In making and moving things, capital and technology are *factors of production*, to use the economist's term. In knowledge and service work, they are *tools of production*. Whether they help productivity or harm it depends on what people do with them, on the purpose to which they are being put, for instance, or on the skill of the user. Thirty years ago we were sure that the computer would result in a massive reduction in clerical and office forces. The investment in data-processing equipment now rivals that in materials-processing technology – that is, in conventional machinery – with the great bulk of it in services. Yet office and clerical forces have grown at a much faster rate since the introduction of information technology than ever before. And there has been virtually no increase in the productivity of service work.

The most telling example are hospitals. When I first began to work with them – in the late 1940s – they were entirely labour-intensive, with little capital investment except in bricks, mortar, and beds. A good many perfectly respectable hospitals then had not yet invested in available and fairly old technologies; they had neither X-ray department nor clinical laboratory nor physical therapy. Today's hospitals are the most capital-intensive facilities around, with enormous sums invested in ultra sound, body scanners, nuclear magnetic imagers, blood and tissue analysers, clean rooms, and a dozen more new technologies. Each of these brought with it the need for additional and expensive people without reducing by a single person the hospital's existing staff. In fact, the worldwide escalation of health-care costs is the result, in large measure, of the hospital's having become an economic monstrosity. Being both highly labour-intensive and highly capital-intensive, it is, by any economist's definition, simply not viable economically. But the hospital has at least significantly increased its performance capacity. In other areas of knowledge or service work there are only higher costs, more investment, and more people.

Only massive increases in hospital productivity can stem the health-care cost explosion. And these increases can only come from 'Working Smarter'.

Neither economist nor technologist gives star billing to Working Smarter as the key to the productivity explosion; the former features capital investment, the latter, technology. But Working Smarter, whether called *scientific management, industrial engineering, human relations, efficiency engineering,* or *task study* (the modest term Frederic W. Taylor himself favoured) – has been the main force behind the productivity explosion. Capital invest-ment and technology were just as copious in the then developed countries in the first hundred years of the Industrial Revolution – i.e., in the century before Taylor – as they have been in the century since. But only when Working Smarter began to have an impact did productivity in making and moving things take off on its meteoric rise. Still, in making and moving things Working Smarter is but one key to increased productivity. In knowledge and service work it is *the* key.

Working Smarter means, however, very different things in knowledge and service work from what it means in making and moving things.

III

When Frederic Taylor started what later became Scientific Management by studying the shovelling of sand, it never occurred to him to ask: '*What* is the task? *Why* do it?' All he asked was '*How* is it done?' Almost fifty years later, Harvard's Elton Mayo (1880–1949) set out to demolish Scientific Management and to replace it with what later came to be called Human Relations. But, like Taylor, he never asked, '*What* is the task? *Why* do it?' In his famous experiments at the Hawthorne Works of Western Electric, he only asked, '*How* can wiring telephone equipment best be done?' In making and moving things the task is always taken for granted.

But the first question in increasing productivity in knowledge and service work has to be: *What* is the task? *What* do we try to accomplish? *Why* do it at all? The easiest – but perhaps also the greatest – increases in productivity in such work come from redefining the task, and especially from eliminating what needs not to be done.

The oldest example is still the best one – mail-order processing at the early Sears, Roebuck. Between 1906 and 1908 Sears eliminated the time-consuming counting of money in incoming mail orders. In those days there was neither paper money nor cheques but only coins. Hence, the money envelopes in the incoming order were weighed automatically: if the weight tallied with the amount of the order within fairly narrow limits, the envelopes were not even opened. Similarly, Sears eliminated the even more time-consuming detailed recording of each incoming order. It scheduled order handling and shipping according to the weight of the incoming mail, assuming forty orders for each pound of mail.

These two steps increased the productivity of the entire mail-order operation ten-fold within two years.*

A major insurance company has recently increased the productivity of claims settlements about five-fold – from an average of fifteen minutes to three minutes per claim – by eliminating detailed checking for all but claims for very large sums. Instead of verifying thirty items – as had always been done – only five are being checked now: whether the policy is still in force; matching its face amount with the amount of the claim; matching the name of the policy holder with the name on the death certificate; matching the name of the beneficiary on the policy with the name of the claimant. What led to this productivity increase was asking the question: 'What is the task?' And then the answer came fairly easily: 'It's to pay death claims as cheaply and as fast as possible' – and all that is now needed to control the process is to work through a small sample, that is, through every fiftieth claim, the traditional way.

A few hospitals have eliminated most of the laborious and expensive admissions processes. They now admit all patients the way they used to admit emergency patients who are brought in unconscious or bleeding and unable to fill out lengthy forms. They asked, 'What is the task?' – and the answer was to identify the patient's name, sex, age, address, and how to bill. This information is found, however, on the insurance identification practically all patients carry.

Another example: a well-known private college has been able to cut its financial-aid staff from eleven full-time clerks to one or two people who work in financial aid for only a few weeks a year. Like other institutions of its kind, the college admits qualified applicants without regard to their ability to pay, with the financial-aid office then determining what tuition reduction an applicant can be given. This was done – and in most colleges is still being done – by laboriously working through a long and detailed form submitted by each applicant. But for 95 out of each 100 applicants financial aid is actually determined by very few factors. Being told the family income; the value of the family home; what, if any, additional sources of income there are – e.g., from a trust fund; and whether there are siblings presently paying college tuition, the computer

*Boris Emmet and John E. Jeucks. *Catalogues and Counters: A History of Sears, Roebuck* (University of Chicago Press, 1950)

figures out in a few seconds how much financial aid will be offered. The two part-timers are needed only to winnow out the five percent of unusual cases – the applicant who is a star athlete or a National Scholarship winner – which are then easily dealt with by the dean and a faculty committee in a few afternoon sessions.

These are all examples of service work. In knowledge work, however, defining the task and getting rid of what needs not be done are even more necessary and produce even greater results.

I know one significant example: the way a major multinational company redefined its strategic planning. For many years a planning staff of forty-five brilliant people carefully prepared 'strategic scenarios' down to minute details. It was first-class work, and stimulating reading, everybody admitted. But it had minimum operational impact. A new CEO asked, 'What is the task?' His answer: 'It isn't to predict the future. It is to give our businesses direction and goals and the strategy to attain these goals.' It took four years of hard work and several false starts. But now the planning people – still about the same number – work through only three questions for each of the company's businesses: What market standing does it need to maintain leadership? What innovative performance does it need to support the needed market standing? What rate of return is the minimum needed to earn the cost of capital? And then the planning people together with the operating executives in each business work out broad strategy guidelines to attain these goals under different assumptions regarding economic conditions. The results are far simpler and far less pretentious than the old-style plans were, and far less elegant. But they have become the 'flight plans' that guide the company's businesses and its senior executives.

Except for this company I have not heard, however, of any case where the questions *What* is the task? and *Why* do it? have so far been asked in respect to knowledge work.

IV

In making and moving things people do one task at a time. Taylor's labourer shovelled sand; he did not also stoke the furnace. Mayo's wiring-room women soldered, they did not also test finished telephones on the side. The Iowa farmer planting corn does not get off his tractor between rows to attend a meeting. Concentration is not unknown in knowledge and service work. The surgeon does not take telephone calls in the operating room; nor should the lawyer while in consultation with a client. But in organizations – and that's where most knowledge and service people work – there is growing splintering. The people at the very top can sometimes concentrate themselves, though far too few even try. But the people who actually do most of the knowledge and service work in organizations – engineers, teachers, salespeople, nurses, middle managers in general – carry a steadily growing load of busy work, additional activities that contribute little or no value and that have little or nothing to do with what these people are qualified and paid for.

The worst case may be the nurse in the American hospital. We hear a great deal about the shortage of nurses. But how could we possibly have one? The number of graduating nurses entering the profession has gone up steadily for a good many years. At the same time the number of bed patients has been going down sharply. The explanation of the paradox: nurses now spend only half their time doing what they have learned and are being paid for – that is, nursing. The other half of their shift is taken by activities that do not require the nurse's skill and knowledge, add neither health-care nor economic value, and have little or nothing to do with patient care and patient well-being – primarily, of course, the ever swelling avalanche of paperwork for Medicare, Medicaid, insurers, the billing office, and the prevention of malpractice suits.

The situation in higher education is not much different. Every study reports that faculty in colleges and universities spend steadily increasing hours in committee meetings rather than in the class-room, in advising students, or in research. But few of these committees would ever be missed. And they would do a better job and in less time if they had three instead of seven members.

Salespeople are just as splintered. In the department store they now spend so much time serving the computer that they have little time serving the customer – the main reason, perhaps, for the steady decline in their productivity as producers of sales and revenues. Field sales representatives spend up to one third of their time filling out reports of all kinds rather than calling on customers. And engineers sit through meeting after meeting when they should be busy at their work stations.

This is not job enrichment; it is job impoverishment. It destroys productivity. It saps motivation and morale. Nurses, every attitude survey shows, bitterly resent not being allowed to do what they went into nursing for and are trained to do – to give patient care at the patient bed. They also – understandably – feel that they are grossly underpaid for what they are capable of doing while the hospital administrator – equally understandably – feels that they are grossly overpaid for the unskilled clerical work they are actually doing.

The cure is fairly easy, as a rule. A few hospitals have taken the paperwork out of the nurses' job and given it to a floor clerk who also answers the telephone calls from friends and relatives of patients and arranges the flowers they send in. All of a sudden, these hospitals had a surplus of nurses. The level of patient care and the hours nurses devote to it went up sharply. Yet the hospitals could cut the number of nurses needed by a quarter or a third, and could thus raise nurses' salaries without incurring a higher nursing payroll.

To do this requires that we ask in respect to every knowledge and service job: 'What do we pay for?' 'What value is this job supposed to add?' The answer is not always obvious or uncontroversial. One department store that raised the question in respect to its salespeople on the floor answered: 'Sales.' Another one in the same metropolitan area and with pretty much the same kind of clientele answered: 'Customer service.' Each answer led to a different restructuring of the jobs on the sales floor. But each store achieved, and fairly fast, substantial increases in the revenues generated by each salesperson and each department, that is, in both productivity and profitability.

V

For all their tremendous worldwide impacts Frederic Taylor and Scientific Management have had a bad press, especially in academia. One reason, perhaps the main one, is the unrelenting campaign America's labour unions waged against both in the early years of this century. The unions actually succeeded in banning every kind of work study in army arsenals and naval shipyards, where in those years practically all defence production was done in this country.

The unions of 1911 did not oppose Taylor because they thought him pro-management or anti-labour (he was neither). His unforgivable sin was his assertion that there is no such thing as skill in making and moving things. All such work, Taylor asserted, was the same. All could be analysed step by step as a series of unskilled operations that then could be put together into any kind of job. Anyone willing to learn these operations would be a 'first-class man', deserving 'first-class pay'. He could do the most highly skilled work and do it to perfection.

But the unions of Taylor's time – and especially the highly respected and extremely powerful unions in arsenals and shipyards – were craft monopolies. Their power base was their control of an apprenticeship of five or seven years to which, as a rule, only relatives of members were admitted. They considered their craft a 'mystery', the secrets of which no member was allowed to divulge. The skilled workers in the arsenals and navy yards in particular were paid extremely well – more than most physicians of those times and triple what Taylor's 'first-class man' could then expect to get. No wonder that Taylor's denial of the mystery of craft and skill infuriated these 'aristocrats of labour' as subversion and pestilential heresy.

Most contemporaries, eighty years ago, agreed with the unions. Even thirty years later the belief in the mystery of craft and skill persisted, and also in the long years of apprenticeship needed to acquire either. Hitler, for instance, was convinced that it would take the U.S. at least five years to train optical craftsmen, and modern war requires precision optics. It would therefore take many years, Hitler was sure, before America could field an effective army and air force in Europe – the conviction that made him declare war on America when Japan attacked Pearl Harbor.

We now know that Taylor was right. The U.S. did indeed have almost no optical craftsmen in 1941. And modern war does indeed require precision optics, and in large quantities. But by applying Taylor's Scientific Management the U.S. trained in a few months semi-skilled workers to turn out more highly advanced optics than the Germans with their craftsmen ever did, and on the assembly line to boot. And by that time Taylor's first-class men with their increased productivity also made a great deal more money than any craftsman of 1911 could ever have dreamed of.

Eventually knowledge work and service work may turn out to be like work making and moving things – that is, 'just work', to use an old Scientific Management slogan. At least this is the position of the more radical proponents of Artificial Intelligence, Taylor's true children or grandchildren. But for the time being, knowledge and service jobs must not be treated as just work. They cannot be assumed to be homogeneous. They must be treated as falling into a number of distinct categories – probably three. Each requires different analysis and different organization. In making and moving things the focus in increasing productivity is on *work*. In knowledge and service work it has to be on *performance*.

To be specific: For some jobs in knowledge and service work performance means quality. One example is the research lab, in which quantity – that is, the number of results – is quite secondary to their quality. One new drug generating annual sales of $500 million and dominating the market for a decade, is infinitely more valuable than twenty 'me-too' drugs each with annual sales of twenty or thirty million. The same holds for basic policy or for strategic decisions. But it also applies to much less grandiose work – the physician's diagnosis, for instance, or packaging design, or to editing a magazine.

Then there is a wide range of knowledge and service jobs in which quality and quantity together constitute performance. The salesperson's performance on the department-store floor is one example. A 'satisfied customer' is a qualitative statement, and indeed not so easy to define. But it is as important as the amounts on the sales tickets, or the quantity of output. In architectural design quality largely defines performance. In the draughtsman's work quality is an integral part of performance. But so is quantity. And the same applies to the engineer; to the sales rep in the local stockbroker's office; to the medical technologist; to the branch manager of the local bank; to the reporter, to the nurse; to the claims adjuster for the automotive insurer – in fact, to a vast range of knowledge and service jobs. Performance in them is always both, quantity and quality. To increase productivity in these jobs therefore always requires work on both.

Finally, there are a good many jobs – filing, handling death claims in the life insurance office, making beds in the hospital – in which performance is similar to performance in making and moving things. Quality is a condition and a restraint. It is external rather than in itself performance. It has to be built into the process. But once this has been done, performance is largely defined by quantity – e.g., the number of minutes it takes to make a hospital bed the prescribed way. These jobs are, in effect, 'production jobs' even though they do not result in making and moving things.

Thus increasing productivity in knowledge and service work requires thinking through into which category of performance a given job belongs. Only then do we know what we should be working on. Only then can we decide what needs to be analysed, what needs to be improved, what needs to be changed. For only then do we know what productivity means in a specific knowledge or service job.

VI

There is more to increasing productivity in knowledge work and service work than defining the task, concentrating on the task, and defining performance. We do not yet know how to analyse the process in jobs in which performance predominantly means quality. We need to ask instead, 'What works?' For jobs in which performance means both quality and quantity, we need to do both: ask what works and analyse the process step by step and operation by operation. In production work we need to define the quality standards and build them into the process, but the actual productivity improvement then comes through fairly conventional industrial engineering, that is, through task analysis followed by putting together the individual simple operations into a complete 'job'.

But the three steps outlined above will by themselves produce substantial productivity increases – perhaps most of what can be attained at any one time. They need to be worked through again and again – maybe every three or five years, and certainly whenever we change work or its organization. But then, according to all the experience we have, the resulting productivity increases will equal, if not exceed, whatever Industrial Engineering, Scientific Management, or Human Relations ever achieved in making and moving things. In other words, they should by themselves give us the 'productivity revolution' we need in knowledge and service work.

But on one condition only: that we actually apply what we have learned since World War II about increasing productivity in making and moving things: the work has to be done in partnership with the people who hold the knowledge and service jobs, the people who are to become more productive. The goal has to be to build responsibility for productivity and performance into every knowledge and service job regardless of level, difficulty, or skill.

Frederic Taylor has often been criticized for never once asking the workers whose jobs he studied; he told them. Nor did Elton

Mayo ever ask – he also told them. But there is also no record of Sigmund Freud's ever asking patients what they thought might be their problem. Neither Marx nor Lenin ever thought of asking the masses. And it did not occur to any High Command in World War I or World War II to ask junior officers or enlisted men in the front lines about weapons, uniforms, or even food (in the American armed forces this became the custom only during Vietnam). Taylor simply shared the belief of his age in the wisdom of the expert. He thought both workers and managers to be 'dumb oxen'. Mayo, forty years later, had high respect for managers, but workers, he thought, were 'immature' and 'maladjusted' and needed the expert guidance of the psychologist.

When World War II came, however, we had no choice; we had to ask the workers. In the plants we had neither engineers nor psychologists nor foremen – they were all in uniform. And when we asked the workers, we found – to our immense surprise, as I still recollect – that the workers were neither dumb oxen nor immature and maladjusted. They knew a great deal about the work they were doing, its logic and rhythm, the tools, the quality and so on. Asking them was the way to get started on productivity and quality.* At first only a few businesses accepted this novel proposition – IBM was perhaps the first one, and for a long time also the only one. Then in the late fifties and early sixties it was picked up by the Japanese, whose earlier attempts to return to prewar autocracy in the plant had collapsed in bloody strikes and near civil war. Nowadays, while still far from being widely practised, it is at least generally accepted in theory that the workers' knowledge of their job is the starting point for improving productivity, quality, and performance altogether.

In making and moving things, partnership with the responsible worker is, however, only the *best* way – after all, Taylor's telling them worked, too, and quite well. In knowledge and service work, partnership with the responsible worker is the *only* way; nothing else will work at all.

---

*I was the first to draw this conclusion in my two early books, *The Future of Industrial Man* (1942) and *The New Society* (1949), in which I argued for the 'responsible worker' as 'part of management'. As a result of their wartime experiences, Edwards Deming and Joseph Juran each developed what we now call 'quality circles' and 'total quality management'. Finally, the idea was forcefully presented by Douglas McGregor in his 1960 book *The Human Side of Enterprise* with its 'Theory X' and 'Theory Y'.

Two more lessons that neither Taylor nor Mayo knew: increased productivity needs continuous learning. It is not enough to redesign the job and then to train the worker in the new way of doing it – which is what Taylor did and taught. That's when learning begins, and it never ends. Indeed, as the Japanese can teach us – it came out of their ancient tradition of Zen learning – the greatest benefit of training is not in learning the new. It is to do better what we already do well. And equally important, an insight of the last few years: knowledge people and service people learn the most when they teach. The best way to improve the productivity of the star salesperson is for him or her to present 'the secrets of my success' at a sales convention. The best way for the surgeon to improve his or her performance is to give a talk about it at the county medical society. The best way for a nurse to improve her performance is to teach her fellow nurses. It is often being said that in the information age every enterprise has to become a learning institution. It also has to become a teaching institution.

Conclusion

Developed economies face economic stagnation if they do not raise the productivity of knowledge and service work. Even Japan – still heavily manufacturing-intensive – can no longer expect increased productivity in making and moving things to sustain economic growth. Even there the great majority of working people are knowledge workers and service workers with productivities as low as those in any other developed country. And when farmers are down to a mere 3 percent of the employed population, as they are in the U.S. and Japan – and in most of Western Europe as well – even record increases in their productivity such as the 4 to 5 percent the U.S. boasts of add virtually nothing to the country's overall productivity, its wealth, its competitiveness.

Raising the productivity of knowledge and service work must therefore be an *economic* priority for developed countries. Whichever country first succeeds in satisfying it will economically dominate the twenty-first century. And the key is raising the productivity of *knowledge* work, on all levels.

But the need to raise the productivity of *service* work may be even greater. It is a *social* priority in developed countries. Unless it is met, the developed world faces increasing social tensions, increasing polarization, increasing radicalization. It may ultimately face a new class war.

In the knowledge society, access to opportunities for careers and advancement is becoming limited to people of advanced schooling, people qualified for knowledge work. But such people will always be a minority. They will always be outnumbered by people who lack the qualifications for anything but fairly low-skilled service work. In their social position such people are comparable to the proletarians of a hundred years ago: the poorly educated, unskilled masses who thronged the exploding industrial cities and streamed into their factories.

When Frederic Taylor started his work on the productivity of making and moving things in the early 1880s, class war between industrial proletarian and 'bourgeois' – its reality but even more the fear of it – obsessed every developed country. Fear of it motivated Taylor to start his work. And the belief in the inevitability of class war was by no means confined to the Left. A generation before Taylor, Benjamin Disraeli, the greatest of the nineteenth-century conservatives, had predicted it. And Henry James, the chronicler of American wealth and European aristocracy, was so frightened by it that he made it the central theme of one of his most haunting novels, *The Princess Casamassima* – it appeared in 1885, two years after Marx's death and four years after Taylor had begun studying the productivity of shovelling sand.

Marx has been proven wrong in his prophecy of the inevitable 'immiseration' of the proletarian leading inevitably to a revolution. But when he made these prophecies they seemed eminently reasonable – indeed, almost self-evident – to well-informed and highly intelligent contemporaries. What defeated Marx and Marxism in the end was the rising productivity of making and moving things – that is, in essence, the work Taylor started. It gave the proletarians the productivity that allowed their being paid a middle-class income and to achieve middle-class status despite lack of skill, wealth, and education. By the time of the Great Depression – when, according to Marx and Marxists the 'Proletarian Revolution' should surely have become triumphant – the proletarian had become bourgeois.

Unless the productivity of service workers is rapidly improved, both the social and the economic position of that large class – as large a group as people making and moving things ever were at their peak –must steadily go down. Real incomes cannot for any length of time be higher than productivity. The service workers may use their numerical strength to get higher wages than their economic contribution justifies. But this only impoverishes all of society with everybody's real income going down and unemployment going up. Or the incomes of the unskilled service workers are allowed to go down in relation to the steadily rising wages of affluent knowledge workers, with an increasing gulf between the two groups, an increasing polarization into classes. In either case service workers must become alienated, increasingly bitter, increasingly see themselves as *a class apart*. And the escape hatch – the productive and therefore well-paid jobs for poorly educated and poorly skilled people in making and moving things – is closing rapidly. By the end of this century the number of such jobs in every developed country will be at most two fifths of what it was at their peak only forty years ago.

We are in a much better position than our ancestors were a century ago. We know what Marx and his contemporaries did not know: *productivity can be raised.* We also know *how to raise it.* And we know this best for the work where the social need is most urgent: unskilled and semi-skilled service work – the jobs in maintenance, whether of factories, schools, hospitals, or offices; in restaurants and in supermarkets; in a host of clerical jobs. This, as has already been stated, is production work – and what we have learned during the past hundred years about increasing productivity applies to such work with a minimum of adaptation. Indeed, in such work substantial productivity increases have already been achieved. Some multinational maintenance companies – both in the U.S. and in Europe – have systematically applied to low-skilled service jobs the approaches this article discusses. They have defined the task; concentrated work on it; defined performance; made the employee a partner in productivity improvement and the first source of ideas for it; and built continuous learning and continuing teaching into the job of every employee and of every work team. They have substantially raised productivity – in some cases, doubled it. This then has allowed them to raise wages. But it has also greatly raised self-respect and pride. It is, incidentally, by no means coincidence that these increases were achieved by outside contractors rather than by the organization (e.g., the hospitals) in which the service people actually do their work. To obtain major productivity increases in production-type service work usually requires contracting out such work to a firm that has no other business, understands this work, respects it, and offers opportunities for advancement for low-skill service workers – e.g., to become its local or regional manager. The organizations in which this work is being done – e.g., the hospital in which the people work who make the beds, or the college whose students they feed – neither understand such work nor respect it enough to devote to it the time and hard work needed to make it productive, no matter how much they pay for it.

The task is known and doable, but the urgency is great. To raise the productivity of service work cannot be done by governmental action or by politics altogether. It is the task of managers and executives in businesses and nonprofit organizations. It is, in fact, the *first social responsibility* of management in the knowledge society.

[1991]

14

The Mystique of the Business Leader

What explains the tremendous interest in business ethics – in the media, in business schools, in business itself? It's not because there has been any sharp change in the behaviour of business people. What has happened is that the behaviour of business and business people has acquired a different meaning in the industrialized world. It suddenly *matters*.

Both the heads of large corporations and the few 'tycoons' have come to be seen as society's leaders. And leaders are expected to set an example. They are not supposed to behave as we know that we behave. They are expected to behave as we know that we ought to behave. The more cynical we have become about the behaviour of earlier leadership groups – politicians, preachers, physicians, lawyers and so on – the more we have come to expect virtue from business and business people.

How this happened no one can explain. After all, it is barely 20 years since the student rebellions of the late '60s in the U.S., Japan, France, and West Germany against business and its 'bourgeois values'. And the turnaround since, to where business and its leaders are now the 'social archetypes' (to use the sociologist's term), has gone even further in Western Europe and

Japan than in the U.S., which is even more remarkable. Such European countries as England, France and Germany used to consider business somewhat dirty, certainly second-rate, and altogether 'infra dig'.

But why this reversal has come to pass is equally mysterious. It would be nice if we could attribute it to the performance of business and business people. And indeed the performance in this century has been spectacular. But the public – as business people constantly bemoan – is singularly unaware of it; it takes it for granted.

None but a very few social historians have even an inkling of the material conditions of the great masses – the domestic servants, the farmers, the shop girls, the manual workers – of 80 years ago and of the changes since. And even these few historians rarely notice that the greatest change has not been in improved material conditions: more than half, perhaps as much as two-thirds, of the fruits of the explosive growth in production and productivity in this century – that is, of the contribution of business and business people – have gone into leisure, education, life-expectancy, and health care, and above all, into opportunities for the individual.

And business and business people in this century have actually lost both in power and in wealth – the two traditional foundations of a leadership position.

No businessman anywhere these days holds even a fraction of the power held 80 years ago by a J. P. Morgan, a John D. Rockefeller, an Alfried Krupp, or by the 10 or 12 private bankers who together constituted the nearly omnipotent 'Court' of the Bank of England before World War I. The gainers in power have been institutions that are either hostile toward or highly critical of business: the labour union, the government bureaucracy, and the greatest gainer of them all – the university. A mere ornament of society 80 years ago, it now holds in every developed country what no earlier society ever granted an institution: the power to grant or to deny access to livelihood and careers through its unregulated monopoly of the all-important university degree.

Neither in absolute nor in relative terms does business wealth today even remotely compare with that of 1900. The wealth of the richest billionaire of today, if adjusted for taxes and inflation, looks puny next to the fortunes of 80 years ago. And for the economy, the 'rich' have actually become irrelevant.

Eighty years ago any one of the 'tycoons', whether in the U.S., in Imperial Germany, in Edwardian England, or in the France of the Third Republic, could – and did – by himself supply the entire capital needed by a major industry. Today the wealth of America's one thousand richest people, taken together, would barely cover one week of the country's capital needs. The only true 'capitalists' in developed countries today are the wage earners through their pension funds and mutual funds.

Whether a leadership position can survive if it is based neither on dominant power nor on dominant wealth remains to be seen. Machiavelli, that shrewd sociologist of leadership, would have doubted it. And business people exist as leaders only as a group. Individually, unlike the members of any earlier leadership group, they are largely anonymous, indeed practically invisible.

How many Americans know the names of the chief executive officers of the Fortune 500? In addition, while the CEO of the big company is a 'big shot' during his six or seven years of tenure – with a private jet, a bevy of secretaries, a flock of PR men, and a private dining room – he is a nobody and has to show his ID to get past the doorman in his own company 24 hours after he has retired.

It is also by no means certain that the leadership position of business and of business people is good for either. At least America's most distinguished economist, Milton Friedman, argues that it is socially irresponsible and economically damaging for business to be concerned with anything but business results – that is, with maximizing profits and thereby raising standards of living, creating capital and providing better and more jobs tomorrow.

But however short-lived, illogical, irrational, even undesirable it may be, it is a fact that business and business people are perceived as the leadership group in today's developed countries.

There is a second and equally important fact, as well. Business executives are inevitably leaders in their organizations, seen as such, perceived as such, judged as such.

'The higher up the monkey goes, the more of his behind he shows,' runs an English schoolboy jingle. What executives do, what they believe and value, what they reward and whom, are watched, seen, and minutely interpreted throughout the whole organization. And nothing is noticed more quickly – and considered more significant – than a discrepancy between what executives preach and what they expect their associates to practise.

Recently I discussed with an elder statesman of Japan's industry the violation of the ban on strategic shipments of American products by a subsidiary of Tokyo's Toshiba. I commented on the fact that the top executives of Toshiba had held themselves 'accountable' and resigned over this matter even though the violator is barely controlled by Toshiba (which holds only 50.1 percent of its stock), is autonomous, and had disregarded published company policy.

'We wouldn't say "accountable",' my friend said. 'We'd say: "It's their fault." If a manager in a company does something wrong to improve the market standing or the profits of the company, you can be sure that he only does what his top management wants him to do and signals him to do.'

The Japanese recognize that there are really only two demands of leadership. One is to accept that rank does not confer privileges; it entails responsibilities. The other is to acknowledge that leaders in an organization need to impose on themselves that congruence between deeds and words, between behaviour and professed beliefs and values, that we call 'personal integrity'.

[1987]

15

Leadership: More Doing Than Dash

Leadership is all the rage just now. 'We'd want you to run a seminar for us on how one acquires charisma,' the human-resources VP of a big bank said to me on the telephone – in dead earnest. Books, articles, and conferences on leadership and on the 'qualities' of the leader abound. Every CEO, it seems, has to be made to look like a dashing Confederate cavalry general or a boardroom Elvis Presley.

Leadership does matter, of course. But, alas, it is something different from what is now touted under this label. It has little to do with 'leadership qualities' and even less to do with 'charisma'. It is mundane, unromantic and boring. Its essence is performance.

In the first place, leadership is not by itself good or desirable. Leadership is a means. Leadership to what end is thus the crucial question. History knows no more charismatic leaders than this century's triad of Stalin, Hitler, and Mao – the misleaders who inflicted as much evil and suffering on humanity as have ever been recorded.

The Undoing of Leaders

But effective leadership doesn't depend on charisma. Dwight Eisenhower, George Marshall, and Harry Truman were singularly effective leaders, yet none possessed any more charisma than a dead mackerel. Nor did Konrad Adenauer, the chancellor who rebuilt West Germany after World War II. No less charismatic personality could be imagined than Abe Lincoln of Illinois, the raw-boned, uncouth backwoodsman of 1860. And there was amazingly little charisma to the bitter, defeated, almost broken Churchill of the interwar years; what mattered was that he turned out in the end to have been right.

Indeed, charisma becomes the undoing of leaders. It makes them inflexible, convinced of their own infallibility, unable to change. This is what happened to Stalin, Hitler, and Mao, and it is a commonplace in the study of ancient history that only Alexander the Great's early death saved him from becoming an ineffectual failure.

Indeed, charisma does not by itself guarantee effectiveness as a leader. John F. Kennedy may have been the most charismatic person ever to occupy the White House. Yet few presidents got as little done.

Nor are there any such things as 'leadership qualities' or a 'leadership personality'. Franklin D. Roosevelt, Winston Churchill, George Marshall, Dwight Eisenhower, Bernard Montgomery, and Douglas MacArthur, were all highly effective – and highly visible – leaders during World War II. No two of them shared any 'personality traits' or any 'qualities'.

What then is leadership if it is not charisma and not a set of personality traits? The first thing to say about it is that it is work – something stressed again and again by the most charismatic leaders: Julius Caesar, for instance, or General MacArthur and Field Marshal Montgomery, or, to use an example from business, Alfred Sloan, the man who built and led General Motors from 1920 to 1955.

The foundation of effective leadership is thinking through the organization's mission, defining it and establishing it, clearly and visibly. The leader sets the goals, sets the priorities, and sets and maintains the standards. He makes compromises, of course; indeed, effective leaders are painfully aware that they are not in control of the universe. (Only misleaders – the Stalins, Hitlers,

Maos – suffer from that delusion.) But before accepting a compromise, the effective leader has thought through what is right and desirable. The leader's first task is to be the trumpet that sounds a clear sound.

What distinguishes the leader from the misleader are his goals. Whether the compromise he makes with the constraints of reality – which may involve political, economic, financial or people problems – are compatible with his mission and goals or lead away from them determines whether he is an effective leader. And whether he holds fast to a few basic standards (exemplifying them in his own conduct) or whether 'standards' for him are what he can get away with, determines whether the leader has followers or only hypocritical time-servers.

The second requirement is that the leader sees leadership as responsibility rather than as rank and privilege. Effective leaders are rarely 'permissive'. But when things go wrong – and they always do – they do not blame others. If Winston Churchill is an example of leadership through clearly defining mission and goals, Gen. George Marshall, America's chief of staff in World War II, is an example of leadership through responsibility. Harry Truman's folksy 'The buck stops here' is still as good a definition as any.

But precisely because an effective leader knows that he, and no one else, is ultimately responsible, he is not afraid of strength in associates and subordinates. Misleaders are; they always go in for purges. But an effective leader wants strong associates; he encourages them, pushes them, indeed glories in them. Because he holds himself ultimately responsible for the mistakes of his associates and subordinates, he also sees the triumphs of his associates and subordinates as his triumphs, rather than as threats. A leader may be personally vain – as General MacArthur was to an almost pathological degree. Or he may be personally humble – both Lincoln and Truman were so almost to the point of having inferiority complexes. But all three wanted able, independent, self-assured people around them; they encouraged their associates and subordinates, praising and promoting them. So did a very different person: Ike Eisenhower, when supreme commander in Europe.

An effective leader knows, of course, that there is a risk: able people tend to be ambitious. But he realizes that it is a much smaller risk than to be served by mediocrity. He also knows that the gravest indictment of a leader is for the organization to collapse as soon as he leaves or dies, as happened in Russia the moment Stalin died and as happens all too often in companies. An effective leader knows that the ultimate task of leadership is to create human energies and human vision.

Earning Trust Is a Must

The final requirement of effective leadership is to earn trust. Otherwise there won't be any followers – and the only definition of a leader is someone who has followers. To trust a leader, it is not necessary to like him. Nor is it necessary to agree with him. Trust is the conviction that the leader means what he says. It is a belief in something very old-fashioned, called 'integrity'. A leader's actions and a leader's professed beliefs must be congruent, or at least compatible. Effective leadership – and again this is very old wisdom – is not based on being clever; it is based primarily on being consistent.

After I had said these things on the telephone to the bank's human-resources VP, there was a long silence. Finally she said: 'But that's no different at all from what we have known for years are the requirements for being an effective manager.'

Precisely.

[1988]

16

People, Work, and the Future of the City

In 20 years Japanese office workers may still commute, packed shoulder to shoulder, to downtown towers. But no one else in the developed world will. Office work, rather than officer workers, will do the travelling. Tomorrow's big city is no longer going to be the office centre.

The exodus is already under way. Citibank handles credit cards in North Dakota, clears cheques in upstate New York and Delaware, and is moving data processing across the Hudson to suburban New Jersey. A large Boston-based mutual-fund group, Colonial Management Associates, has moved nationwide customer service and customer accounting to a Denver suburb. Insurance companies are rapidly shifting their labour-intensive work – claims handling, customer correspondence, record keeping – to the outskirts of metropolitan areas. And office parks especially built for back-office operations are now springing up in the suburbs as fast as shopping malls sprang up there in the '60s and '70s.

Acquiring Wheels

The modern big city is the creation of the nineteenth century's ability to move people. Everyone in Dickens's London walked to work except the owners, who lived over their shops or their countinghouses. But then, beginning in mid-century, people began to acquire wheels – the railroad first, then the omnibus and the streetcar (horse-drawn, of course, for many decades), the subway and the elevated train, the automobile, the bicycle. Suddenly large masses of people could move over great distances to where the work was. And the elevator added vertical mobility. It was this ability to move people that, more than anything else, made possible large organizations, businesses, hospitals, government agencies, and universities.

By 1914, every single one of the means to move people into an office-centred large city – and to enable the office workers to live outside it – had been developed. But they did not have their full impact until after World War II. Until then only two cities had skyscrapers – New York and Chicago. Now every mid-sized city worldwide boasts a 'skyline'. And even in mid-sized cities people commute.

This trend has clearly reached its end, has indeed widely overshot the mark. Tokyo's office workers have to live more than two hours away just to get a seat on the morning train. In Los Angeles, traffic at six every weekday morning is bumper to bumper in all directions – people trying to get to their desks by 8:30 or 9. Things are not much better in Boston or New York or Philadelphia. London's Piccadilly Circus is chaos 24 hours a day, and so are those marvels of nineteenth-century city planning, the *Grands Boulevards* of Paris. Rome and Madrid are worse still.

Office workers in the world's big cities do not have eight-hour days; they have 12-hour days. And all attempts in the past 30 years to relieve the traffic jams and their frustrations through new public transit have been total failures despite countless billions spent on them.

Yet none of this is necessary any more; indeed, commuting to office work is obsolete. It is now infinitely easier, cheaper and faster to do what the nineteenth century could not do: move information, and with it office work, to where the people are. The tools to do so are already here: the telephone, two-way video, electronic mail, the fax machine, the personal computer, the modem, and so on. And so is the receptivity: witness, for example, the boom in fax machines in the past 18 months.

We already know how office work will be done in the future.

Contrary to what futurists predicted 25 years ago, the trend is not toward individuals working in their homes. People greatly prefer to work where other people are. But even in Japan – where the need for community and companionship at work is greater than in the West – the exodus of such clerical work as data processing from downtown has begun.

But, equally important, clerical work increasingly will become 'uncoupled', the way much physical office work – cleaning, maintaining equipment, running the cafeteria – already has been. Rather than being employees of the institution whose office work they do, more and more clerical workers will be employed by specialized and independent contractors. A growing amount of such work already is being done by people hired, trained, placed, and paid by temporary-help firms – with more and more of the 'temporaries' actually holding down full-time, permanent assignments in the client companies. A good many of the new type of office parks provide a trained clerical force and the supervision for it. They provide office work rather than office space. And, according to some reports that is where the demand is.

Office workers doing clerical and maintenance work are the largest single work group in the developed world's big cities – accounting for as much as half the working population. What, then, will the city of tomorrow look like when it is no longer an 'office city'? It will, one can safely say, be a 'headquarters city'.

Twenty-five years ago a number of large U.S. companies – General Foods, IBM, General Electric – moved out of Manhattan and into suburbia, lock, stock, and barrel. At that time we did not know that we could move information. Thus, to free office workers from the need to commute, companies isolated top management people and professionals and imposed on them constant travelling into the city for business meetings.

Big companies tomorrow are almost certain to keep their management people – at least their senior ones – where other senior management people are: in the city. And so will government agencies and other large organizations. But this means that the big city will also house the purveyors of specialized skills and knowledge – the lawyer, the accounting firm, the architect, the consultant, the advertising agency, the investment banker, the financial analyst, and so on. But even these people will have their office work done outside the city.

A very big law firm is completing plans to have only one law library, in one suburban location. It will serve all 10 of its offices in the U.S. and overseas through a computer network supplemented by fax machines and two-way video. Within two or three years the firm expects to vacate all the space now occupied by the current 10 libraries – two floors each in every location.

We may be at the very end of the tremendous boom in office construction and office rents that was triggered when Napoleon III created the modern city's prototype in 1860 Paris and which has reached such a frenzy in all major Free World cities these past 20 years. (I, for one, am perfectly reconciled to the Japanese buying up more and more of the large office buildings in downtown America.) The big city of tomorrow is far more likely to resemble the preindustrial city than the nineteenth-century city that still shapes today's New York or Paris.

But will even those who work in the urban headquarters live in the cities? Where will the largest number of them – managers and professionals in particular – make their homes?

In continental Europe, where middle managers and professionals still tend to live in the city, the shift from office city to headquarters city may well prevent their moving out. But it is doubtful that the exodus to the suburbs will be reversed or even greatly slowed in the U.S., in Britain, or in Japan, where middle-class people with children have already moved out of the core cities. And surely the headquarters city will have even less work for the poor and unskilled than the office city has. This will be a particular problem in the U.S., where welfare payments have drawn so many of the least-skilled and least-schooled into the inner-city jungle.

What will the tax base of the headquarters city be, and can it remain a commercial centre? Luxury shops do not depend on the office worker. But most other shops in the city do, especially department stores and only in Japan do people not working in the city regularly come in to shop there. What about restaurants and hotels? Will theatres and opera houses become transmitters of shows through videotape and cable TV rather than places people go to? Will the big-city hospital become a centre of teaching, of information, and of diagnosis for the suburban and exurban hospitals where the patients will be?

A Lecture to 10,000

And what about the large university? The costs of higher education in all developed countries are nearly as out of control as the costs of health care. The only way, perhaps, to cap them may be to convert the university into a place from which learning flows to where the *students* are – something already done by the successful Open University in Britain.

Several times a year I lecture to 10,000 or more students, yet fewer than 100 are in the room with me. The rest see me via satellite in more than 100 'downlinks' and discuss their questions with me via telephone.

There is a great deal said and written these days about the technological impacts of information. But perhaps its social impacts are greater still, and more important.

[1989]

17

The Rise and Fall of the Blue-Collar Worker

Whether high-paying jobs are growing or declining in the American economy is being hotly debated. But as important as the numbers is the fact that the new high-paying jobs are not where the old ones used to be.

For 30 years, from the end of World War II to the mid-1970s, high-paying jobs in all developed countries were concentrated in unskilled blue-collar work. Now a majority of the new high-paying jobs are in knowledge work: technicians, professionals, specialists of all kinds, managers. The qualification for the high-paying jobs of 20 years ago was a union card. Now it is formal schooling. The long and steep rise of the 'working man' – in numbers, in social standing, in income – has turned overnight into fast decline.

There is no parallel in history to the rise of the working man in the developed countries during this century. Eighty years ago American blue-collar workers, toiling 60 hours a week, made $250 a year at most, or one-third the price of that 'low-priced miracle', Henry Ford's Model T. And they had no 'fringes', no seniority, no unemployment insurance, no Social Security, no paid holidays, no overtime, no pension – nothing but a cash wage of less than one dollar a day. Today's employed blue-collar worker in a unionized mass-production industry (steel, automotive, electrical machinery, paper, rubber, petroleum) working 40 hours a week earns about $50,000 a year – half in cash wages, half in benefits. Even after taxes, this equals seven or eight new small cars, such as the South Korean Excel, or 25 times the worker's 1907 real income (if food were used as the yardstick, the increase would be even larger). And the rise in social standing, and especially in political power, has been greater still.

Society's Stepchildren

And now it is suddenly all over. There also is no parallel in history to the abrupt decline of the blue-collar worker during the past 15 years. As a proportion of the working population, blue-collar workers in manufacturing have already decreased to less than a fifth of the American labour force from more than a third. By the year 2010 – less than 25 years away – they will constitute no larger a proportion of the labour force of every developed country than farmers do today – that is, a twentieth of the total. The decline will be greatest precisely where the highest-paid jobs are. Blue-collar automobile employment in the U.S., 15 or 20 years hence, will hardly be more than half of what it now is, even if there are no imports at all – and automobile blue-collar employment is already down 40 percent from its peak, less than 10 years ago. No wonder the unions do not regard the fast growth of high-paying knowledge jobs as a compensation for the steady decline in the numbers, power, prestige, and income of their constituents. Yesterday's blue-collar workers in manufacturing were society's darlings; they are fast becoming stepchildren.

This transformation was not caused by a decline in production. U.S. manufacturing output is steadily expanding, growing as fast as gross national product or a little faster. The decline of the blue-collar worker is not a matter of 'competitiveness', of 'government policies', of the 'business cycle', or even of 'imports'. It is structural and irreversible.

There are two major causes. First is the steady shift from labour-intensive to knowledge-intensive industries – e.g., a drop in pouring steel and a steady rise in making pharmaceuticals. All the growth in U.S. manufacturing output in the past two decades – and it has about doubled – has been in knowledge-intensive industries. Equally important is the worldwide spread in the past 40 years of two American inventions (or discoveries), 'training' and 'management'. In a complete reversal of all that economic history and theory had taught, these two methods enable a country with the labour costs of an 'underdeveloped' economy to attain, within a very short period, the productivity of a fully 'developed' one.

The first to understand this were the Japanese after World War II. By now everybody does – the South Koreans, for instance, or the Brazilians. The most telling example are the 'maquiladoras', the plants on the Mexican side of the U.S.–Mexican border, where unskilled and often illiterate people produce labour-intensive parts and goods for the U.S. market. It takes three years at most for a maquiladora to attain the labour productivity of a well-run American or Japanese plant even in turning out highly sophisticated products – and it pays workers less than $2 an hour.

This means that manufacturing industry in developed countries can survive only if it shifts from being labour-intensive to being knowledge-intensive. Machine operators getting high wages for doing unskilled, repetitive work are being replaced by knowledge-workers getting high wages for designing, controlling, and servicing process and product, or for managing information. This shift also fits in with demographics. In every developed country more and more young people, and especially young males, stay in school beyond the secondary level and are no longer available for blue-collar jobs, even for well-paying ones.

These are changes so sharp and so sudden as, for once, to deserve being called 'revolutionary'. Yet their impact is different from what everyone expected, and different also from what economic and political theory had taught.

This applies particularly to U.S. unemployment. In Britain and Western Europe the decline in blue-collar jobs in manufacturing has indeed, as unions predicted, resulted in stubborn unemployment. But in the U.S. the decline has had marginal effects at most. Even the massive job losses in the steel and automotive industries have barely left a trace in national unemployment rates. To be sure, the current 6½ percent unemployment rate for both adult men and adult women is probably somewhat above the rate of 'natural unemployment' (the rate needed for normal job changes) – but not by much, considering the age structure of the working population. And the 4½ percent unemployment rate for married men is, if anything, below the natural rate and constitutes virtual 'full employment'. 'Hidden unemployment' – that is, people who have given up looking for a job – is very big in union propaganda but probably quite scarce outside of it. A larger proportion of American adults than ever before in peacetime history – almost two-thirds – is in the labour force and working. One explanation for the low unemployment rates is surely that American workers are singularly adaptable and mobile – far more so than anyone would have thought possible. But, equally significant, blue-collar labour in manufacturing may also have already shrunk to a point where it only marginally affects total employment and unemploy-ment rates, consumer spending, purchasing power and the economy as a whole. This would mean that we should stop looking at manufacturing employment as the economy's bellwether and should look at manufacturing output instead; as long as its volume continues to rise, the industrial economy is healthy almost regardless of employment.

Equally novel is the behaviour of wage costs in the U.S. That unions give priority to the maintenance of nominal wages rather than accept lower wage rates to gain higher employment has been one of the axioms of modern economics. It still holds in Europe. But America's unions have shown an amazing willingness to make sizeable concessions on wages – and even on work rules – to prevent plant closings and massive layoffs. In the U.S., at least, the principal cost-rigidity inhibiting the 'self-correction' of a market economy surely no longer lies in wage costs (as economics has assumed since Keynes) but in the cost of government.

Every labour economist and every labour leader would have expected the decline of the blue-collar worker to lead to 'labour militancy' on a grand scale. Some politicians still expect it – for instance, the Rev. Jesse Jackson in the U.S., the 'Militants' in the British Labour party, and the 'Radicals' among the German Social Democrats. But so far there has been labour militancy in only one developed country: Canada. Elsewhere there is much bitterness among the rank and file. But it is the bitterness of resignation, of impotence rather than of rebellion. In a way, the blue-collar worker has conceded defeat.

And this may underlie the most startling, and least expected, development: the political one. It is almost an axiom of politics that a major interest group actually increases its political clout for a long time after it has begun to lose numbers or income. Its members join ranks, learn to hang together lest they hang separately, and increasingly act and vote in concert. The way in which farmers in every developed country have maintained political power and increased their subsidies despite their rapid decline in numbers since World War II is a good example.

Political Strength Eroded

But though it is only 10 or 15 years since the decline of the blue-collar workers first began, their political strength has already been greatly eroded. In the midst of World War II, John L. Lewis of the United Mine Workers defied the country's most popular president –and won. Thirty years later, another coal miners' leader – this time in Britain – forced a prime minister to resign. But in 1981 President Reagan broke the powerful and deeply entrenched air traffic controllers union; and a few years later British Prime Minister Margaret Thatcher broke the union that had driven her predecessor into political exile. And both President Reagan and Prime Minister Thatcher had overwhelming popular support. The labour vote may still be needed for a 'progressive' candidate to be nominated. But then, in the election, labour's endorsement has become a near-guarantee of defeat, as shown by Walter Mondale's debacle in the U.S. presidential election of 1986, by the German election this January, and by numerous British by-elections.

In little more than a decade before World War I, the blue-collar worker rose from impotence to become a dominant economic and social power in Western Europe, and his party the largest single political factor. The U.S. followed suit 10 years later. This transformed the economy, the society and the politics of every developed country, transcending even two World Wars and tyrannies beyond precedent. What then will the decline of the blue-collar worker – and its counterpoint, the rise of the knowledge-worker – mean for the rest of this century and the next one?

[1987]

18

On Ending Work Rules and Job Descriptions

In all the hundreds of books, articles, and speeches on American competitiveness – or the lack thereof – work rules and job restrictions are rarely mentioned. Such rules forbid a foreman to do any production work, whether taking the place of a worker who goes to the restroom, repairing a tool, or helping when the work falls behind. They forbid electricians to straighten a stud when installing a fuse box. They forbid workers' moving from one job to another, thus restricting them to narrow, repetitive tasks, e.g., spray-painting the door panel of a car. And they narrowly restrict what a worker may be trained for. Yet all available evidence indicates that work rules and job restrictions are the main cause of the 'productivity gap' of American (and European) manufacturing industry.

To be sure, productivity is not the sum of competitiveness. But when it comes to making things, productivity is the foundation. And it is precisely those American and European industries in which making things is most hedged in by work rules and job restrictions – steel, automobiles, consumer electronics, rubber, and so on – that have done the poorest against the competitors from East Asia.

'Double-Breasting'

The best evidence for the effect of work rules and job restrictions is found in America's building industry. It alone of all major industries anywhere has – working side by side – union shops with tight job restrictions and nonunion shops without them. Both shops are often owned by the same company – it's called 'double-breasting' in the industry – with the same people running them. The time it takes to do an individual job, e.g. connecting a drainpipe, is exactly the same in both. Yet the crew working under work rules and job restrictions needs two-thirds more people to do the same job in the same time.

A 'double-breasted' contractor recently ran a study on two nearly identical projects done by his company, one by a union crew, the other by a nonunion crew. The nonunion crew worked an average of 50 minutes out of every hour. The union crew worked 35; the rest of the time it was forced to wait – for someone to come back from the restroom or for a journeyman to become available to do work an apprentice could easily have done but was not allowed to touch. The unionized crew also had to work short-handed for 40 minutes until a man qualified to drive a truck had come back from the shop with a replacement part. When that happened on the nonunion project, the foreman ran the errand and the work continued.

The result: the unionized crew required a crew of eight, the non-union job was done by five workers. Interestingly, the large Japanese contractors who are considered models of efficiency work with roughly the same productivity, all observers agree, as American nonunion contractors.

Work rules and job restrictions also explain in large measure the higher productivity of the Japanese-owned plants in the U.S. and Europe. The best-documented example is an English one. In Nissan's plant in the Midlands a worker turns out 24 cars a year. At English Ford in Dagenham outside London a worker turns out 6! Half of that difference may be Nissan's buying many more parts on the outside than does Ford. This still leaves a productivity differential of 2 to 1. Yet the time it takes an individual worker to do any one operation – positioning the engine on the chassis, for instance – is pretty much the same in both plants. But Dagenham has 125 job classifications, each restricting the workers to one small task: Nissan has 5 classifications.

Similarly, the much-publicized higher productivity of the Japanese-owned auto plants in the U.S. – Honda in Marysville, Ohio, for instance, or Toyota in Fremont, California – is largely, perhaps entirely, the result of their having only three to five job classifications. GM, Ford, and Chrysler are each burdened with about 60. Again, the time it takes the individual worker to do any one operation is pretty much the same all around. And yet the Japanese-owned plants turn out 30 percent to 50 percent more per worker per day.

A recent book on the productivity gap, *Tough Words for American Industry* by Hajime Karatsu, one of Japan's leading manufacturing engineers (Productivity Press, Cambridge, Massachusetts), predicts that the American market for manufactured goods eventually will be supplied by competition between Japanese-owned companies producing in U.S. plants, and American-owned companies importing the same goods into the U.S. from 'offshore' plants in Singapore or on the Mexican side of the border. In some industries, e.g., consumer electronics, this is already happening. The main – perhaps the only – reason is that the Japanese, being newcomers, are largely exempt in their American plants – even the unionized ones – from the work rules and job classifications that control the U.S. plants of their American competitors.

One of the leading multinationals recently studied its consumer electronics production in the U.S., Europe, Japan, Singapore, South Korea, and Hong Kong; it also studied the productivity of its main Japanese and Korean competitors in the same areas. The time it takes to do any given task was actually somewhat shorter in its U.S. plants than it was in the best plant of its principal Japanese competitor. But, overall, its American and European plants were outproduced by the plants – both its own and those of its competitors – in East Asia. The only explanation: in the U.S. and in Europe the company's plants operate with more than 100 job classifications; the plants in East Asia – its own as well as those of its competitors – have at most 7.

The vehicle for work rules and job restrictions is, of course, the labour contract. But don't just blame the unions. Managements are equally at fault. One major reason for proliferation of work rules and job restrictions is the narrow focus on dollars per hour with which Western managements conduct labour negotiations –

and their tunnel vision is shared by economists, politicians, the press, and the public.

As a result, managements accepted, often eagerly, tighter work rules and more restrictive job classifications in exchange against a few pennies less wage per hour. Companies that all along paid attention to the total cost of work done rather than solely to immediate wage dollars per hour – IBM is one example – do not, it seems, suffer from a 'productivity gap' either in their American or in their European plants.

But also Western managements typically – again IBM would be one major exception – rejected any other form of job security such as an annual wage, responsibility for retraining and 'outplacing' redundant workers, and so on. This virtually forced the unions into pushing for work rules and job restrictions. In the end, of course, work rules and job restrictions have proven more costly; and in Western Europe and increasingly in the U.S., a good deal of expensive job security has been imposed by law on top of work rules and job restrictions, thus giving Western manufacturing companies the worst of both worlds.

But, then, conventional measurements available to both managements and unions also conceal the cost of work rules and job restrictions. It is captured neither by the industrial engineer's time-and-motion study nor by cost accounting. It shows up only in 'systems' figures such as the total number of cars produced per worker per year. And until recently such figures simply did not exist. The cost of rules and restrictions were thus dismissed as 'intangible' by both managements and unions.

How do we get out of the work-rule hole we have dug for ourselves? Both American managements and American union leaders – though not, so far, very many of their counterparts in Europe – increasingly realize that they must get out, and fast. U.S. Steel has more than doubled productivity per worker in the past eight years, in large measure by cutting work rules and job classifications, and is now among the world's most productive steelmakers – a few years ago it was near the bottom. And the United Steel Workers Union acquiesced in the rules and classifications cuts, even though it had to accept substantial cuts in jobs and members.

The Alternatives

At Ford, a joint union-management effort is under way to raise productivity by cutting job classifications in one of the company's biggest plants. Still, it is not easy for the rank and file to accept both abandonment of what for 40 years it has been taught to consider 'gains', and sizeable reductions in the number of jobs, especially in industries, with low or no job growth to begin with.

In both a GM division in the U.S. and at Ford in England the membership rejected cuts in job classifications even though their own union leaders had strongly urged acceptance. But what are the alternatives? One is the disappearance of the unions. America's building industry has moved pretty far down that road. Or are we going to end up with the weird paradox foreseen by Mr Karatsu, the Japanese manufacturing engineer: newcomers from Japan and Korea produce in the U.S. and Europe while American and European manufactures are being forced by work rules and job restrictions to go 'offshore' to supply their own home markets?

[1988]

19

Making Managers of Communist Bureaucrats

'To rebuild and run the Hungarian business in which we are buying a 49% stake,' reports the CEO of a Western consumer-goods company, 'we'll need a dozen experienced Hungarian executives. We had over a hundred applicants, each appearing well qualified by job title and position. But only three or four turned out to have the experience and skills needed.'

Businesses in Central Europe seem to employ at least twice as many managers and professionals as do comparable businesses in the West. But there is an extreme scarcity of managerial skills and experience.

Many Central European managers have received excellent educations: Central Europe's technical schools have maintained high standards. But then these people spent their working lives as paperpushers – writing regulations or endless reports or negotiating with the ministry and the central planners about quotas, production targets, overhead allocation, prices. Or they made their careers as 'fixers': chasing promised parts that hadn't arrived; scurrying to find a few extra tons of materials, a little extra food for their workers or foreign exchange to pay for a machine tool from abroad.

In fact, the abler a person was, the more likely he or she was to be shifted into paperpushing or fixing, and kept there. The skills needed to make a business perform are not in great demand in a Stalinist economy. Stalinism knows record keeping but not cost analysis or cost accounting. Financial management of any kind is totally absent. But so are pricing, market research, marketing, product innovation, product and customer service, quality control. No major design work on either one of East Germany's two automobiles, the Trabant and the Wartburg, has been done since the mid-1960s, 25 years ago.

Commute From West

Indeed people with experience and skills are so scarce that Commerzbank, third-largest of West Germany's big banks, is not even trying to find East Germans for the branches it is putting into every sizeable East Germany town. It is staffing them with West German employees who will commute for 18 months or two years until their East German replacements have been trained. 'Our new East German customers expect competent service,' explains one of Commerzbank's top people, 'and that requires a seasoned banker.'

Even two years' training, I suspect, isn't going to produce an executive seasoned enough to run a regional banking centre in a big industrial city like Leipzig. But skills can be taught and can be learned. There is furious skill-learning going on all over Central Europe. Hungary for instance, has opened an executive management centre in Budapest – that teaches in English! Skills can sometimes also be supplied from the outside. The scarcity of people in Eastern Europe with the needed managerial and professional skills is a very big problem. But it should be surmountable, over time at last.

Infinitely more difficult but also infinitely more critical will be the needed revolution in the managerial culture of Central Europe. It means undoing 40 years of wrong values, wrong incentives and wrong policies.

For 40 years no one in a Stalinist country has been permitted to report the truth. An old Soviet story – going back to the early years of the Five Year Plans 60 years ago – tells of the plant manager who needed an accountant. He asked each applicant: 'How much is two and two?' He gave the job to the one who answered: 'How much do you need it to be, Comrade Manager?'

And that's still the right answer, despite *glasnost* and *perestroika*. There is no other explanation for the near-famine in the Soviet Union today than that last fall's glowing reports of record harvests were what Moscow 'needed them to be'. And the regimes of Central Europe, especially the hard-liners in East Germany and Czechoslovakia, were even more economically Stalinist than the Russians, and stayed Stalinist longer. How can people now be expected to tell the truth when no one has been able to make a career for 40 years unless he was willing to lie and to be lied to? But a functioning economy is based on reliable information and on reports that can be trusted.

In a Stalinist system decisions are made at the highest possible level. This is the essence of a 'Plan' (and, of course, a main reason why centralized planning did not work). What to make and how much, what the product should look like and how much it should cost, are all laid down in the Plan. But so also is the number of people employed, their pay and their bonuses, their job titles and their promotions. All this is decided on high with minimum or no input from the people who then are supposed to carry out the Plan. These people can sabotage the Plan – and they do. But they cannot decide.

As a result no one is in the habit of decision-making, trained in it, tested in it. Nothing so much frightens people in former Communist countries, visitors report, as to be asked to make a decision. They are paralysed by the fear of making a mistake. They hold endless meetings, call for more and more studies and in the end find a good reason why someone higher up should take the responsibility. Yet it is the essence of a market economy – and its strength – that decisions are made close to market and customer, all the way down to the salesman who decides whether to stop calling on an unreceptive prospect, and to the supervisor who decides whether to stop the line to correct a malfunction. This is almost inconceivable to people who have lived and worked 40 years under a Stalinist regime.

Central Europe desperately needs midde-sized enterprises. The greatest opportunities, especially for providing badly needed new jobs, lie in services and in consumer goods. These are both areas in which middle-sized, locally managed businesses flourish. The bankrupt, giant government businesses can in most cases be salvaged only if broken up into smaller and more manageable units. If instead they are 'privatized' as they are – as now strongly advocated by government people in Czechoslovakia, East Germany and Poland – they will simply shift from being unproductive government monopolies to being unproductive non- government monopolies. And there would then be no economic turn-around, no free-market economy, only continued economic stagnation.

But where will the people come from to manage middle-sized enterprises? Stalinism can tolerate a farm woman's selling a few apples off a push cart. It cannot and does not tolerate middle-sized enterprises. To be effectively controlled, enterprises must be big and super-big. There is the huge ministry, employing tens of thousands which centrally runs all of the country's machine-tool factories. There is the *Kombinat*, only slightly smaller, the large holding company which centrally runs all the country's clothing factories. And then there are large conglomerates for which Stalinism has special affection. The former Bata shoe factory in Zlin in Central Czechoslovakia – until World War II the world's most efficient and most profitable footwear manufacturer – still makes shoes. But it now also includes a dozen totally unrelated businesses, including machinery manufacturers and even an aeroplane maker.

Sixty years ago Central Europe was chock-full of the kind of firms, the Germans call '*Mittelstand*', that is, successful middle-sized businesses, usually family-owned and family-managed. But only a few old people at or past retirement age even remember them now. The last ones in East Germany were expropriated more than 30 years ago; in Czechoslovakia and Hungary, as well as Poland, they were gone 10 years earlier.

And even if the needed entrepreneurs were to emerge, would they be allowed to do their work? After 40 years of Stalinist indoctrination there is deep prejudice against such people. That they try to make a profit is bad enough. Worse, much worse, they are independent. And for 40 years independent people have been virtual outlaws, 'They all want capitalism,' said a Belgian Mittelstand industrialist who had just come back from a long trip to Hungary and East Germany. 'But they don't want capitalists; they want functionaries.'

What Is a Market Economy?

There is, finally, an even bigger problem of managerial culture than any discussed so far: the lack of understanding of what free enterprise and a market economy are all about.

An American marketing executive this spring visited the Czech provincial city in which she had been born and raised and which she left, 22 years ago, fresh out of college, when the Russian tanks crushed the 'Prague Spring' in 1968. 'I was immediately asked,' she reports, 'to hold a seminar on marketing for the top people in the city's five big factories. I started out by telling them how our company in the U.S. operates. We have 2500 employees and are number three in a small but highly competitive and fast-moving market. I soon realized that I made no sense to my audience.

'So I stopped and said: "I have the feeling that you define a competitive market as one in which prices are kept high enough for every competitor to make a good profit."

' "That's exactly right," they all said. "After all, in a market economy a business has to make a profit."

' "No," I said, "in a market economy it has to earn a profit." And there was a look of utter bewilderment on every face.'

Very few, if any. people in Central Europe still believe in communism as a political, a social, an economic or a moral system. They want political freedom. They want the incomes and the goods that they know only a market economy can provide. But do they yet know – and how could they possibly know? – that in a market economy there is no 'profit' but only 'profit and loss'; no 'reward', but only 'risk and reward'; and that freedom is not just the absence of restraint but self-discipline and responsibility?

[1990]

20

China's Nightmare: No Jobs for the Millions

There are no unemployment figures in China, but huge numbers of people are grossly underemployed. They may nominally be on a payroll, but there is no work for them.

The crushing shortage of jobs in China is rarely ever mentioned, and least of all by the Chinese. Yet it may be the greatest obstacle to economic growth and performance. This reluctance to discuss the problem was exemplified recently during a week-long symposium in Beijing on economic and enterprise reform that I took part in. The symposium was organized by the World Bank at the behest of China's prime minister, Zhao Ziyang. However, the 30 Chinese members of the symposium – all senior government members – pushed exploration of the job shortage onto the handful of attending 'foreign experts'.

After years of spectacular advances, China's agricultural output is now stagnating because there are far too many people tilling the land. Reducing the peasant population from about 800 million to 400 million would almost certainly double farm output. Yet even 400 million would still represent 40 percent of the total population, or at least five times as much as developed countries now employ on the land to produce vast surpluses.

Imaginative Experiments

The Chinese are promoting 'village industries' to help unemployed peasants. These may be the most imaginative social experiments going on anyplace today, but at their most successful they could employ only thousands, not millions.

But where would those millions of underemployed peasants go? There are neither jobs nor housing for them in the overcrowded, desperately job-short cities. Indeed, the first demand of urban workers on the enterprises that employ them is that they start new businesses (called 'collectives', and pay substantially lower wages) to provide jobs for their own jobless children.

Overpopulation has been the curse of China for 200 years and in large part has been responsible for the social convulsions periodically ravaging the country from the Taiping Rebellion of the 1850s to Mao Tse-tung's 'Cultural Revolution' 20 years ago. But despite draconic, not to say brutal, birth control imposed by the present regime, population is still growing, and with it the need for jobs.

Hence the Chinese are caught on the horns of a fearful dilemma between the imperative of economic performance and the imperative of jobs. Only very rapid economic growth and stellar economic performance can ultimately provide jobs. But fast growth and economic performance, whether on the land or in industry, require giving priority to productivity and profit, along with the willingness to close inefficient plants and lay off their employees – and also the willingness to fire or demote inefficient or lazy workers.

Yet the present regime owes much of its popular support to the promise of lifetime employment regardless of performance. In the short run – and that may mean 10 years – emphasis on economic performance thus must aggravate the job pressures that already are a central problem. This would hit hardest those people least able to fend for themselves, the least skilled, least productive, least energetic and least trained – in a country that knows neither labour mobility nor training.

Adding to the difficulty are the different priorities of the central and local governments. The emphasis in Beijing is of necessity on economic performance; all the talk is of the need for more profit, higher productivity, more plant discipline. For the central government, a vastly increased supply of consumer goods – and of goods of vastly improved quality – must be the first priority. Without the incentives that only an increased consumer-goods supply can provide, the economic drive, both on the farm and in the cities, would soon falter; it shows signs of slowing down now.

But in the provinces, the cities and the villages, jobs are the first priority. The constant pressure on local governments to provide jobs explains, for instance, why there are now 30 million bicycles in government warehouses that are so shoddy they are unsaleable even though the bicycle is China's main vehicle. Provincial and city governments forced local manufacturers to keep on making the bicycles long after they had become unsaleable – the alternative would have been layoffs. Similar surpluses of unsaleable poor-quality goods, made only because the goods provided employment for large numbers of unskilled and untrained people, are said to be building up in tractors, black-and-white TV sets and light trucks.

Equally difficult is the second dilemma confronting the Chinese policymakers: the choice between economic growth and inflation. Growth will require dismantling the spider's web of regulations, controls, and negotiations that paralyses economic activity and forces managers to spend three-quarters of their time negotiating with myriad government and party agencies. Prices and wages are so grossly distorted that no one really knows what an enterprise, an industry, or a village community actually produces, let alone at what cost.

For instance, businesses are charged a 5 percent interest rate on all the money they take in – yet the inflation rate is 8 percent or 9 percent, so that businesses actually are subsidized by a negative rate of interest (there are persistent stories of businesses that borrow from the state bank at 5 percent and smuggle the money to Hong Kong, where it yields up to three times that). Since the real cost of money in China – a country with a critical shortage of capital formation – is probably close to 20 percent, the much-vaunted 'profits' of Chinese enterprises are pure fiction; I doubt there is a single Chinese business that is actually in the black. All other prices – for raw materials, finished goods, housing, or labour – are similarly out of touch with reality.

Worse still, all costs – for raw material, finished goods, wages, taxes, shares in the fictitious profits, rents, and so on – are constantly negotiated by each enterprise with a multitude of governments, party agencies, and works councils. Enterprises commonly pay four different prices for the same raw material: one price for the 30 percent supplied by the central government, another for the 30 percent supplied by the provincial government, a third for the 10 percent supplied by the city, and yet another price for the last 30 percent obtained in barter deals from customers. In each of these deals there are different 'concessions' – a higher tax rate for the central government; employing more people for the provincial and local authorities; or better-quality goods at lower prices for the barter partners.

There will be little economic growth unless this nightmare of regulations and negotiations is replaced by the discipline of a market economy. There will be only more unsaleable goods like the 30 million shoddy bicycles – and no incentive for farmers or workers. But removing controls is almost certain to bring sharp price increases. In relation to incomes, China's prices are actually quite high. But in relation to any cost – and especially to the cost of a bloated and singularly inefficient labour force – they are kept artificially low. 'Eventually' a market economy will, of course, correct the imbalance. But 'eventually' may mean four or five years, perhaps even longer, as China is still desperately short of trained and skilled people able to exploit the opportunities of a free economy.

But five years of inflation? Every Chinese policy maker knows that it was not Mao but inflation that ultimately defeated Chiang Kai-shek 40 years ago. Hence few people dare even talk of anything but 'gradual decontrol', even though it has never worked before anywhere. The first step in 'gradual decontrol' will be taken next spring when rents in government housing are nudged from 1 percent to 2 percent of a worker's monthly salary – still no more than a fraction of true cost, and probably not even enough to cover the cost of the utilities, such as electricity, that currently are provided without any charge. If this rent increase does not cause trouble, the next step may be one that was urged on the prime minister by the 'foreign experts' at the Beijing symposium: raising the interest rate for money that is being charged businesses and villages. But in all likelihood the rise at first will be only to a fraction of the true cost.

No One Wants to Yield

There is a good deal of discussion today, inside and outside China, of the political obstacles to that country's economic reform: the resistance of an entrenched bureaucracy to anything that threatens its power, and the Stalinists and Maoists who, while temporarily beaten, are only waiting for the reformers to stumble. Even the strongest advocates of rapid and radical economic reform are not willing to yield an iota of political control and domination by government and party for the sake of economic performance and growth.

But the crucial issues, the ones on which the success, and perhaps even the survival, of the present regime ultimately may depend, may be tactics rather than ideology or political strategies: China's ability to balance economic performance with the pressure for jobs, and decontrol with avoidance of inflation.

[1987]

Part III

MANAGEMENT

21

Tomorrow's Managers: The Major Trends

The greatest challenge to American business in the '90s, especially to the large company, may well be its management people. And we are totally unprepared for it.

One reason why there will be a problem is the sharp turn in the structure of management. For 35 years, from the end of World War II until the early '80s, the trend ran toward more and more layers of management and more and more staff specialists. The trend now goes in the opposite direction.

Restructuring the organization around information – something that will, of necessity, have to be done by all large businesses – invariably results in a drastic cut in the number of management levels and, with it, in the number of 'general' management jobs. Even the General Motors of 1995 is likely to have only 5 or 6 management levels, as against the 14 or 15 it has now. The 3 or 4 levels between operating divisions and the corporate top will, for instance, be eliminated altogether, and with them large numbers of staff people who now 'report' to these levels.

And 'restructuring' by the 'raiders' has shown in every single case that even a large company can get along without 'service staffs' –that is, people who analyse and advise rather than do. Yet, 'service staffs' have been the major growth area in American big business since Harold Geneen 30 years ago began to run a large and diversified ITT with staff specialists from the top.

The total number of managerial and professional people in the America of the mid-1990s is almost certainly going to be larger than it is today if only because we can expect fairly rapid growth in production, information, and customer service. But proportionately many more of the managerial and professional people in the latter '90s are going to be in 'lower-' rather than in 'middle-', let alone 'upper-' level jobs. Proportionately more will be in operations and in functional and technical work rather than in 'general' management, let alone in 'staff' work. And many more will be on their 'terminal' job at a fairly early age rather than on a 'promotion track'.

It is not only information that is causing these changes. During the last 20 years demographics almost guaranteed rapid promotion, at least into middle management, as the baby boomers moved into a near-vacuum created by 20 years of falling birth rates between 1925 and 1945. Now, especially in the big companies, two people stand on every rung of a promotional ladder that is itself getting shorter.

Business, and especially the big company, will have to change its personnel policies, its compensation policies, its promotion policies. Even more difficult, it will have to change the expectations and the vision of its management group. And it will have to do this at a time when it has lost a good deal of the trust and confidence of that group. In many – and, again, especially in big – companies, middle managers and professionals have become alienated from their company, and especially from its top management. They're distrustful of and sometimes openly hostile to it.

The reversal of the trend toward layers of management and headquarters staff – the trend that had propelled the careers of the people who are in management jobs today – would have been upsetting enough. It means a drastic change in their expectations and in their views of both the company and themselves. In many cases it means loss of a job when 'lifetime employment' had virtually been taken for granted. And it means the anxiety of a job hunt and a painful relocation.

What made all this traumatic, however, was that the 'restructuring' was done largely through financial manipulation: mergers, acquisitions and divestitures, leveraged buyouts, asset-stripping, and hostile takeovers. Middle managers and professionals feel, as a result, that their lives and careers are being sacrificed to enrich a few speculators who 'have never done any productive work'.

Bitterness

It isn't just Iowa farmers who fuel the populist upsurge that is so pronounced an element in the 1988 presidential campaign. It's equally management and professional people in the big corporations. 'I thought slavery had been abolished,' one middle manager, a highly competent engineer who had been 'relocated' by two hostile takeovers in a row, said with great bitterness in one of my seminars. 'But we are nothing but chattels now to be sold to the highest bidder.'

What has hurt particularly are the 'golden parachutes' that make top-management people rich in a hostile takeover or a leveraged buyout while their middle-management associates lose their jobs. Every middle manager in this country knows the E. F. Hutton story: the bosses whose mistakes caused the brokerage firm's downfall walked away with huge bonuses when the company was sold to Shearson Lehman while the local managers and salesmen who had kept the firm afloat through a decade of poor decisions at the top lost their jobs, their stock options, and, in some cases, even their severance pay.

But what hurts the most is that the new masters of American business (at least as perceived by middle managers and professionals) – the raiders, the junk-bond underwriters, the arbitrageurs and stock-exchange players – are so openly contemptuous of management people, of their focus on work rather than on 'deals', of their working for a salary rather than to become rich, and especially of their belief in the company as something to be proud of, as something to 'belong' to.

'Can we restore middle-management loyalty?' is a constantly asked question today. 'No' is the answer. Loyalty is a two-way street. And middle-management people do not feel that they have deserted the company; they feel strongly that the company has deserted them.

What's more, they now know they do not need to depend on the big company. Being let go by a GE or a Citibank is very painful, but it is rarely fatal. The overwhelming majority of middle-level people who were fired by big companies have found new jobs – and often better ones – within a year at the most. They are particularly in demand in small, entrepreneurial businesses.

The executive recruiters, in turn, who a few short years ago confined themselves to looking for top-management personnel, are increasingly willing to take on middle-management clients. 'I doubt,' says a leading executive recruiter, 'that there is a single middle manager or middle professional under 50 at a big company such as IBM or GE, AT&T or Sears Roebuck, who does not have his resume ready. And not one of them hangs up on me when I call.' And what top managements call 'disloyalty', middle-management people call 'taking responsibility for one's family and career'.

But just as yesterday's 'loyalty' will not be restored, yesterday's expectation of 'lifetime employment' for middle management will likewise not come back. Companies from now on will increasingly be run with the clear realization that what they call 'profit' is a genuine cost (something I have said for 30 years). A business, a division, a market, a product line has to earn the cost of capital or it will eventually be shut down or abandoned. This means that, increasingly, bigness will not be used or misused to finance the losers and to perpetuate yesterday. Thus, both employer and employee can expect more rather than less instability in managerial and professional employment.

Adjustments

These trends demand changes in compensation. Many companies have 'dual ladders of advancement' that offer pay and recognition other than promotion into management ranks for individual professional contributors. These will have to be substantially improved. But we also need policies that encourage staying in a job rather than being promoted out of it. We need emphasis on assignments to task-force teams, which will be the only way, in most cases, in which professional specialists can acquire a 'view of the whole' now that they will no longer be routinely promoted into managerial positions.

Altogether, we need policies that compensate people for performance rather than for rank – to the point where ten years hence we may routinely pay a top-flight professional more than the manager to whom he or she reports, just as we pay a football star more than we pay the coach.

But above all we will have to reconsider the relationship between employer and managerial or professional employee. Increasingly, we will be forced by middle-management pressure to restructure the job as a 'property right'. And a 'property right' is something that can be taken away only by 'due process'. Actually, we are halfway there even though company lawyers still do not want it to be true.

Increasingly, dismissed managers and professionals sue, and many many more threaten to do so. In every case I know of, the plaintiff has either won or received a generous out-of-court settlement. A few more years and it will be accepted legal doctrine that an individual manager or professional cannot be dismissed unless there is (a) proven malperformance on his or her part against clear, preset performance standards; (b) a clear removal procedure including, except in the grossest violations, a number of formal warnings; (c) appeal of the decision to, and its review by, impartial authority; and (d) proper compensation.

The sooner employers institute such 'due process' themselves, rather than wait for the courts to force them, the sooner they will regain the trust and allegiance of their managerial and professional employees.

But at the same time we need to safeguard the company's ability to lay off managerial and professional people, and especially to lay them off when it is not their performance, but economic conditions or business decisions (e.g., a merger or a divestiture) that causes them to become redundant. This certainly means higher severance pay than American companies have traditionally offered; we are already moving in that direction.

It would be less expensive and have greater motivational impact to do what some companies (e.g., Herman Miller, the office-furniture maker) are already doing: provide for all managerial and professional employees 'silver parachutes', that is, extra compensation in the event of the firm's being sold, acquired, or merged.

More effective, probably, would be nonfinancial measures, foremost among them 'outplacement' services for managerial and professional people who lose their jobs for any reason except gross malfeasance. Most laid-off managers find new jobs themselves rather than through a company's 'out-placement' service. But for most, especially people with long years of service with a company, the shock of being let go is severe – and that would be greatly assuaged by an effective 'outplacement' service furnished by the company.

For 50 years, ever since the union movement of the '30s, 'employee relations' in American business has meant relationships with and policies for rank-and-file workers. Increasingly, the employees to be concerned with will be the ones that most companies today take for granted (as companies in the '30s took the blue-collar worker for granted): managerial and professional people.

[1988]

22

How to Manage the Boss

Most managers, including of course most chief executives, have a boss. Few people are as important to the performance and success of a manager as the boss. Yet while management books and courses abound in advice on how to manage subordinates, few if any even mention managing the boss.

Few managers seem to realize how important it is to manage the boss or, worse, believe that it can be done at all. They bellyache about the boss but do not even try to manage him (or her). Yet managing the boss is fairly simple – indeed generally quite a bit simpler than managing subordinates. There are only a few Dos, and even fewer Don'ts.

- The first Do is to realize that it is both the subordinate's duty and in the subordinate's self-interest to make the boss as effective and as achieving as possible. The best prescription for one's own success is, after all, still to work for a boss who is going places. Thus the first Do is to go to the boss – at least once a year – and ask: 'What do I do and what do my people do that helps *you* do your job? And what do we do that hampers *you* and makes life more difficult for *you*?'

The Correct Definition

This sounds obvious – but it is rarely done. For even effective executives tend to misdefine a 'manager' as someone who is responsible for the work of subordinates – the definition of 50 years ago – and thus tend not to perceive that they have any responsibility for the boss's performance and effectiveness. But the correct definition of a manager – as we have known it for at least 40 years – is someone who is responsible for the performance of all the people on whom his own performance depends.

The first person on whom a manager's performance depends is the boss, and the boss is thus the first person for whose performance a manager has to take responsibility. But only by asking, 'what do I do to help you or to hamper you?' – the best way to ask is without beating about the bush – can you find out what the boss needs and what gets in the boss's way.

- Closely related is the need for awareness that your boss is a human being and an individual; no two persons work alike, perform alike, or behave alike. The subordinate's job is not to reform the boss, not to reeducate the boss, not to make the boss conform to what the business schools and the management books say bosses should be like. It is to enable a particular boss to perform as a unique individual. And being an individual, every boss has idiosyncrasies, has 'good words' and 'bad words', and, like the rest of us, needs his own security blanket.

To manage the boss requires thinking through such questions as: Does this individual who is my boss want me to come in once every month – but no more often – and spend 30 minutes presenting the performance, the plans, and the problems of my department? Or does this individual want me to come in every time there is anything to report or to discuss, every time there is the slightest change, every time we make a move? Does this individual want me to send the stuff in as a written report, in a nice folder, complete with tabs and a table of contents? Or does this individual want an oral presentation? Is this individual, in other words, a reader or a listener? And does this boss require (as do for instance most financial executives) 30 pages of figures on everything as his security blanket – and should it be tables or graphs? Does this individual need the information to be there when he gets to the office in the morning, or does this boss (as do a good many operating people) want it at the end of the day, say around 3:30 on Friday afternoon? And if there is disagreement among the management group, how does this boss want to have it handled? To have us iron it out and report our consensus (as did General Eisenhower and as President Reagan clearly did)? Or for us to report our disagreements in full detail and with complete documentation (as did both Gens. George Marshall and MacArthur)?

• What are the things the boss does well? What are his strengths? And what are the boss's limitations and weaknesses –the areas in which the subordinate needs to support, to buttress and to supplement the boss? A manager's task is to make the strengths of people effective and their weaknesses irrelevant – and that applies fully as much to the manager's boss as it applies to the manager's subordinates. If for instance the boss is good at marketing but uncomfortable with financial figures and analysis, managing the boss means to bring him into the marketing decision but to prepare the financial analysis beforehand and in depth.

Managing the boss means, above all, creating a relationship of trust. This requires confidence on the part of the superior that the subordinate manager will play to the boss's strengths and safeguard the boss against his or her limitations and weaknesses.

Keep the Boss Aware

• The final Do: Make sure the boss understands what can be expected of you, what the objectives and goals are on which your own energies and those of your people will be concentrated, what your priorities are, and, equally important, what they are not. It is by no means always necessary that the boss approve – it is sometimes not even desirable. But the boss must understand what you are up to, must know what to expect and what not to expect. Bosses, after all, are held responsible by their own bosses for the performance of their subordinates. They must be able to say: 'I know what Anne (or Joe) is trying to do.' Only if they can say this will they be able to delegate to their subordinate managers.

And now two Don'ts:

• Never expose the boss to surprises. It is the job of the subordinate to protect the boss against surprises – even pleasant ones (if any such exist). To be exposed to a surprise in the organization one is responsible for is humilation, and usually public humiliation. Different bosses want very different warnings of possible surprises. Some – again Ike is a good example – want no more than a warning that things may turn out differently. Other bosses – President Kennedy for example – demand a full, detailed report even if there is only a slight chance of a surprise. But all bosses need to be protected against surprises. Otherwise they will not trust a subordinate – and with good reason.

• Never underrate the boss! The boss may look illiterate: he may look stupid – and looks are not always deceptive. But there is no risk at all in overrating a boss. The worst that can happen is for the boss to feel flattered. But if you underrate the boss he will either see through your little game and will bitterly resent it. Or the boss will impute to you the deficiency in brains or knowledge you imputed to the boss and will consider you ignorant, dumb, or lacking in imagination.

But the most important thing is not what to do or what not to do. It is to accept that managing the boss is the responsibility of the subordinate manager and a key – maybe the most important one – to his or her own effectiveness as an executive.

[1986]

23

What Really Ails the U.S. Auto Industry

General Motors, Ford, and Chrysler have improved car quality so much that several of their models are now as well made as anything the Japanese offer. And through their discounts and financing deals they now offer the lowest prices. Yet they still steadily lose market share to the Japanese.

Detroit has also sharply reduced costs; some new Ford plants in the U.S. and in Mexico may now be the world's lowest-cost producers. Yet the Big Three are losing money hand over fist while the leading Japanese companies are profitable. All three – again with Ford in the lead – have sharply reduced the time it takes to develop a new design and bring it to market. But in the meantime the Japanese have reduced their lead-times even further, so that the time gap between Detroit and the Japanese has hardly narrowed at all.

There are a great many different diagnoses of Detroit's sickness: 'fat' instead of 'lean' manufacturing; union work rules: management's short-term vision; departmental parochialism, and so on. But the root of Detroit's problems goes much deeper. Detroit still operates on the assumption that the U.S. car market is homogeneous in its values and expectations but sharply segregated by income into four or five 'socioeconomic' groups. This theory of the market shapes how Detroit sees the market, how it organizes itself, and how it designs, makes, merchandises, and distributes its products. But this theory became obsolete at least 15 years ago.

Sloan's Legacy

Both the homogeneity of the market's values and expectations and its socioeconomic segmentation were first discerned by Alfred P. Sloan right after World War I. Sloan built GM on this insight into the world's biggest and for many decades its most profitable manufacturing enterprise. And both Chrysler and Ford – Chrysler during its rise in the '20s and '30s, Ford during its rebirth after World War II – built themselves in GM's image and on Sloan's socioeconomic market segmentation.

The Sloan theory of the U.S. market worked for more than 40 years – a good deal longer than such theories usually last. But it ceased to be valid in the '60s. Ford's Edsel should have been a roaring success. It was researched, designed, and marketed as the ultimate socioeconomic car for the newly affluent 'middle-middle' market. Instead, it was rejected by every socioeconomic group. The marketing success of that period was the Volkswagen Beetle – the symbol of the 'youth culture' and a low-priced car for affluent people. The 1973 petroleum crunch then finished off socioeconomic segmentation in the car market. It made driving a small, fuel-efficient car fashionable, if not patriotic, and a status symbol for the upper-middle class.

Many older Americans, those over 55 or so, still buy cars according to socioeconomic segmentation. But Detroit is losing the younger ones and with them the future. Up to half of them buy 'lifestyle' cars – primarily non-Detroit cars. Income is, of course, still important. But where it was the determinant in automobile buying from 1920 until 1965 or 1970, it has now become a restraint – in the U.S., in Western Europe, and in Japan. The determinant increasingly is 'lifestyle'; that is, values and expectations a potential customer largely selects for himself. And lifestyle is as elusive and qualitative a concept as socioeconomic segmentation was tangible and rigorously quantitative.

Equally important: Sloan's theory of the market assumed one car per family. But the American family today owns two as a rule. There is nothing 'typical' about the choice of the second car. In the same upper-middle socioeconomic group – all two-career professional families – there may be a family whose two cars are a Buick and a Dodge minivan; the family with two compacts, one American, one Japanese; the family whose two cars are a big Mercedes and a Ford Escort; and the couple, both professors at the state university, who drive 'His' and 'Hers' BMWs. Which of the four is 'typical'?

A market of socioeconomic segments is stable. It makes sense, then, to have long lead times for a new design. A lifestyle market is fuzzy and extremely volatile. One has to *plan* long-range and for every possible (or impossible) contingency so as to be able to *act* with extreme speed when opportunity knocks.

The lifestyle market is the one the Japanese take for granted, the market that they see, plan for, are prepared for. For their automobile industry barely existed when socioeconomic market segmentation prevailed: it emerged only after World War II and entered the U.S. only in the '70s. Japanese cars are therefore designed from the beginning as lifestyle cars, and the cars for one lifestyle market are designed to look very much alike regardless of price. All Toyota 'family cars', for example, from the low-price Corolla to the luxury Lexus, have the same look of comfortable solidity. They differ mainly in options and accessories rather than in style or in the way they handle.

But the Japanese are also organized to be opportunistic, which means that they continuously plan for every conceivable contingency so that they can move with lightning speed whenever an opportunity opens. When the success of Honda's Acura showed that there was a substantial market for a luxury car among baby boomers reaching middle age, Toyota and Nissan both already had detailed plans for such a car – and this enabled them to have it produced and out in the market in less than three years.

The Japanese also try to design parts so that they can be combined in any number of ways even though this considerably increases the cost of tools and dies – rank heresy for any American automobile producer. This made it possible, for instance, for Mazda to bring out in no time at all its sports car, the Miata – the marketing sensation of 1989. Though it looks entirely different from any other Mazda car, 80 percent of its parts are standard. This then enabled Mazda to make good money on the Miata even though it probably has sold fewer than a hundred thousand units, at which volume any American manufacturer would lose his shirt.

Detroit knows how to design successful lifestyle cars. In fact, every truly successful American car since World War II has been a lifestyle car: the Jeep as it was transformed after World War II from army roughneck into a high-performance and comfortable 'outdoors' vehicle; the Rambler, American Motors' original compact, which was designed as the second car of the newly affluent; Ford's Mustang and Thunderbird; the Dodge minivan. But despite these successes Detroit remains in the grip of Sloan's socioeconomic market segmentation. GM set up the Saturn Division a few years back as a new and separate lifestyle-based business. But when the Saturn car was unveiled last year, it turned out to be just another socioeconomic car for the already over-crowded 'middle-middle' segment.

Forty-five years of unbroken success are indeed hard to slough off. Everybody in Detroit management has grown up with socioeconomic market segmentation as an article of faith, if not as a law of nature. Worse: the way the Big Three are structured all but forces them into a socioeconomic straitjacket.

Sloan decentralized GM in the early '20s into divisions, each of which serves one socioeconomic segment. He similarly organized distribution in dealerships, each serving one of these segments. Despite countless reorganizations, this is still how GM, Ford, and Chrysler function. As a result, planning, design and marketing are either socioeconomically determined – that is, run counter to the way the market now actually works – or, if one of the Big Three designs a lifestyle car it is then subordinated to the socioeconomic axiom.

One example: the Chevrolet Cavalier is arguably the best second car on the American market – small enough to park easily and big enough for the entire family and a lot of luggage. But in order to give each GM division a 'popular' car, it was parcelled out among them. Several divisions thus offer and advertise the same car under different names, through different dealers, and at different prices. Thus GM customers are confused and complain that GM cars have lost all product differentiation. GM customers also tend to settle for the cheapest version with the fewest options and accessories and thus with the lowest profit margin for GM.

The Cavalier's main competitor, Toyota's Corolla, is marketed, advertised, and sold as one model by one group of dealers and with a full array of options and accessories. As a result, Corolla customers tend to buy the biggest package of options and accessories, which is where the profits are. And the Toyota dealers can also give much better service because they have so much more volume.

Teams vs. Traitors

The socioeconomic bent of the American automobile industry also explains in large measure its long lead times in developing new models and in reacting to market changes. Instead of being divided into autonomous market-segment divisions, the Japanese companies are decentralized into powerful, autonomous companywide functions, such as engineering, manufacturing, and marketing. It is easy for them to form companywide teams to work on designs outside the existing product scope. In Detroit, however, where market-segment divisions dominate, people who work on such teams risk being considered traitors by the division on whose payroll they are.

How can Detroit free itself from the straitjacket of its past success? It may require the complete restructuring of the traditional divisions and of the traditional dealer system as well. It may even require that GM, the biggest (and for more than 50 years, the most successful) company, be split into two or more competing businesses (which, incidentally, was advocated by some GM executives right after World War II). And until Detroit restructures itself to fit today's rather than yesterday's American automobile market, and today's American society, no amount of improvement in manufacturing processes, quality management, or interfunctional and interdepartmental teamwork is likely to restore it to health and to leadership.

[1991]

24

Manage by Walking Around – Outside!

Everyone knows how fast technology is changing. Everyone knows about markets becoming global and about shifts in the work force and in demographics. But few people pay attention to changing distributive channels. Yet, how goods and services get to customers and where customers buy are changing fully as fast as technology, markets and demography. And they are changing fast all over the world.

The bulk of consumer electronics – radios, TVs, VCRs calculators – were sold in Britain 15 years ago by thousands of independent, locally owned 'mom-and-pop' shops. Today the bulk of these goods is sold by four national chains. The mom-and-pop shop had to carry major manufacturers' brands and relied on the manufacturers' advertising. The four big chains carry their own private brands and do their own advertising.

In the U.S. office furniture – chairs, desks, filing cabinets – was bought 15 years ago in specialized office-furniture stores. Increasingly these goods are now being bought in discount stores and 'buying clubs'.

The recent Japanese promise to repeal the law that protects their mom-and-pop shops and keeps out big stores and chains, has been hailed as a great American victory. But in Japan's metropolitan areas (where 60 percent of the population live and shop), a majority of the mom & pop shops have already been converted into franchises of huge chains such as 7-Eleven or Mister Donut.

Six or seven years ago, mutual funds were distributed in the U.S. through two channels: indirectly, through brokerage houses and directly, through TV advertising. These two channels still carry something like three-fifths of all mutual funds sold. But one of the big mutual-fund groups (which six years ago sold exclusively through brokers) now sells 15 percent of its products through regional banks, 15 per cent through insurance agencies and another 15 percent through professional and trade associations.

Independent Outsiders

The hospital became a major market only 25 years ago. But then the hospital itself bought the goods it used. Now a steadily growing share is bought by independent outsiders to whom the hospital contracts maintenance, patient feeding, billing, physical therapy, the pharmacy, X-ray, the medical lab, and so on.

Increasingly even large users do not themselves buy their computers. They are bought instead by computer management firms that design, buy, install, and run their clients' information systems. A major computer maker, Digital Equipment Corp., now has its own computer-management subsidiary.

Where customers buy is changing fast too.

Many major department store chains are in serious trouble. Some once great stores – Bonwit Teller, for instance, or B. Altman, only recently New York's fashion leaders – are out of business. Others, such as Bloomingdale's, are in bankruptcy. But one chain, Seattle-based Nordstrom, has been doing well. The department stores that are in trouble are all organized and run as downtown stores with suburban branches. Nordstrom has only suburban stores. We may be seeing the first result of the slow but steady move of office work out of downtown and into the suburbs where the office workers live.

The big 'wire houses', the New York-based stockbrokers such as Merrill Lynch and Shearson Lehman, did exceptionally well only a few years ago. Now they are losing sales and profits. But some large 'regional' houses (i.e., brokers not headquartered in New York) such as A. G. Edwards in St Louis, are doing fine. And so are some 'institutional brokers' such as New York-based Sanford Bernstein.

The wire houses serve both the 'retail customer' – the individual investor – and the 'wholesale customers' – the pension funds. A. G. Edwards serves primarily the retail market, Sanford Bernstein exclusively the institutional market. Traditionally large stock-brokers were successful in serving both markets. But in no other line of business do retail customers and wholesale customers shop in the same place. Are the securities markets now segmenting themselves the way every other market has?

Changes in distributive channels may not matter much to GNP and macroeconomics. But they should be a major concern of every business and every industry. Yet they are very difficult to predict. What's worse: They do not show up in reports and statistics until they have gone very far. They are what statisticians call 'changes at the margin'. And by the time such changes become statistically significant, it is usually too late to adapt to them, let alone to exploit them as opportunities.

The one way to be abreast of them is to go out and look for these changes. Here again are a few examples:

Alfred P. Sloan built General Motors into the world's premier manufacturing company, in the '20s and '30s, by actually working with customers. Once every three months he would disappear from Detroit without telling anyone where he was going. The next morning he would show up at a dealer's lot in Memphis or Albany, would introduce himself, and would ask the dealer's permission to work as a salesman for a couple of days or as an assistant service manager. During that week he would work like this in two more dealerships in two other cities. The following Monday he'd be back in Detroit, firing off memoranda on changing customer behaviour and changing customer preferences on dealer service and on company service to the dealer, on market trends and style trends.

GM in those years had the most up-to-date and comprehensive customer research in American industry. And yet – at least so I was told by the then head of customer research at GM – Sloan, by actually working in the field, spotted more and more important trends than did customer research, and spotted them earlier.

The late Karl Bays made American Hospital Corp. the leader in its industry during the 1970s. He himself credited his success largely to his going out into the field. Twice a year he would take for two weeks each the place of a salesman on vacation. When the salesman came back, Bays said (with a twinkle in his eye) 'the customer always complained about the incompetence of his replacement and about the dumb questions I asked.' But selling, Bays said, was not the point of the exercise; learning was.

Another variant: two men who together took over a small and lacklustre chain of fashion shops in the mid-'50s built it into one of America's retail giants. For 30 years, until their retirement, each spent every Saturday in a different shopping mall. They did not visit their own stores. They spent the day in other companies' stores – some fashion stores, some bookshops, some stores for household goods and so on, watching shoppers, watching sales people, chatting with store managers. And they insisted that every one of their senior executives do likewise, including the lawyer, the controller, and the vice president for personnel.

As a result, the company foresaw in the early '60s the coming of the 'youth culture' and built or remodelled stores to attract teenagers. A few years later, when everyone talked of the 'greening of America', the company realized that the youth culture was passé and changed merchandise and stores to attract the young adult. And another 10 years later, well before 1980, the company saw and understood the emergence of the two-earner family.

Dumb Questions

To be able to anticipate changes in distributive channels and in where customers buy (and how, which is equally important) one has to be in the marketplace, has to watch customers, and noncustomers, has to ask 'dumb questions'. It is almost 40 years since I first advised executives to 'walk around' – that is, to get out of their offices, visit and talk to their associates in the company. This was the right advice then; now it is the wrong thing to do, and a waste of the executive's scarcest resource, his time. For now we know how to build upward information into the organization. To depend on walking around actually may lull executives into a false sense of security; it may make them believe that they have information when all they have is what their subordinates wanted them to hear.

The right advice to executives now is to walk outside.

[1990]

25

Corporate Culture: Use It, Don't Lose It

Changing the corporate culture has become the latest management fad. Every business magazine carries articles about it. And not a week goes by without my being asked to run a seminar on the subject.

There is indeed a need to change deeply ingrained habits in a good many organizations. Electric-power and telephone companies always had their profits guaranteed by public regulation. Now they find themselves up against cutthroat competition. Customers demand just-in-time delivery. Consumers are increasingly picky about quality and service. Employees sue at the drop of a hat alleging discrimination and sexual harassment. And with product lives shrinking, there is an urgent need in most mechanical industries in the U.S. (and even more in those of Europe) to change drastically the way new products and new models are conceived, designed, made and marketed, with the process eventually being telescoped into months from years.

Form and Content

What these needs require are changes in behaviour. But 'changing culture' is not going to produce them. Culture – no matter how defined – is singularly persistent. Nearly 50 years ago, Japan and Germany suffered the worst defeats in recorded history, with their values, their institutions and their cultures discredited. But today's Japan and today's Germany are unmistakably Japanese and German in culture, no matter how different this or that behaviour. In fact, changing behaviour works only if it can be based on the existing 'culture'.

Japan is the best example. Alone of all non-Western countries it has become a modern society, because her reformers, a hundred years ago, consciously based the new 'Westernized' behaviour on traditional Japanese values and on traditional Japanese culture. The modern Japanese corporation and university are thoroughly 'Western' in their form. But they were used as containers, so to speak, for the traditional and thoroughly un-Western culture of the mutual obligations and loyalties of a clan society – e.g., in the lifetime commitment of company to employee and employee to company, or in organizing industry in *keiretsu*, groups of autonomous firms held together as 'vassals' by mutual dependence and mutual loyalty.

The reformers of India and China, by contrast, felt that they had to change their countries' cultures. The only results have been frustration, friction, confusion – and no changes in behaviour.

Another example: Konrad Adenauer in the 1920s was a vocal critic of Weimar Germany, for its 'bourgeois' values, its greed, its materialism, its worship of money and business. When he became chancellor of a defeated Germany after World War II he deliberately and uncompromisingly strove to restore the pre-Hitler 'bourgeois' Germany he so thoroughly detested. When criticized – and he was harshly attacked by well-meaning 'progressives' both in Germany and in the West – he answered: 'Pre-Hitler Germany, no matter how deficient, is the only culture Germans alive today know that still worked: we have no choice but to use it to build the new, the post-Hitler Germany.'

But there is also a good – and American – business example: the railroads. In the late 1940s, the American railroads were losing money hand over fist. Worse still, they were losing market share to trucks and aeroplanes even faster. Yet they were clearly needed – and so Uncle Sam, everybody agreed, would have to take them over. And most of the passenger business did indeed have to be taken over by government agencies. But passenger business was never more than one-tenth of railroad traffic.

The railroads' real business, freight traffic, remained totally private in the U.S. – the only country in the world where this is the case. Moreover, the American railroads are the only ones that make money. Every other railroad system is virtually bankrupt. And the railroads in the U.S. carry a significant share of the country's freight – a little more than one-third of long-distance traffic – with no other system carrying more than 5 percent to 8 percent (and neither the British nor the Japanese railroads carry even that much). The American railroads based this turnaround on the existing values of their managers, their clerks, their train crews – on the railroaders' dedication to technical standards, for instance.

If you have to change habits, don't change culture. Change habits. And we know how to do that.

The first thing is to define what results are needed. In the hospital emergency room, for instance, each patient should be seen within one minute after arrival by a competent person – e.g., an emergency-room nurse. The new model of the washing machine or of the laptop computer has to be ready for market testing within 15 months of its predecessor's introduction. Every customer inquiry, including every complaint, has to be settled within 24 hours (the standard of a well-run mutual-funds firm).

The next – and most important – step is *not* a 'training session' or a management conference, let alone a lecture by the big boss. It is to ask: 'Where within our own system do we *do* this already?'

The American railroads began their turnaround around 1948 or 1949 when executives at the Union Pacific, the Chesapeake & Ohio and the Norfolk & Western first asked: 'What is the most important result we need?' They all answered: 'To get back on the railroad the shipment of finished automobiles from factory to dealer.' Then they asked: 'Is anyone on any railroad actually doing this?'

The moment the question was asked, they all realized that one subsidiary of the Chesapeake & Ohio – the one serving Flint, Michigan, home of the Buick Division of General Motors – was actually increasing its share of finished-automobile shipments while every other railroad in the country was losing automobile business. Yet all these people in Flint had done was to find out what traditional railroad services Buick needed and was willing to pay for – and then to provide the service with true excellence.

Marshall Field in Chicago was one of the first of the high-class big-city department stores to get into trouble, in the 1970s – and one of the first ones to get out of trouble too. Three or four successive CEOs tried to change the culture – to no avail. Then a new CEO came in who asked, 'What do we have to produce by way of results?' Every one of his store managers knew the answer, 'We have to increase the amount each shopper spends per visit.' Then he asked, 'Do any of our stores actually do this?' Three or four – out of 30 or so – did it. 'Will you then tell us,' the new CEO asked, 'what you people *do* that gives you the desired results?'

In every single case these results were achieved not by doing something different but by systematically doing something everyone had known all along should be done, had in the policy manuals, and had been preaching – but only the few exceptions had been practising.

The next step, therefore, is for top management to make sure that the effective behaviour as it develops out of the organization's own culture is actually being practised. This means, above all, that senior management systematically asks, again and again: 'What do we in senior management, and in this company as a whole, do that helps you to produce the results that all of us are agreed are the necessary ones?' And: 'What do we do that hampers you concentrating on these necessary results?' People who successfully managed to get old and entrenched organizations to do the needed new things ask these questions at every single meeting with their associates – and take immediate action on what they hear.

Iraq vs. Grenada

Finally, changing habits and behaviour requires changing recognitions and rewards. People in organizations, we have known for a century, tend to act in response for being recognized and rewarded – everything else is preaching. The moment people in an organization are recognized – for instance by being asked to present to their peers what made them successful in obtaining the desired results – they will act to get the recognition. The moment they realize that the organization rewards for the right behaviour they will accept it.

The best example: the way the American military services worked together in the recent Iraq campaign. In the invasion of Grenada in 1983 there was no cooperation at all between the services – if there had been the slightest opposition, the invasion would have ended in disaster. The military immediately organized all kinds of conferences, pep sessions, lectures and so on, to preach cooperation. Still, less than a year and a half ago, the Panama invasion almost foundered because the services still did not cooperate.

Only a year later, in Iraq, cooperation worked as no service cooperation ever worked before. The reason: Word got around, I am told, that henceforth the appraisal of an officer's cooperation with other services – as judged by those other services – would be a material factor in promotion decisions.

[1991]

26

Permanent Cost Cutting: Permanent Policy

Scores of large organizations – businesses of all kinds but also government agencies, hospitals, and universities – have sharply cut staffs these past few years. But few have realized the expected cost savings. In some cases costs have even gone up. In many more performance has suffered. And there are growing employee complaints about stress and work loads.

Cutting staffs to cut costs is putting the cart before the horse. The only way to bring costs down is to restructure the work. This will then result in reducing the number of people needed to do the job, and far more drastically than even the most radical staff cutbacks could possibly do. Indeed, a cost crunch should always be used as an opportunity to rethink and to redesign operations.

Eliminate Operations

To start cost cutting managements usually ask: 'How can we make this operation more efficient?' It is the wrong question. The question should be: 'Would the roof cave in if we stopped doing this work altogether?' And if the answer is 'probably not,' one eliminates the operation. This is unpopular, to be sure. Someone is bound to argue: 'We needed this procedure only 18 months ago and may need it again 18 months hence.' But eliminating an entire operation is by far the most effective way to cut costs, and the only one likely to produce by itself permanent cost savings. It is by no means accidental that the only places where cost cutting done during the past few years has produced real savings are where an entire operation was eliminated – in the commercial bank, for instance, that closed down an unprofitable merchant-banking subsidiary.

And it is always amazing how many of the things we do will never be missed. One example – a fairly typical one – is the old manual order-entry system used until the task was computerized five years ago, but still maintained 'just in case'. Another is the system of duplicate patient files that many hospitals maintain, one for billing, one for patient-care, each run on a different computer with a different program. Altogether, up to one-third of all clerical and control operations are likely to be found unneeded, because they either never served a purpose or because they have outlived it. And nothing is less productive than to make more efficient what should not be done at all.

The next question in respect to the two-thirds of operations that will be found to serve a need is: 'What contribution to the business should each make? What purpose does it serve?' Managements usually think the answer to be obvious. But more often than not, no one has an answer; or the answer is patently wrong; or, worst of all, there is more than one.

'Why do we check all our sales peoples' expense accounts?' 'To keep them honest, of course.' But that is hardly a business objective. The right answer is: 'To keep sales expenses under control.' And this is best done – and at a fraction of the cost – by determining expense standards based, for instance, on a sales person's need to travel and on the number of nights spent away from home. All that is needed to arrive at these standards is for a small number of experienced sales people to keep a record of their actual expenses twice a year for one week.

The previous system in the company – the system that thought its purpose was morality – kept 11 clerks busy the year round. The new system employs not even one full-time person. And it further enabled the company – a large national wholesaler of builders' supplies – to cut its sales force to 158 people from 167, despite a steady growth in sales volume. Sales people have more time to sell, when they no longer misuse selling time filling out lengthy 'swindle sheets'.

Just as common as the wrong answer to the question of what purpose a given operation serves, are two or more answers. But a well-designed and cost-effective operation serves one purpose only. To combine two or more in one operation means inefficiencies and sky-high costs.

'We have two objectives in supplying our 2800 national distributors,' said the builders'-supply people in answer to the question of what their big logistics operation contributed. 'We make sure that none of our distributors is ever out of stock. And we make sure that we don't pile up excess inventory.' What was needed were two separate operations.

One would make sure that the distributors are always stocked adequately with the fast-moving standard items that together account for about half of the firm's dollar sales. This is being done by stocking the distributors with 15 percent to 20 percent more of these items than they will sell during the next three weeks. There is no central inventory of these items any more, and no inventory control. The stock level for every distributor is determined by systematic spot checks, taken every other week, of the actual retail sale of a 3 percent sample of distributors – that is of 84 distributors throughout the country. This requires only seven or eight sales trainees, and has been found, incidentally, to be a most effective training tool.

A second operation then handles the 20 percent of 'speciality' products – mostly big-ticket items – that together account for the other half of the firm's dollar sales (and for a substantially larger part of its profits). These are stocked in one central warehouse located at the hub of an air freight company, and shipped free of charge by overnight air delivery anyplace in the country within six hours of receipt of the order.

The old system cost almost 1 percent of the company's sales (and that in a business where a 6 percent return on sales is considered outstanding!). The new systems together cost less than one-third as much. And where the old system kept 53 people busy the two new systems together employ 20. Yet the new systems give both better service and better inventory control.

The question of *how* to organize the restructured organization for maximum performance and minimum cost comes only at the very end. More computers to handle more data faster is rarely the right answer. To be sure, the end product will be in many cases expressed by a computer program. But the task is to define what information is needed rather than how to manipulate it.

This may mean – as it did in one of my earlier examples – switching from inside to outside data, in order to find out the actual retail sales of one's customers to the ultimate consumers. It may mean – especially in operations aimed at controlling a process – shifting from counting to statistics and sampling. Not only is sampling much cheaper than counting, it is far more reliable. Statistical analysis alone can provide the crucial information on which effective control rests: the difference between fluctuations within the permissible range of normal, and the 'exception', that is the genuine malfunction, which calls for immediate remedy.

Cutting costs is only the beginning. If all that is being done is to cut costs without putting in adequate cost prevention, a recurrence of excess costs a few short years hence, can be guaranteed. For costs never drift down. Cost prevention requires steady work on productivity improvement of every operation, year in and year out – with a 3 percent annual improvement a minimum goal. It requires that every operation and every activity be put, every third year or so, to the question: 'Do we really need to do this or should it be abandoned?' It requires that new operations and activities – and especially new staff operations – be entered only if an old operation is abandoned or at least pruned back.

Each operation and activity should also be questioned – again every three years – as to the purpose it serves and the contribution it makes to the business. And each, finally, should be subjected to the question: What is the simplest way to achieve this purpose?

Excess Fat

By now most of us have learned the hard way that dieting off fat is a good deal more difficult than not putting it on in the first place. Excess costs are excess fat. Cutting costs rarely gets much support from the work force itself: it means, after all, laying off people. Without active work-force participation, however, none of the measures needed for effective cost control are easy to implement. Indeed one reason why so many of the cost-cutting efforts of past years have failed to cut costs is that they were imposed from above on a work force that saw in them a threat to their own jobs and incomes. Cost prevention, however, can count on active, and indeed, enthusiastic work-force support. Employees know where the fat is. They also know that low, controlled costs mean better and more secure jobs.

A great deal more cost-cutting is still needed, especially in big organizations (and by no means only in American ones – the big Japanese companies, e.g., the big banks, are far more overstaffed still). But cost-cutting should always be used as the first step toward building permanent cost prevention into the organization.

[1989]

27

What the Nonprofits Are Teaching Business

The Girl Scouts, the Red Cross, the pastoral churches – our nonprofit organizations – are becoming America's management leaders. In two areas, strategy and the effectiveness of the board, they are practising what most American businesses only preach. And in the most crucial area – the motivation and productivity of knowledge workers – they are truly pioneers, working out the policies and practices that business will have to learn tomorrow.

Few people are aware that the nonprofit sector is by far America's largest employer. Every other adult – a total of 80 million-plus people – works as a volunteer, giving on average nearly five hours each week to one or several nonprofit organizations. This is equal to 10 million full-time jobs. Were volunteers paid, their wages, even at minimum rate, would amount to some $150 billion, or 5 percent of GNP. And volunteer work is changing fast. To be sure, what many do requires little skill or judgment: collecting in the neighbourhood for the Community Chest one Saturday afternoon a year, chaperoning youngsters selling Girl Scout cookies door to door, driving old people to the doctor. But more and more volunteers are becoming 'unpaid staff', taking over the professional and managerial tasks in their organizations.

Not all nonprofits have been doing well, of course. A good many community hospitals are in dire straits. Traditional churches and synagogues of all persuasions – liberal, conservative, evangelical, fundamentalist – are still steadily losing members. Indeed, the sector overall has not expanded in the last 10 or 15 years, either in terms of the money it raises (when adjusted for inflation) or in the number of volunteers. Yet in its productivity, in the scope of its work and in its contribution to American society, the nonprofit sector has grown tremendously in the last two decades.

The Salvation Army is an example. People convicted to their first prison term in Florida, mostly very poor black or hispanic youths, are now paroled into the Salvation Army's custody – about 25,000 each year. Statistics show that if these young men and women go to jail the majority will become habitual criminals. But the Salvation Army has been able to rehabilitate 80 percent of them through a strict work programme run largely by volunteers. And the programme costs a fraction of what it would to keep the offenders behind bars.

Underlying this programme and many other effective nonprofit endeavours is a commitment to management. Twenty years ago, management was a dirty word for those involved in nonprofit organizations. It meant business, and nonprofits prided themselves on being free of the taint of commercialism and above such sordid considerations as the bottom line. Now most of them have learned that nonprofits need management even more than business does, precisely because they lack the discipline of the bottom line. The nonprofits are, of course, still dedicated to 'doing good'. But they also realize that good intentions are no substitute for organization and leadership, for accountability, performance, and results. Those require management and that, in turn, begins with the organization's mission.

As a rule, nonprofits are more money-conscious than business enterprises are. They talk and worry about money much of the time because it is so hard to raise and because they always have so much less of it than they need. But nonprofits do not base their strategy on money, nor do they make it the centre of their plans, as so many corporate executives do. 'The businesses I work with start their planning with financial returns,' says one well-known CEO who sits on both business and nonprofit boards. 'The nonprofits start with the performance of their mission.'

Starting with the mission and its requirements may be the first lesson business can learn from successful nonprofits. It focuses the organization on action. It defines the specific strategies needed to attain the crucial goals. It creates a disciplined organization. It alone can prevent the most common degenerative disease of organizations, especially large ones: splintering their always limited resources on things that are 'interesting' or look 'profitable' rather than concentrating them on a very small number of productive efforts.

The best nonprofits devote a great deal of thought to defining their organization's mission. They avoid sweeping statements full of good intentions and focus, instead, on objectives that have clear-cut implications for the work their members perform – staff and volunteers both. The Salvation Army's goal, for example, is to turn society's rejects – alcoholics, criminals, derelicts – into citizens. The Girl Scouts help youngsters become confident, capable young women who respect themselves and other people. The Nature Conservancy preserves the diversity of nature's fauna and flora. Nonprofits also start with the environment, the community, the 'customers' to be; they do not, as American businesses tend to do, start with the inside, that is, with the organization or with financial returns.

Willowcreek Community Church in South Barrington, Illinois, outside Chicago, has become the nation's largest church – some 13,000 parishioners. Yet it is barely 15 years old. Bill Hybels, in his early twenties when he founded the church, chose the community because it had relatively few churchgoers, though the population was growing fast and churches were plentiful. He went from door to door asking, 'Why don't you go to church?' Then he designed a church to answer the potential customers' needs: for instance, it offers full services on Wednesday evenings because many working parents need Sunday to spend with their children. Moreover, Hybels continues to listen and react. The pastor's sermon is taped while it is being delivered and instantly reproduced so that parishioners can pick up a cassette when they leave the building because he was told again and again, 'I need to listen when I drive home or drive to work so that I can build the message into my life.' But he was also told: 'The sermon always tells me to change my life but never how to do it.' So now every one of Hybels's sermons ends with specific action recommendations.

A well-defined mission serves as a constant reminder of the need to look outside the organization not only for 'customers' but also for measures of success. The temptation to content oneself with the 'goodness of our cause' – and thus to substitute good intentions for results – always exists in nonprofit organizations. It is precisely because of this that the successful and performing nonprofits have learned to define clearly what changes *outside* the organization constitute 'results' and to focus on them.

The experience of one large Catholic hospital chain in the Southwest shows how productive a clear sense of mission and a focus on results can be. Despite the sharp cuts in Medicare payments and hospital stays during the past eight years, this chain has increased revenues by 15 percent (thereby managing to break even) while greatly expanding its services and raising both patient-care and medical standards. It has done so because the nun who is the CEO understood that she and her staff are in the business of delivering health care (especially to the poor), not running hospitals.

As a result, when health care delivery began moving out of hospitals for medical rather than economic reasons about ten years ago, the chain promoted the trend instead of fighting it. It founded ambulatory surgery centres, rehabilitation centres, X-ray and lab networks, HMOs, and so on. The chain's motto was: 'If it's in the patient's interest, we have to promote it; it's then our job to make it pay.' Paradoxically, the policy has filled the chain's hospitals; the freestanding facilities are so popular they generate a steady stream of referrals.

This is, of course, not so different from the marketing strategy of successful Japanese companies. But it is very different indeed from the way most Western businesses think and operate. And the difference is that the Catholic nuns – and the Japanese – start with the mission rather than with their own rewards, and with what they have to make happen outside themselves, in the marketplace, to deserve a reward.

Finally, a clearly defined mission will foster innovative ideas and help others understand why they need to be implemented – however much they fly in the face of tradition. To illustrate, consider the Daisy Scouts, a programme for five-year-olds which the Girl Scouts initiated a few years back. For 75 years, first grade had been the minimum age for entry into a Brownie troop, and many Girl Scout councils wanted to keep it that way. Others, however, looked at demographics and saw the growing number of working women with 'latchkey' kids. They also looked at the children and realized that they were far more sophisticated than their predecessors a generation ago (largely thanks to TV).

Today the Daisy Scouts are 100,000 strong and growing fast. It is by far the most successful of the many programmes for preschoolers that have been started these last 20 years, and far more successful than any of the very expensive government programmes. Moreover, it is so far the only programme that has seen these critical demographic changes and children's exposure to long hours of TV viewing as an opportunity.

Many nonprofits now have what is still the exception in business – a functioning board. They also have something even rarer: a CEO who is clearly accountable to the board and whose performance is reviewed annually by a board committee. And they have what is rarer still: a board whose performance is reviewed annually against preset performance objectives. Effective use of the board is thus a second area in which business can learn from the nonprofit sector.

In U.S. law, the board of directors is still considered the 'managing' organ of the corporation. Management authors and scholars agree that strong boards are essential and have been writing to that effect for more than 20 years, beginning with Myles Mace's pioneering work. Nevertheless, the top managements of our large companies have been whittling away at the directors' role, power, and independence for more than half a century. In every single business failure of a large company in the last few decades, the board was the last to realize that things were going wrong. To find a truly effective board, you are much better advised to look in the nonprofit sector than in our public corporations.

In part, this difference is a product of history. Traditionally, the board has run the shop in nonprofit organizations – or tried to. In fact, it is only because nonprofits have grown too big and complex to be run by part-time outsiders, meeting for three hours a month, that so many have shifted to professional management. The American Red Cross is probably the largest nongovernmental agency in the world and certainly one of the most complex. It is responsible for worldwide disaster relief; it runs thousands of blood banks as well as the bone and skin banks in hospitals; it conducts training in cardiac and respiratory rescue nationwide; and it gives first-aid courses in thousands of schools. Yet it did not have a paid chief executive until 1950, and its first professional CEO came only with the Reagan era.

But however common professional management becomes – and professional CEOs are now found in most nonprofits and all the bigger ones – nonprofit boards cannot, as a rule, be rendered impotent the way so many business boards have been. No matter how much nonprofit CEOs would welcome it – and quite a few surely would – nonprofit boards cannot become their rubber stamp. Money is one reason. Few directors in publicly held corporations are substantial shareholders, whereas directors on nonprofit boards very often contribute large sums themselves, and are expected to bring in donors as well. But also, nonprofit directors tend to have a personal commitment to the organization's cause. Few people sit on a church vestry or on a school board unless they deeply care about religion or education. Moreover, nonprofit board members typically have served as volunteers themselves for a good many years and are deeply knowledgeable about the organization, unlike outside directors in a business.

Precisely because the nonprofit board is so committed and active, its relationship with the CEO tends to be highly contentious and full of potential for friction. Nonprofit CEOs complain that their board 'meddles'. The directors, in turn, complain that management 'usurps' the board's function. This has forced an increasing number of nonprofits to realize that neither board nor CEO is 'the boss'. They are colleagues, working for the same goal but each having a different task. And they have learned that it is the CEO's responsibility to define the tasks of each, the board's and his or her own.

For example, a large electric co-op in the Pacific Northwest created ten board committees, one for every member. Each has a specific work assignment: community relations, electricity rates, personnel, service standards, and so on. Together with the co-op's volunteer chairman and its paid CEO, each of these one-person committees defines its one-year and three-year objectives and the work needed to attain them, which usually requires five to eight days a year from the board member. The chairman reviews each member's work and performance every year, and a member whose performance is found wanting two years in a row cannot stand for reelection. In addition, the chairman, together with three other board members, annually reviews the performance of the entire board and of the CEO.

The key to making a board effective, as this example suggests, is not to talk about its function but to organize its work. More and more nonprofits are doing just that, among them half a dozen fair-sized liberal arts colleges, a leading theological seminary, and some large research hospitals and museums. Ironically, these approaches reinvent the way the first nonprofit board in America was set up 300 years ago: the Harvard University Board of Overseers. Each member is assigned as a 'visitor' to one area in the university – the Medical School, the Astronomy Department, the investment of the endowment – and acts both as a source of knowledge to that area and as a critic of its performance. It is a common saying in American academia that Harvard has the only board that makes a difference.

The weakening of the large corporation's board would, many of us predicted (beginning with Myles Mace), weaken management rather than strengthen it. It would diffuse management's accountability for performance and results; and indeed, it is the rare big-company board that reviews the CEO's performance against preset business objectives. Weakening the board would also, we predicted, deprive top management of effective and credible support if it were attacked. These predictions have been borne out amply in the recent rash of hostile takeovers.

To restore management's ability to manage we will have to make boards effective again – and that should be considered a responsibility of the CEO. A few first steps have been taken. The audit committee in most companies now has a real rather than a make-believe job responsibility. A few companies – though so far almost no large ones – have a small board committee on succession and executive development, which regularly meets with senior executives to discuss their performance and their plans. But I know of no company so far where there are work plans for the board and any kind of review of the board's performance. And few do what the larger nonprofits now do routinely: put a new board member through systematic training.

Nonprofits used to say, 'We don't pay volunteers so we cannot make demands upon them.' Now they are more likely to say, 'Volunteers must get far greater satisfaction from their accomplishments and make a greater contribution precisely because they do not get a paycheque.' The steady transformation of the volunteer from well-meaning amateur to trained, professional, unpaid staff member is the most significant development in the nonprofit sector – as well as the one with the most far-reaching implications for tomorrow's business.

A midwestern Catholic diocese may have come furthest in this process. It now has fewer than half the priests and nuns it had only 15 years ago. Yet it has greatly expanded its activities – in some cases, such as help for the homeless and for drug abusers, more than doubling them. It still has many traditional volunteers like the Altar Guild members who arrange flowers. But now it is also being served by some 2,000 part-time unpaid staff who run the Catholic charities, perform administrative jobs in parochial schools, and organize youth activities, college Newman Clubs, and even some retreats.

A similar change has taken place at the First Baptist Church in Richmond Virginia, one of the largest and oldest churches in the Southern Baptist Convention. When Dr Peter James Flamming took over five years ago, the church had been going downhill for many years, as is typical of old, inner-city churches. Today it again has 4,000 communicants and runs a dozen community outreach programmes as well as a full complement of in-church ministries. The church has only nine paid full-time employees. But of its 4,000 communicants, 1,000 serve as unpaid staff.

This development is by no means confined to religious organizations. The American Heart Association has chapters in every city of any size throughout the country. Yet its paid staff is limited to those at national headquarters, with just a few travelling trouble-shooters serving the field. Volunteers manage and staff the chapters, with full responsibility for community health education as well as fund raising.

These changes are, in part, a response to need. With close to half the adult population already serving as volunteers, their overall number is unlikely to grow. And with money always in short supply, the nonprofits cannot add paid staff. If they want to add to their activities – and needs are growing – they have to make volunteers more productive, have to give them more work and more responsibility. But the major impetus for the change in the volunteer's role has come from the volunteers themselves.

More and more volunteers are educated people in managerial or professional jobs – some preretirement men and women in their fifties, even more baby boomers who are reaching their mid-thirties or forties. These people are not satisfied with being helpers. They are knowledge workers in the jobs in which they earn their living, and they want to be knowledge workers in the jobs in which they contribute to society – that is, their volunteer work. If nonprofit organizations want to attract and hold them, they have to put their competence and knowledge to work. They have to offer meaningful achievement.

Many nonprofits systematically recruit for such people. Seasoned volunteers are assigned to scan the newcomers – the new member in a church or synagogue, the neighbour who collects for the Red Cross – to find those with leadership talent and persuade them to try themselves in more demanding assignments. Then senior staff (either a full-timer on the payroll or a seasoned volunteer) interviews the newcomers to assess their strengths and place them accordingly. Volunteers may also be assigned both a mentor and a supervisor with whom they work out their performance goals. These advisers are two different people, as a rule, and both, ordinarily, volunteers themselves.

The Girl Scouts, which employs 730,000 volunteers and only 6,000 paid staff for 3½ million girl members, works this way. A volunteer typically starts by driving youngsters once a week to a meeting. Then a more seasoned volunteer draws her into other work – accompanying Girl Scouts selling cookies door-to-door, assisting a Brownie leader on a camping trip. Out of this step-by-step process evolve the volunteer boards of the local councils and, eventually, the Girl Scouts' governing organ, the National Board. Each step, even the very first, has its own compulsory training programme, usually conducted by a woman who is herself a volunteer. Each has specific performance standards and performance goals.

What do these unpaid staff people themselves demand? What makes them stay – and, of course, they can leave at any time. Their first and most important demand is that the non-profit have a clear mission, one that drives everything the organization does. A senior vice president in a large regional bank has two small children. Yet she just took over as chair of the state chapter of Nature Conservancy, which finds, buys, and manages endangered natural ecologies. 'I love my job,' she said, when I asked her why she took on such heavy additional work, 'and of course the bank has a creed. But it doesn't really know what it contributes. At Nature Conservancy, I know what I am

The second thing this new breed requires, indeed demands, is training, training, and more training. And, in turn, the most effective way to motivate and hold veterans is to recognize their expertise and use them to train newcomers. Then these knowledge workers demand responsibility – above all, for thinking through and setting their own performance goals. They expect to be consulted and to participate in making decisions that affect their work and the work of the organization as a whole. And they expect opportunities for advancement, that is, a chance to take on more demanding assignments and more responsibility as their performance warrants. That is why a good many nonprofits have developed career ladders for their volunteers.

Supporting all this activity is accountability. Many of today's knowledge-worker volunteers insist on having their performance reviewed against preset objectives at least once a year. And increasingly, they expect their organizations to remove non-performers by moving them to other assignments that better fit their capacities or by counselling them to leave. 'It's worse than the Marine Corps boot camp,' says the priest in charge of volunteers in the midwestern diocese, 'but we have 400 people on the waiting list.' One large and growing midwestern art museum requires of its volunteers – board members, fundraisers, docents, and the people who edit the museum's newsletter – that they set their goals each year, appraise themselves against these goals each year, and resign when they fail to meet their goals two years in a row. So does a fair-sized Jewish organization working on college campuses.

These volunteer professionals are still a minority, but a significant one – perhaps a tenth of the total volunteer population. And they are growing in numbers and, more important, in their impact on the nonprofit sector. Increasingly, nonprofits say what the minister in a large pastoral church says: 'There is no laity in this church; there are only pastors, a few paid, most unpaid.'

This move from nonprofit volunteer to paid professional may be the most important development in American society today. We hear a great deal about the decay and dissolution of family and community and about the loss of values. And, of course, there is reason for concern. But the nonprofits are generating a powerful countercurrent. They are forging new bonds of community, a new commitment to active citizenship, to social responsibility, to values. And surely what the nonprofit contributes to the volunteer is as important as what the volunteer contributes to the nonprofit. Indeed, it may be fully as important as the service, whether religious, educational, or welfare related, that the nonprofit provides in the community.

This development also carries a clear lesson for business. Managing the knowledge worker for productivity is the challenge ahead for American management. The nonprofits are showing us how to do that. It requires a clear mission, careful placement and continuous learning and teaching, management by objectives and self-control, high demands but corresponding responsibility, and accountability for performance and results.

There is also, however, a clear warning to American business in this transformation of volunteer work. The students in the programme for senior and middle-level executives in which I teach work in a wide diversity of businesses: banks and insurance companies, large retail chains, aerospace and computer companies, real estate developers, and many others. But most of them also serve as volunteers in nonprofits – in a church, on the board of the college they graduated from, as scout leaders, with the YMCA or the Community Chest or the local symphony orchestra. When I ask them why they do it, far too many give the same answer: Because in my job there isn't much challenge, not enough achievement, not enough responsibility; and there is no mission, there is only expediency.

[1989]

28

Nonprofit Governance: Lessons for Success

Despite the almost limitless diversity in their mission and size, the majority of American nonprofits have the same governance structure. They have an unpaid, outside, part-time board. And, they have a paid full-time executive officer, called variously *president, executive director, executive secretary, senior pastor, administrator, executive vice-president,* or *general manager.* Despite their almost limitless diversity, nonprofits are alike also in that in many – maybe the majority – this governance structure malfunctions as often as it functions. Boards are criticized as being 'rubber stamps' for the executive. But, the same boards also 'meddle'. Board members complain that the executive officer 'usurps' the board's policy-making function. Executive officers in turn complain that the board wastes endless hours discussing operational trivia. Board members complain that they get no information. Executive officers and their staffs complain about the hours, days, and weeks wasted preparing reports on matters well beyond the board's competence and ken. And, there is confusion across the nonprofit spectrum – in churches and trade associations, hospitals, universities, community services, learned societies, and foundations – as to what governance the institution needs, what the task of each organ of governance should be, and how they should work together. Indeed, no subject provokes more heated debate in the nonprofit world than that of governance.

Yet, we know the answers – or at least enough of them to do the job. A small but growing number of nonprofits are truly well managed. For many nonprofits, it is probably true – at least their board members so believe – that they are a good deal less well managed than the average business. However, the small but rapidly growing group of nonprofits that have organized their governance is beyond doubt better managed than some businesses with a reputation for first-rate management. These institutions have both a functioning board and a functioning executive. Some of these leaders in the nonprofit sector are colleges and universities, some are community services, some are churches, and some are hospitals. Some are very large national or international organizations; others are local and at best middle sized. Yet, all have reached pretty much the same conclusions in regard to nonprofit governance. Their solutions are thus generic and should apply across the nonprofit spectrum.

Clear and Functioning Governance Structure

The first lesson to be learned is that nonprofits need a clear and functioning governance structure. They have to take their governance seriously, and they have to work hard on it. They need effective leadership and management a good deal more than even businesses do – for three reasons.

First, they lack the bottom line that a business has. They must therefore have a clear mission that translates into operational goals and that provides guides for effective action. Of course, businesses also deteriorate if they do not have a clear mission; they become diffuse, and their efforts splinter. But, in good times a business can muddle through for a while with no other lodestar than the financial bottom line. A nonprofit institution will start to flounder almost immediately unless it clearly defines its mission and emphasizes that mission again and again. This is doubly true for the nonprofit that relies on donors, volunteers, or both.

Second, the nonprofit needs a clear definition of the 'results' that it seeks to obtain. Again, a business can, though only for a few short years, steer by the financial bottom line alone.

Last, a business earns its money for its performance; the money is its own. In contrast, the money of the nonprofit, whether obtained from donors or from the taxpayer, is given against promises. Nonprofits are not owners; they are trustees of the money that they spend.

Nonprofits thus need both strong organs of accountability – for mission, for results, for allocation of resources and their productivity – and a clear process for discharging these responsibilities. They need effective, strong, directed governance and a clear governance structure.

These are truisms. Everyone nods and says *of course*, but far too few nonprofits listen, let alone act.

Effective Board and Effective Executive

Nonprofits need both an effective board and an effective executive. Practically every nonprofit will accept one or the other half of this assertion. But, a good many will not accept that both are needed. Yet, neither the board-dominated nor the executive-dominated nonprofit is likely to work well, let alone succeed in perpetuating itself beyond the tenure of an autocrat, whethei that individual be board chairperson or executive officer.

In a good many businesses, especially in large publicly held ones, boards have become slumber parties. They only wake up when there is a serious crisis and usually when it is way too late. In the large and successful petroleum companies that grew out of Rockefeller's Standard Oil Trust, but also in companies in Europe and Japan, boards have traditionally been a legal fiction. Some nonprofits, too – large private universities or large churches dominated by a powerful, charismatic pastor – have reduced their boards to a purely ceremonial role. And, boards as a part of governance are not known altogether in the canon law of the Catholic church (although American Catholic dioceses are increasingly setting up lay committees that in effect are governing boards), in the Salvation Army, and in the typical labour union (which is surely also a nonprofit institution).

But, most nonprofits could not emasculate the board even if they wanted to. One reason is that the board often actively leads in raising money. Another, more important one is that board members are committed to the nonprofit's cause. If they have no legitimate function and no real job to do, they will do mischief; they will 'meddle'. The nonprofit has no choice but to work on making its board an effective organ of governance. Only an effective board composed of independent but committed outside people can give the nonprofit the clear focus on mission, the definition of results, and the accountability for the money entrusted to it that it needs. Without these, any nonprofit will soon decline into nonperformance.

At the same time, every nonprofit, except maybe the very small and purely local one, must also have an effective executive officer. Its success in this century has made the American nonprofit too big, too complex, too important to be managed by its board.

The community hospital in the small New England town where I lived in the 1940s was still run by its board. It did not even have a chief medical officer or a nursing supervisor. But, it also had no emergency room, no ambulance service, no X-ray department, no physical therapy unit, no clinical lab, no social workers, and not even a well-baby clinic. To be sure, it was no longer simply a place where the poor could die in a little dignity, as it had been two decades before. But, its job was primarily to provide private physicians with beds for their patients, not to be a 'health care centre'. Similarly, none of the churches in the town at that time tried to provide anything but two services on Sunday mornings and Sunday school to go with them. And, it was not until World War II that the American Red Cross – the world's largest volunteer organization – went beyond disaster relief and took on blood banks and health and safety education.

Indeed, the most noteworthy feature of the American nonprofit institution is not its size. It is the explosive growth in the scope of nonprofit work and the parallel growth in the demands placed on the competence of the nonprofit institution. These demands go way beyond what good intentions and generosity can supply. Increasingly, they demand professionalism of a high order. The more a nonprofit institution relies on volunteers, the more professional its management has to be. An organization has far too many things to do for it to be able to operate without professional, full-time staff. Furthermore, if performance standards are to have any results, they must be coupled with executive accountability.

Board and Executive Officer as Colleagues

Nonprofits waste uncounted hours debating who is superior and who is subordinate – board or executive officer. The answer is that they must be colleagues. Each has a different part, but together they share the play. Their tasks are complementary. Thus, each has to ask, What do I owe the other? not – as board and executive officers still tend to do – What does the other one owe me? The two have to work as one team of equals.

Double-Bridge Team

The double-bridge team is a model for the board-executive team in nonprofit institutions. In the double-bridge team, neither player is more important; they are equals, and they are equally indispensable. The job for the stronger player is to adjust to the style, strengths, and personality of the weaker partner. The executive officers in nonprofit organizations are the stronger players. It is their job to adjust both what they do and how they do it to the personalities and strengths of their chairpersons.

In more than eleven years with one of the country's largest community services organizations, the chief executive has worked with four board chairpersons, each of whom served for three years. The first was strongly outside focused, a good speaker and skilful in public relations. The successor was inside focused, effective with local chapters and happy working with them but somewhat publicity-shy and awkward on the platform. The next chairperson saw her main task as one of raising money, and she worked hard on getting much-needed business support. The fourth and last chairperson – still in the job today – is concerned primarily with the recruiting, training, and motivating of volunteers. Each chairperson's priority was a legitimate one, and each brought enthusiasm and considerable skill to the tasks on which he or she concentrated. All, in other words, deployed themselves properly. But, each had results only because the executive officer positioned herself in the areas in which her partner, the board chair, was weak or had little interest – the inside during the tenure of the first chairperson; the outside during the tenure of the second one; operations during the third chairperson's term; programmes, outside relations, and money raising during the last years.

Tasks of Board and Executive Officer

What are the respective tasks of the board and the executive officer? The conventional answer is that the board makes policy and the executive officer executes it. The trouble with this elegant answer is that no one knows (or has ever known) what policy is, let alone where its boundaries lie. As a result, there is constant wrangling, constant turf battles, constant friction.

Effective nonprofits do not talk much about policy. They talk about work. They define what work each organ is expected to perform and what results each organ is expected to achieve. One work assignment for the board may be to raise so many dollars in contributions in the coming year. Conversely, it may be the work assignment of the executive officer to recruit a given number of new volunteers the next year and to introduce two new programmes successfully. Or, the board may commit itself to a certain number of community appearances by each of its members – one of the work assignments of the board members of a major rural cooperative. The board's work assignment may include a specified number of board-conducted, in-depth audits of individual hospital functions and of intensive meetings with major department heads. For the vestry in a large and rapidly growing evangelical church or the lay board in a Catholic diocese, the work assignment may be to specify, design, supervise, and edit the materials that the church uses to recruit and train volunteer workers. For the board of a theological seminary, it may be a half-day at each of its bimonthly meetings spent reviewing one of the school's educational programmes. In the effective nonprofit institution, every board committee – indeed, every board member – accepts a work programme with specific achievement goals. So, too, does the executive officer.

This has two implications, both still anathema to many nonprofits and their boards. First, the performance of the entire board, each board committee, and each board member and the performance of the executive officer and all key people on the staff is regularly appraised against preestablished performance goals. (This appraisal is best done by a small group of former board members.) Second, board members and executives whose performance consistently falls below goals and expectations will resign or at least not stand for reelection.

Boards Should Meddle

Boards should meddle. To begin with, there is no way to stop them, and if you can't lick them, you had better join them! Board members of a nonprofit organization should be committed to the cause. They should be deeply interested and involved in it, they should know the programmes and the people who work on them, and they should *care*. But also, nonprofit boards are usually organized in such a way that 'meddling' is part of their job. They work in committees, each with a specific mandate, such as fund-raising, or physical facilities, or youth activities. This forces them to work directly – that is, without going through the executive officer – with people working in the particular area of the committee's concern. It thus forces them to 'meddle'. They had therefore better be organized so as to meddle constructively.

In one of the country's oldest nonprofit boards, the Board of Overseers of Harvard University, which was set up more than three hundred years ago, members act as 'visitors' to one of the university's academic departments or schools. They meet regularly with the department, interview faculty and students, and appraise the department's performance. A good many people in academe consider the Harvard board the most effective, if not the only effective, American university board.

However, the board's meddling must strengthen rather than divide the institution. This requires first that there be no restrictions on contacts between board members and staff members. Restrictions are in any case ineffective, and they only make board members and staff members suspicious. They invite politicking. Nevertheless, the executive officer needs always to be informed of any contact between a board committee or board member and a staff member. The Harvard board achieves this by having each visitor submit a formal and written report, which is discussed first with the academic department and then presented to the president and the full board. Equally effective but simpler is a commitment – entered into by board and staff members alike – to have each staff member report any board contact immediately to the executive officer, preferably in writing and with a copy for the board member.

This may seem petty. It is. But the executive officer's fear of 'meddling' and the resentment of board members at being 'isolated' from the organization are, in my experience, the main cause of guerilla warfare between the two organs of governance in the nonprofit institution. It is almost impossible to cure. But, it can be prevented by a little elementary hygiene.

Who Is Responsible?

Who should be responsible for an effective board, for the relationship between board and executive officer, and for the structure of governance in the nonprofit institution? The standard answer is, the board's chairperson. There is only one thing wrong with this: it does not work. What works is to assign responsibility for the effective governance of the organization to the executive officer and to make it one of his or her key duties. I know the arguments against this: it is risky. There is danger of the board's becoming the executive officer's creature and a *roi fainéant*, a shadow king. It would indeed be greatly preferable if the board chairperson were to take on the duty.

Alas, I have not seen a single one who was willing to do so. It simply takes too much time. Wherever I have seen the job done, it required five years of hard, persistent work. And, that goes well beyond what a part-time outsider can spare, no matter how committed he or she may be. Making the organs of governance effective in the nonprofit institution and creating the proper relationship between them should therefore be considered a priority task of executive officers, and it should receive serious consideration when executive officers are hired and appraised.

Lessons

The lessons from nonprofits that have developed a working and effective governance structure will not come as a great surprise to many people in the nonprofit world, but they will still not be particularly popular. Indeed, they may be quite unpalatable to board members and executive officers alike. They clash with the widespread view that nonprofits are governed by good intentions. In fact, nonprofits have to be governed by performance.

At the same time, these lessons contradict the equally widespread belief that all a nonprofit institution needs is to be managed in a 'more businesslike' way. No, nonprofits have to be committed to a cause, they have to have a mission, and they have to be imbued with passion. Nevertheless, the growing number of nonprofits that have worked out an effective governance structure and the lessons they offer should come as a relief to the many dedicated people in the nonprofit world who complain – some to the point of despair – about the chasm between the good intentions and the performance of their institution, whether it is a church, university, hospital, or community service. It is indeed fairly simple to make nonprofits effective. It does not require miracles – it needs will and work.

[1990]

29

The Nonprofits' Outreach Revolution

A major American growth area over the past 10 to 20 years is not even recorded in the economic figures: the 'Third Sector', comprising nonprofit, nongovernmental community services – both national and local, secular and religious.

- About 2.5 million volunteers work for the American Heart Association – a 50 percent increase in three years.
- The Girl Scouts enrol one in four American girls between the ages of six and nine. While the number of school-age girls in the U.S. has dropped by one-fifth in the past 20 years, Girl Scout membership has remained the same – a little short of 2.5 million. And while the organization used to be disproportionately white 20 years ago, it now enrols proportionately just as many black girls of elementary-school age as it does white ones.
- Local 'pastoral' churches – Protestant and Catholic, evangelical and mainstream – that focus on the needs and concerns of their individual members, particularly those of the baby-boom generation, are growing even faster than the large national nonprofit organizations. There are now at least 10,000

such churches with memberships of 2,000 or more – twice the number of such churches 10 years ago.

A Bad Word

Not all Third Sector institutions have done that well. Traditional churches, regardless of denomination, still steadily lose members. Many large universities simply spend more. But many nonprofits have become vastly more productive during the past 10 years. This is because the Third Sector has discovered management.

Twenty years ago 'management' was a bad word in nonprofit institutions; it meant 'big business'. Far too many of these institutions then believed that good intentions and a noble cause are all that is needed to produce results – and quite a few, of course, still do. But more and more are learning that good intentions by themselves only spawn bureaucracy.

Twenty years ago nonprofit institutions tended to believe that they did not have to 'manage' because they did not have a 'bottom line'. More and more of them have since learned that they have to manage *especially* well precisely because they lack the discipline of the 'bottom line'.

The need to research the people who should be customers but aren't is, of course, preached by every marketing text. But few businesses actually do it.

Similarly, while every management text talks of making the board into a working organ of the company, it is rarely done in business. But in nonprofit institutions, aspiring board members are now being asked: 'For what contribution should we hold you accountable once you are on our board. What specific work will you take on?' A dozen such organizations subject their boards to annual performance reviews against preset objectives – something practically unheard of in business.

In addition, nonprofit institutions – and not only the big national ones – increasingly put the entire staff, from the chief executive officer on down, into constant training, with each person serving as a trainer on one subject and as a learner on others. They increasingly apply management-by-objectives – all staff members are expected to commit themselves to specific objectives against which their performance is evaluated. And – something unheard of 20 years ago – nonperformers are no longer being tolerated because they 'mean well' and 'serve in a good cause'. Increasingly they are being 'outplaced', compassionately but firmly.

In general, there has been a shift from emphasis on the 'good cause' to emphasis on accountability and results. The greatest and most important change has been with respect to the volunteers – their role, their treatment, their numbers:

- The church outside Chicago has a big youth ministry, a music ministry, ministries to young marrieds, parents, singles, seniors, and big and growing community services: to teenage mothers, to alcoholics and drug addicts, to cancer patients, to newcomers to the community, and so on. It pays decent salaries, but to only 160 people. Each adult member of the congregation, however, is invited after a few months of membership to join the 'unpaid staff'. He then is carefully screened to determine where he should serve and undergoes months of training. Each unpaid staffer's performance is regularly reviewed by two seasoned fellow workers.

- The Salvation Army keeps a tight rein on the 25,000 Florida parolees. But only 100 paid staffers are assigned to this task; they supervise and train volunteers and take care of crises. The work itself is done by 250 to 300 volunteers.

- A midwestern Catholic diocese serving 200,000 families now has less than half the number of priests it had 20 years ago but double the number of community services. The 140 priests preach, say Mass, hear confessions, and baptize, confirm, marry, and bury people. Virtually everything else is done by 2,000 lay people, each expected to give at least three hours of work a week and to spend an additional two or three hours a week in training sessions, both as trainer and trainee. Each lay person's performance is appraised by senior officials twice a year – and anyone whose rating falls below 'highly satisfactory' twice in a row is asked to resign.

Of course, plenty of volunteers still do only what volunteers have always done: go door to door in the neighbourhood, collecting money. But even those foot soldiers are increasingly carefully selected, trained, and supported with sophisticated solicitation material. They are increasingly being managed as unpaid staff rather than as well-meaning amateurs.

And increasingly volunteers are taking over the professional and executive work in the nonprofit organizations. The 1,800 local chapters of the American Heart Association, for instance, are managed and run by volunteers. A growing number of volunteers are professional men and women; 20 or 30 years ago, they tended to be housewives. For a senior business executive, board membership in a nonprofit organization has almost become a 'must'.

The number of active volunteers working for nonprofits has grown fast these past 10 years. A lot of older people, retired or semiretired, have found volunteer work to be satisfying and a way to put a lifetime's experience to work. But there is even more demand for participation on the part of affluent baby boomers.

Millions of Adults

The substantial increase in the 'market penetration' of the Girl Scouts was possible only because the organization could increase the number of volunteers to more than 700,000 from 530,000 while cutting paid staff substantially. Many of these additional Girl Scout volunteers are young professional women. And practically all of the 35- to 34-year-olds in the Executive Management Programme of the Claremont Graduate School are active as volunteers in community-service organizations.

There are no statistics on the total number of people who serve as volunteers in nonprofit organizations. But they are almost certain to constitute our largest single 'employment'. The 10,000 very large churches alone have at least two million active volunteers; 1.5 million adults (not counting blood donors) work as volunteers for the Red Cross. The total for all nonprofits probably exceeds 80 million.

Government has become too big, too complex, too remote for each citizen actively to participate in it. Yet we no longer believe, as did the 'liberals' and 'progressives' these past hundred years, that community tasks can – nay, should – be, left to government. As a volunteer the individual can again find active, effective citizenship, can again make a difference, can again exercise control. This is a uniquely American achievement; it may well be America's most important contribution today.

[1988]

Part IV

THE ORGANIZATION

30

The Governance of Corporations

Fifteen years after it was first chronicled, the 'unseen revolution' has transformed corporate ownership in the United States and is now visible to all. The 20 largest pension funds (13 of them funds of state, municipal, or nonprofit employees) hold around one-tenth of the equity capital of America's publicly owned companies. All told, institutional investors – that is, primarily pension funds – control close to 40 percent of the common stock of the country's large (and many midsize) businesses. The largest and fastest-growing funds, those of public employees, are no longer content to be passive investors. Increasingly, they demand a voice in the companies in which they invest – for instance, a veto over board appointments, executive compensation, and critical corporate charter provisions.

Equally important, and still largely overlooked, pension funds also hold 40 percent or so of the medium-term and long-term debt of the country's bigger companies. Thus these institutions have become corporate America's largest lenders as well as its largest owners. As the finance texts have stressed for years, the power of the lender is as great as the power of the owner – sometimes greater.

The rise of pension funds as dominant owners and lenders represent one of the most startling power shifts in economic history. The first modern pension fund was established in 1950 by General Motors. Four decades later, pension funds control total assets of $2.5 trillion, divided about equally between common stocks and fixed-income securities. Demographics guarantee that these assets will grow aggressively for at least another ten years. Barring a prolonged depression, pension funds will have to invest $100 billion to $200 billion in new resources every year throughout the 1990s.

America's failure, until quite recently, to recognize (let alone address) this power shift accounts in large measure for much of the financial turbulence of the 1980s – the hostile takeovers, the leveraged buyouts, and the general restructuring frenzy. Two problems in particular demand attention: for what should America's new owners, the pension funds, hold corporate management accountable? And what is the appropriate institutional structure through which to exercise accountability?

Actually, the United States is quite late among developed countries in concentrating ownership of large companies in a small number of institutions. In Germany, the country's three major banks have long controlled around 60 percent of the share capital of the large companies, partly through direct holdings, partly through the holdings of their customers that, under German law, the banks manage and vote on. In Japan, the majority of large companies are members of a small number (ten at most) of industrial groups, the now-familiar *keiretsu*. In a keiretsu, 20 percent to 30 percent of the share capital of each member company is held by the other members and by the group's bank and trading company, and practically all credit to the member companies is provided by the group's bank. In Italy, half of the country's large businesses have been owned or controlled by the state since the 1930s. (IRI, the biggest state holding company, is the second-largest company in all of Europe.) The rest of Italy's big businesses are under the control of five or six huge conglomerates such as the Fiat Group.

Ownership in the United States is quite different. It is indeed unique. In Europe and Japan, stock ownership is a means to nonfinancial ends. A German bank's income from the companies to which it is the *hausbank* comes through commercial relationships rather than through its ownership stake. Deutsche Bank,

Germany's largest financial institution, gets many times as much in fees from client companies for mundane services such as letters of credit as it receives from them in stock dividends. The keiretsu's first concern is power – power in the market, power over suppliers and subcontractors, power and influence with ministries and civil servants. As for tangible benefits, a keiretsu company profits far more from the business it gets from the other members than from their dividends. The government holdings in Italy constitute the largest concentration of economic power in any market economy. They serve primarily political objectives. The companies are run to provide jobs in politically important regions, to create lucrative executive positions for the party faithful, and to supply campaign funds for the parties in power.

Neither the German banks nor the Japanese keiretsu nor Italy's government nor its conglomerates has much interest in share prices or capital gains. They do not intend to sell. The American pension fund by contrast, has no commercial ties to the companies in which it invests or to which it lends. It is not a 'business' at all, but an 'asset manager'. There are, as we shall see, important lessons to be learned from developments in Europe and in Japan, both as to what to do and what not to do. But in the United States, the rapid shift of ownership and credit power to these new and quite different owners poses totally new and very different problems.

Pension funds first emerged as the premier owners of the country's share capital in the early 1970s. But for 15 or 20 years thereafter, the realities of pension fund ownership were ignored. In part this was because the pension funds themselves did not want to be 'owners'. They wanted to be passive 'investors' and short-term investors at that. 'We do not buy a company,' they asserted. 'We buy shares that we sell as soon as they no longer offer good prospects for capital gains over a fairly short time.' Moreover, the development was totally at variance with American tradition and with what everybody took for granted – and many still take for granted – as the structure of the U.S. economy. Long after pension funds had become the largest holders of equity capital, the United States was still referred to as the country of 'people's capitalism' in which millions of individuals each owned small pieces of the country's large companies. To be sure, employees have become the owners of America's means of production. But their ownership is exercised through a fairly small number of very large 'trustees'.

Finally, though, the fog has begun to lift. The trustees of pension funds, especially those representing public employees, are waking up to the fact that they are no longer investors in shares. An investor, by definition, can *sell* holdings. A small pension fund may still be able to do so. There are thousands of such small funds, but their total holdings represent no more than a quarter or so of all pension fund assets. The share holdings of even a midsize pension fund are already so large that they are not easily sold. Or more precisely, these holdings can, as a rule, be sold only if another pension fund buys them. They are much too large to be easily absorbed by the retail market and are thus permanently part of the circular trading among institutions.

Ownership in the United States is far less concentrated than in Germany, Japan, or Italy – and will remain far less concentrated. Hence the U.S. pension fund still has more elbow room than the big bank in Germany, the keiretsu in Japan, or the industrial conglomerate in Italy. But some large U.S. pension funds each own as much as 1 percent or even 2 percent of a big company's total capital. All pension funds together may own 35 percent of the company's total capital. (For example, pension funds own 75 percent of the equity of the Chase Manhattan Bank.) The 1 percent holder cannot sell easily. And the 40 percent holder, that is, the pension fund community at large, cannot sell at all. It is almost as committed as the German hausbank to a client company or the Japanese keiretsu to a member company. Thus the large funds are beginning to learn what Georg Siemens, founder of Deutsche Bank and inventor of the hausbank system said a hundred years ago when he was criticized for spending so much of his and the bank's time on a troubled client company: 'If one can't sell, one must care.'

Pension funds cannot be managers as were so many nineteenth-century owners. Yet a business, even a small one, needs strong, autonomous management with the authority, continuity, and competence to build and run the organization. Thus pension funds, as America's new owners, will increasingly have to make sure that a company has the management it needs. As we have learned over the last 40 years, this means that management must be clearly accountable to somebody and that accountability must be institutionally anchored. It means that management must be accountable for *performance* and *results* rather than for good intentions, however beautifully quantified. It means that accountability must involve financial accountability, even though everyone knows that performance and results go way beyond the financial 'bottom line'.

Surely, most people will say, we know what performance and results mean for business enterprise. We should, of course, because clearly defining these terms is a prerequisite both for effective management and for successful and profitable ownership. In fact, there have been two definitions offered in the 40 years since World War II. Neither has stood the test of time.

The first definition was formulated around 1950, at about the same time at which the modern pension fund was invented. The most prominent of the period's 'professional managers', Ralph Cordiner, CEO of the General Electric Company, asserted that top management in the large, publicly owned corporation was a 'trustee'. Cordiner argued that senior executives were responsible for managing the enterprise 'in the best-balanced interest of shareholders, customers, employees, suppliers, and plant community cities'. That is, what we now call 'stakeholders'.

Cordiner's answer, as some of us pointed out right away, still required a clear definition of results and of the meaning of 'best' with respect to 'balance'. It also required a clear structure of accountability, with an independent and powerful organ of supervision and control to hold management accountable for performance and results. Otherwise, professional management becomes an enlightened despot – and enlightened despots, whether platonic philosopher kings or CEOs, neither perform nor last.

But Cordiner's generation and its executive successors did not define what performance and results produce the best balance, nor did they develop any kind of accountability. As a result, professional management, 1950s-style, has neither performed nor lasted.

The single most powerful blow to Cordiner-style management was the rise of the hostile takeover in the late 1970s. One after the other of such managers has been toppled. The survivors have been forced to change drastically how they manage or at least to change their rhetoric. No top management I know now claims to run its business as a 'trustee' for the 'best-balanced interests' of 'stakeholders'.

Pension funds have been the driving force behind this change.

Without the concentration of voting power in a few pension funds
and the funds' willingness to endorse hostile transactions, most of
the raiders' attacks would never have been launched. A raider who
has to get support from millions of dispersed individual stock-
holders soon runs out of time and money.

To be sure, pension fund managers had serious doubts about
many buyouts and takeovers, about their impact on the companies
in play, and about their value to the economy. Pension fund
managers – especially the moderately paid civil servants running
the funds of public employees – also had serious aesthetic and
moral misgivings about such things as 'greenmail' and the huge
fortunes earned by corporate raiders, lawyers, and investment
bankers. Yet they felt they had no choice but to provide money for
takeovers and buyouts and to tender their shares into them. They
did so in droves.

One reason for their support was that these transactions kept
alive the illusion that pension funds could in fact sell their shares –
that is, that they were 'investors' still. Takeovers and LBOs also
offered immediate capital gains. And since pension fund portfolios
have by and large done quite poorly, such gains were most
welcome – though, as will be discussed shortly, they too were more
illusion than reality.

What made takeovers and buyouts inevitable (or at least created
the opportunity for them) was the mediocre performance of
enlightened-despot management, the management without clear
definitions of performance and results and with no clear accountability to somebody. It may be argued that the mediocre performance of so many of America's large corporations in the last 30
years was not management's fault, that is resulted instead from
wrong-headed public policies that have kept American savings
rates low and capital costs high. But captains are responsible for
what happens on their watches. And whatever the reasons or
excuses, the large U.S. company has not done particularly well on
professional management's watch – whether measured by competitiveness, market standing, or innovative performance. As for
financial performance, it has, by and large, not even earned the
minimum-acceptable result, a return on equity equal to its cost of
capital.

The raiders thus performed a needed function. As an old
proverb has it, 'If there are no grave diggers, one needs vultures'.
But takeovers and buyouts are very radical surgery. And even if

radical surgery is not life-threatening, it inflicts profound shock. Takeovers and buyouts deeply disturb and indeed alienate middle managers and professionals, the very people on whose motivation, effort, and loyalty a business depends. For these people, the takeover or dismantling of a company to which they have given years of service is nothing short of betrayal. It is a denial of all they must believe in to work productively and with devotion. As a result, few of the companies that were taken over or sold in a buyout performed any better a few years later than they had performed under the old dispensation.

But weren't takeovers and buyouts at least good for shareholders? Perhaps not. In a typical transaction, shareholders (and this means primarily the pension funds) received, say, $60 for a share that had been quoted on the stock exchange for an average of $40 in the year before the deal. This 50 percent premium is proving to have been an illusion in many cases. Perhaps $25 of the $60 was not solid cash but the value put by the raider or the raider's investment banker on convertible warrants, unsecured loans, or junk bonds. These noncash nonsecurities, which were bought by many of the same institutions that sold shares, are rapidly losing value. Many pension funds immediately did sell these now-depreciating pieces of paper. But they sold them to other pension funds or institutional investors – there are no other buyers. Thus the net financial value of these transactions to the pension fund community at large remains suspect indeed.

Today nearly all CEOs of large U.S. companies proclaim that they run their enterprises 'in the interest of the shareholders' and 'to maximize shareholder value'. This is the second definition of performance and results developed over the past 40 years. It sounds much less noble than Cordiner's assertion of the 'best-balanced interest', but it also sounds much more realistic. Yet its life span will be even shorter than yesterday's professional management. For most people, 'maximizing shareholder value' means a higher share price within six months or a year – certainly not much longer. Such short-term capital gains are the wrong objective for both the enterprise and its dominant shareholders. As a theory of corporate performance, then, 'maximizing shareholder value' has little staying power.

Regarding the enterprise, the cost of short-term thinking hardly needs to be argued. But short-term capital gains are also of no benefit to holders who cannot sell. The interest of a large pension fund is in the value of a holding at the time at which a beneficiary turns from being an employee who pays into the fund into a pensioner who gets paid by the fund. Concretely, this means that the time over which a fund invests – the time until its future beneficiaries will retire – is on average 15 years rather than 3 months or 6 months. This is the appropriate return horizon for these owners.

There is however, one group that does – or at least thinks it does – have an interest in short-term gains. These are the employers with 'defined benefit' pension plans. Until now, in a classic case of the tail wagging the dog, the interests of these employers have dominated how the pension fund community approaches its role as owner. In a defined-benefit plan, retiring employees receive fixed annual payments, usually a percentage of their wages during the last three or five years on the job. The employer's annual contribution fluctuates with the value of the fund's assets. If in any given year that value is high (compared with the amount needed on an actuarial basis to cover the fund's future pension obligations) the employer's contribution is cut. If the fund's asset value is low, the contribution goes up.

We owe the defined-benefit trust to mere accident. When General Motors management proposed the pension fund in 1950, several powerful board members resisted it as a giveaway to the union. The directors relented only when promised that, under a defined-benefit plan, the company would have to pay little or nothing. An ever-rising stock market, so the argument went, would create the assets needed to pay future pensions. Most private employers followed the GM model, if only because they too deluded themselves into believing that the stock market rather than the company would take care of the pension obligation.

Needless to say, this was wishful thinking. Most defined-benefit plans have done poorly, precisely because they have been chasing inappropriate short-term gains. The other kind of plan, the 'defined contribution' plan under which the employer contributes each year a defined percentage of the employee's annual salary or wages, has done better in a good many cases. Indeed, defined-benefit plans are rapidly losing their allure. Because they have not delivered the promised capital gains, a great many are seriously underfunded. From now on, as a result of new accounting standards, such underfunding has to be shown as a liability on the employing company's balance sheet. This means that even in a mild recession (in which both a company's earnings and the stock market are down), a good many companies will actually be pushed to, if not over, the brink of insolvency. And what many of them have done in good years – that is, to syphon off the actuarial surplus in the pension fund and show it as 'net income' in their income statement – is unlikely to be permitted much longer.

Company after company is therefore going out of defined-benefit plans. By the end of the decade, they will have become marginal. As a result, short-term gains as an objective for the major owners of American business will no longer dominate. They are already playing second fiddle. Public-employee funds are defined-contribution plans, and they constitute the majority of the biggest funds. Being independent of corporate management, they, rather than the pension funds of private businesses, are taking the lead and writing the new script.

We no longer need to theorize about how to define performance and results in the large enterprise. We have successful examples. Both the Germans and the Japanese have highly concentrated institutional ownership. In neither country can the owners actually manage. In both countries industry has done extremely well in the 40 years since its near destruction in World War II. It has done well in terms of the overall economy of its country. It has also done exceedingly well for its shareholders. Whether invested in 1950, 1960, 1970, or 1980, $100,000 put into something like an index fund in the stock exchanges of Tokyo or Frankfurt would today be worth a good deal more than a similar investment in a New York Stock Exchange index fund.

How, then, do the institutional owners of German or Japanese industry define performance and results? Though they manage quite differently, they define them in the same way. Unlike Cordiner, they do not 'balance' anything. They maximize. But they do not attempt to maximize shareholder value or the short- term interest of any one of the enterprise's 'stakeholders'. Rather, they *maximize the wealth-producing capacity of the enterprise*. It is this objective that integrates short-term and long-term results and that ties the operational dimensions of business performance – market standing, innovation, productivity, and people and their development – with financial needs and financial results. It is also this objective on which all constituencies depend for the satisfaction of their expectations and objectives, whether shareholders, customers, or employees.

To define performance and results as 'maximizing the wealth-producing capacity of the enterprise' may be criticized as vague. To be sure, one doesn't get the answers by filling out forms. Decisions need to be made, and economic decisions that commit scarce resources to an uncertain future are always risky and controversial. When Ralph Cordiner first attempted to define performance and results – no one had tried to do so earlier – maximizing the wealth-producing capacity of the enterprise would indeed have been pretty fuzzy. By now, after four decades of work by many people, it has become crisp. All the elements that go into the process can be quantified with considerable rigour and are indeed quantified by those archquantifiers, by the planning departments of large Japanese companies and by many of the German companies as well.

The first step toward a clear definition of the concept was probably taken in my 1954 book, *The Practice of Management*, which outlined eight key objective areas for a business. These areas (or some variations thereof) are still the starting point for business planning in the large Japanese company. Since then, management analysts have done an enormous amount of work on the strategy needed to convert objectives into performance.

Financial objectives are needed to tie all this together. Indeed, financial accountability is the key to the performance of management and enterprise. Without financial accountability, there is no accountability at all. And without financial accountability, there will also be no results in any other area. It is commonly believed in the United States that the Japanese are not profit conscious. This is simply not true. In fact, their profitability goals as measured against the cost of capital tend to be a good deal higher than those of most American companies. Only the Japanese do not start with profitability; they end with it.

Finally, maximizing the wealth-producing capacity of the enterprise also helps define the roles of institutional owners and their relationship to the enterprise. German and Japanese management structure and style differ greatly. But institutional owners in both countries support a management regardless of short-term results as long as the company performs according to a business plan that is designed to maximize the enterprise's wealth-producing capacity – and that is agreed upon between management and whatever organ represents the owners. This makes both sides focus on results. It makes management accountable. But it gives a performing company's management the needed continuity and security.

What we have is not the 'final answer'. Still, it is no longer theory but proven practice. And its results, to judge by German and Japanese business performance, are clearly superior to running the enterprise as a 'trustee' for stakeholders or to maximize short-term gains for shareholders.

The one thing that we in the United States have yet to work out – and we have to work it out ourselves – is how to build the new definition of management accountability into an institutional structure. We need what a political scientist would call a constitution – provisions that spell out, as does the German company law, the duties and responsibilities of management and that clarify the respective rights of other groups, especially the shareholders. *What* we have to do the Germans and the Japanese can show us. *How* we do it will have to be quite different to fit U.S. conditions.

In both Germany and Japan, managements are supervised closely and judged carefully. In Germany, a senior executive of the hausbank sits on the board of each company in which the bank has substantial holdings, usually as chairperson of the supervisory board. The bank's representative is expected to move fast whenever management fails to perform to exacting standards. In Japan, the chief executives of the major companies in a keiretsu – headed either by the CEO of the group's bank or by the CEO of the group's trading company – function as the executive committee of the whole group. They meet regularly. The top executives of the Mitsubishi group, for instance, meet every other Friday for three or four hours. They carefully review the business plans of each group's companies and evaluate the performance of each group's managements. Again and again, though usually without fanfare, chief executives who are found wanting are moved out, kicked upstairs, or shifted to the sidelines.

The analysis and scrutiny of management's performance is organized as systematic work in both countries. In Germany, it is done by the *sekretariat* of the big banks – invented in the 1870s by Deutsche Bank, which modelled it on the Prussian general staff. The sekretariat works constantly on the companies for which its bank is the hausbank and on the board of which one of the bank's executives sits. Since the bank also handles the commercial banking business of these companies, the sekretariat has access to both their financial and business data. There is no sekretariat in Japan. But the same function is discharged by the large and powerful planning departments of the keiretsu's main bank and of the keiretsu's trading company. They too have access to commercial and business data in addition to financial information.

Even the largest U.S. pension fund holds much too small a fraction of any one company's capital to control it. Law wisely limits a corporate pension fund to a maximum holding of 5 percent of any one company's stock, and very few funds go anywhere near that high. Not being businesses, the funds have no access to commercial or business information. They are not business-focused, nor could they be. They are asset managers. Yet they need the in-depth business analysis of the companies they collectively control. And they need an institutional structure in which management accountability is embedded.

In an American context, the business analysis – call it the business audit – will have to be done by some kind of independent professional agency. Certain management consulting firms already do such work, though only on an ad hoc basis and usually after a company has gotten into trouble, which is rather late in the process. The consulting divisions of some of the large accounting firms also perform business analysis assignments. One of them, KPMG Peat Marwick, actually offers a systematic business audit to nonprofit organizations, which it calls a resource-development system. And several firms have recently come into being to advise pension funds – mostly public funds – on the industries and companies in which they invest.

I suspect that in the end we shall develop a formal business-audit practice, analogous perhaps to the financial-audit practice of independent professional accounting firms. For while the business audit need not be conducted every year – every three years may be enough in most cases – it needs to be based on predetermined standards and go through a systematic evaluation of business performance: starting with mission and strategy, through marketing, innovation, productivity, people development, community relations, all the way to profitability. The elements for such a business audit are known and available. But they need to be pulled together into systematic procedures. And that is best done, in all likelihood, by an organization that specializes in audits, whether an independent firm or a new and separate division of an accounting practice.

Thus it may not be too fanciful to expect that in ten years a major pension fund will not invest in a company's shares or fixed-income securities unless that company submits itself to a business audit by an outside professional firm. Managements will resist, of course. But only 60 years ago, managements equally resisted – in fact, resented – demands that they submit themselves to a financial audit by outside public accountants and even more to publication of the audit's findings.

Still, the question remains: Who is going to use this tool? In the American context, there is only one possible answer: a revitalized board of directors.

The need for an effective board has been stressed by every student of the publicly owned corporation in the last 40 years. To run a business enterprise, especially a large and complex enterprise, management needs considerable power. But power without accountability always becomes flabby or tyrannical and usually both. Surely, we know how to make boards effective as an organ of corporate governance. Having better people is not the key; ordinary people will do. Making a board effective requires spelling out its work, setting specific objectives for its performance and contribution, and regularly appraising the board's performance against these objectives.

We have known this for a long time. But American boards have on the whole become less, rather than more, effective. Boards are not effective if they represent good intentions. Boards are effective if they represent strong owners, committed to the enterprise.

Almost 60 years ago, in 1933, Adolph A. Berle, Jr., and Gardner C. Means published *The Modern Corporation and Private Property*, arguably the most influential book in U.S. business history. They showed that the traditional 'owners', the nineteenth-century capitalists, had disappeared, with the title of ownership shifting rapidly to faceless multitudes of investors without interest in or commitment to the company and concerned with only short-term gains. As a result, they argued, ownership was becoming divorced from control and a mere legal fiction, with management becoming accountable to no one and for nothing. Then, 20 years later, Ralph Cordiner's *Professional Management* accepted this divorce of ownership from control and tried to make a virtue out of it.

By now, the wheel has come full circle. The pension funds are very different owners from nineteenth-century tycoons. They are not owners because they want to be owners but because they have no choice. They cannot sell. They also cannot become owner-managers. But they are owners nonetheless. As such, they have more than mere power. They have the responsibility to ensure performance and results in America's largest and most important companies.

[1991]

31

Four Marketing Lessons for the Future

Of the top marketing lessons for the highly competitive '90s, the most crucial one may well be that buying customers doesn't work. Witness two spectacular marketing failures of the past few years: the collapse of the Hyundai Excel and the fiasco caused by the discounts and bonuses offered by the Big Three U.S. auto makers.

The Excel was the *Wundercar* of 1987–88. Fifteen months after the Korean car's introduction into the U.S. market, it was selling at an annual rate of more than 400,000 cars – the fastest growth of any automobile anywhere in history. But by mid-1990, only two years later, the Excel had all but disappeared.

There was nothing wrong with the car. But the company had greatly underpriced it to shoot itself into the U.S. market. As a result, it had no profits to plough back into promotion, service, dealers or improvements to the car itself. Hyundai, copying the Japanese, attacked the undefended low end of the market. But the Japanese learned long ago that to do so requires a substantial profit cushion, if only in the home market. They always quote to me what Henry Ford is supposed to have said, all of 80 years ago: 'We can sell the Model T at such a low price only because it earns such a nice profit.'

Few New Buyers

GM and Chrysler – and Ford to a lesser degree – also tried to buy customers in the late '80s; the results have been equally disastrous. Faced with growing defections of customers to the Japanese, the Big Three offered round after round of special incentives: discounts, cash bonuses, low-interest or no-interest financing. Each offer brought immediate sales and was hailed as a success. But the moment it expired sales collapsed, and to a lower level than before the latest special offer.

The offers attracted few, if any, new buyers; customers who had already decided to buy a domestic car simply waited for the next special offer to come along. Potential customers, however, were turned off. 'If they can sell cars only by giving them away,' was the reaction, 'they can't be much good.' Thus the American public brushed aside the very real improvements the Big Three have made in the past five years in quality, service, and styling.

As a result, GM and Chrysler have lost substantial market standing to the Japanese – and Ford has barely held its own. The Big Three have also weakened themselves financially. Compared to its archrival, Toyota, even GM no longer has very deep pockets.

How to define the market is the second lesson – the lesson of what was both a major marketing success and a major marketing fiasco: the conquest of the American market by the fax machine.

Seven or even five years ago, these machines were found only in a few large offices. Today they are ubiquitous and are rapidly spilling out of the office and into the home. The fax machine is American in invention, technology, design, and development. And U.S. manufacturers had fax machines all ready to be sold. Yet not one fax machine offered for sale in the U.S. today is American-made.

The Americans did not put the fax machines on the market, because market research convinced them that there was no demand for such a gadget. But we have known for decades that one cannot conduct market research on something not in the market. All one can do then is ask people: 'Would you buy a telephone accessory that costs upwards of $1,500 and enables you to send, for $1 a page, the same letter the post office delivers for 25 cents?' The answer, predictably, will be 'no'.

The Japanese, instead, looked at the market rather than market research. It told them that economics are a poor guide to the information and communications markets. Not one of the successes in these markets since the early '50s can be explained in economic terms, whether the mainframe computer, the PC, the copying machine, the car telephone, or the VCR. None reduces costs or increases profits. Even more important, the Japanese defined the market differently. They did not ask, 'What is the market for this *machine*?' Instead, they asked, 'What is the market for what it does?' And they immediately saw, when looking at the growth of courier services such as Federal Express in the '70s and early '80s, that the market for the fax machine had already been established.

Another lesson born of failure: the precipitate decline of the big-city American department store. The cock of the walk in 1980, it is in severe trouble, if not in bankruptcy, 10 years later. The decline is not – as is widely believed – the result of financial manipulation and miscalculation burdening the stores with crushing debt. If department stores today had the same share of the market they had 10 years ago, they could carry the debt. What brought them low is the most common of all marketing sins: ignoring the people who should be customers but aren't.

No one has better customer data than the big department store or studies them more assiduously. But these data are all about people who already shop at the store. During the '80s the department stores, by and large, held on to their old customers. But their share of new customers was shrinking steadily – especially their share of the most significant group, the educated and affluent two-earner families. They never learned that these people shop together, shop in the evenings, and are far more value-conscious than the traditional department store customer. Sooner or later the total number of customers always goes down, and with it the customer base, if an industry's or business's share of new customers declines. By then it is in serious trouble.

Marketing starts with *all* customers in the market rather than with *our* customers. Even a powerful business rarely has a market share much larger than 30 percent. This means that 70 percent of the customers buy from someone else. Yet most businesses or industries pay no more attention to this 70 percent than the department stores did.

The final lesson is that of the success of the new 'pastoral' churches by exploiting demographic changes as marketing opportunity.

Traditional churches and synagogues in the U.S. have been losing members steadily for 40 years, whether 'mainstream' or 'dissident'; liberal, conservative, evangelical, or fundamentalist; Protestant, Catholic, or Jewish; white, black, or racially integrated. But during the past 15 years new kinds of congregations have been growing fast. They range across all denominations and across the theological spectrum from ultraliberal to rockbound fundamentalist – and many have no discernible theology at all. But they do have one thing in common. They saw a major opportunity in America's demographic changes – in the emergence of a large population of elderly people, but especially in the emergence of the new educated, affluent two-earner family.

Both groups were bored with the traditional churches and increasingly stayed home. Traditional churches saw them as 'noncustomers'; the pastoral churches saw them as 'potential customers'. They asked what these customers need and want in a church. They focus, as a result, on the individual's spiritual wants; and on the individual's need for a freely chosen but close community. And they try to satisfy the desire of the affluent younger people to be put to work in the church and to hold responsible positions in its governance.

Large Pastoral Congregations

Fifteen years ago there were few such churches around, and most were quite small. Today there are some 20,000 large pastoral churches, each with a membership of 2,000 people or more – and some 5,000 of them have congregations in excess of 4,000 or 5,000.

None of these marketing lessons are new. Anyone who has taken a marketing course these past 30 years or who has read a marketing text should know them. We have known all along that buying customers boomerangs; that one can use market research only on what is already in the market; that the customer rather than the maker defines a market; that those who should be customers but aren't are a critical group to watch; that change has to be exploited as opportunity, and that demographic change offers the greatest – and the least risky – opportunity.

But the right marketing *knowledge* won't be much help in this turbulent, competitive, fast-changing decade. It requires the right marketing *action*.

[1990]

32

Tomorrow's Company: Dressed for Success

The big companies dominate the headlines. But midsized businesses are fast replacing them as the engines driving the American economy.

Between 1985 and 1990 American manufactured-goods exports rose by more than 80 percent in volume; those to Japan actually doubled. Yet, only two of the nation's biggest companies, Boeing and General Electric – selling airplanes and aircraft engines, respectively – significantly increased exports. The rest of the growth – the fastest ever recorded in peacetime America, and one of the fastest in any country's history – was contributed by medium-sized firms with sales (in 1990 dollars) of more than $75 million to less than $1 billion.

Since the 1987 stock market crash, big businesses across the board have steadily cut employment. Indeed, for the first time since the Great Depression, big businesses have been laying off white-collar people in large numbers. Yet, until the second half of last year, total employment still grew faster than population. Labour-force participation remained the highest in our history (and the highest ever recorded in peacetime for a developed country), and unemployment remained at a boom-time low. At least 75 percent of America's almost explosive employment growth since 1975 took place in midsized businesses.

Handicaps Disappeared

During the past decade or two, midsized business has become more competitive and big business less competitive. The handicaps under which midsized business used to labour have largely disappeared. Above all, now that a managerial or professional job in the big company no longer promises life-time security as it did only 10 years ago, midsized companies are fast becoming the employers of choice for many of the ablest young people.

But more important than the strengthening of the midsized firm is the decline in the advantage of being big.

The manufacturing companies that dominated their industries during the past hundred years – GE, Siemens, and Philips; Procter & Gamble, Unilever, and Nestle; Du Pont, Hoechst, and ICI; International Harvester and International Paper; the Standard Oil companies, Shell, and Texaco; GM, Ford, Fiat, and Daimler-Benz – were all built on the same conceptual foundation. And so was the Bell Telephone System. To each industry, the theory asserted, belongs one clearly delineated technology. It generates all the knowledge needed to lead the industry. In turn, whatever knowledge comes out of the industry's specific technology will become a saleable product for the company. And there is, the theory asserted further, very little if any overlap between different technologies and between different industries based on them.

This theory still underlay the rise of the very big companies of the post-World War II period, such as IBM in the U.S. and Matsushita, Hitachi, and Toyota in Japan. It also underlay the rise since 1950 of such pharmaceutical giants as Hoffmann-La Roche, Merck and Pfizer. One of them, only 20 years ago, defined its business as 'the application of biochemistry to supplying whatever products are needed in health care.' And Citibank's strategy for becoming the world's first financial institution that is both trans-national and a 'universal bank' was based on the same theory of the business.

A parallel theory underlay the rise of the large retailers, such as Sears Roebuck in the U.S., Marks & Spencer in Britain, and the department-store chains in the U.S., Western Europe, and Japan. They assumed homogeneous but totally distinct mass markets, again with little overlap between them. Everything bought by a customer within one of these markets would belong in the same value category, in terms of price or quality or lifestyle appeal.

This theory enabled the successful retailer to change from being a 'distributor' of goods designed by outside makers into being a 'buyer' who creates and designs the goods he sells – the pioneers were Sears and Marks & Spencer in the '20s and early '30s. Again, the theory still worked in the postwar period. Kmart, for instance, was built on it.

No new theories on which a big business can be built have emerged. But the old ones are no longer dependable. Technologies are no longer discrete. They overlap and crisscross each other. No industry or company can be fed out of one technological stream. However brilliant its work, even AT&T's magnificent Bell Labs can no longer supply everything the telecommunications industry needs, nor can IBM's equally magnificent labs supply all the software or semiconductor designs that IBM's computers need. Health-care products, competing with one another, now come out of organic chemistry and pharmacology, genetics and molecular biology, physics and electronic engineering.

Conversely, one technology no longer feeds only one industry. Much of what the research labs of the big companies are now discovering finds its major application outside of the company and even outside of the industry – in the case of Bell Labs, for instance, outside of telecommunications. Above all, 'industry' is becoming a very fuzzy term indeed.

Twenty-five years ago, computers and telephones were separate industries. Now AT&T has decided that telecommunications leadership requires acquiring a major computer company – NCR, a century-old maker of cash registers and a leader in computerized office equipment. Twenty-five years ago, copiers, printing machinery, typewriters, and computers were separate industries, each with its own technology and its own markets. Xerox now offers a machine that is a copier, high-speed printer, word processor, and fair-sized computer all in one.

Similarly, the assumptions on which the big retails have been operating no longer hold. There is increasing segmentation in all markets, and increasing overlap and crisscrossing between them. No one, for instance, in the office-furniture market could tell any more what is industrial, wholesale, and retail.

Big businesses are not going to disappear. On the contrary, we will need quite a few big businesses, some even bigger than anything we have today. Information and money are becoming increasingly global. New challenges, such as the environment, demand the kind of transnational work that only very big enterprises can perform. And there are many products and services that can be supplied efficiently only by big organizations: building a big power plant or a pipeline; producing passenger jets; making paper; running long-distance telephone service, or making automobiles and trucks that can be serviced throughout the world or at least across a continent – the list is endless.

Global competition in high technology almost certainly requires bigness. The competitors threatening America's global position in high-tech industries, whether semiconductors, computers, factory automation or high-resolution TV, are not lonely garage mechanics. They are multibillion-dollar giants. And the only American companies that have successfully fought them so far are very big companies – IBM, Intel, Motorola, and Xerox, for example.

The challenge, therefore, is for the corporation to learn how to be competitive despite being big. This means becoming market-driven. It means building into the company's system an organized abandonment of yesterday's products and technologies. It means organizing the whole business around innovation. Big businesses will have to become not only better but different. 'Synergy' will be out. The more clearly a business (especially a big one) is focused on one product range or on one market, the better it is likely to do.

Another implication: Whatever diversification a big business needs – e.g., to gain access to a different technology or a different market – is better achieved through strategic alliances, such as partnerships, joint ventures, and minority participations, than through acquisitions or grass-roots developments.

Finally, decentralization is no longer enough for a multiproduct, multitechnology, multimarkets company; the various units have to be set up as truly separate businesses. This is what GE, for instance, is trying to do in setting up 13 'Strategic Business Units'. One might go a step further and organize the big business the way GE's European counterpart, Siemens in Germany, is organized: as a 'group' in which each business is a separate company with its own CEO and board.

The Right Size

Big diversified companies of tomorrow may not even have 'central management'. They may emulate the two most successful builders of large business empires in the past two decades, the American investor Warren Buffett and the Anglo-American Hanson PLC. Both operate as 'investors' that 'supervise'. They make sure that their individual businesses have the right plan, the right strategy, and the management they need. But they do not 'manage'.

Still, bigness will no longer be desirable in itself. It will have to serve a function. For 100 years superior performance went with being the biggest in a given industry. From now on it will increasingly mean being the *right* size. And in most fields this will mean being midsized – as the leaders in American exports of manufactured goods already are.

The shift from the big to the midsized enterprise as the economy's centre of gravity is a radical reversal of the trend that dominated all developed economies for more than a century. It has been all but ignored so far by economists, politicians and the media: It may well, however, have been the most important economic event of the past 20 years. One of its consequences is that to be competitive despite being big is fast becoming the new management challenge.

[1991]

33

Company Performance: Five Telltale Tests

The pressure for short-term earnings on the part of security analysts and asset managers is unlikely to abate in the foreseeable future. Businesses, thus, have to accommodate themselves to it. But most chief executive officers have learned by now that short-term earnings are quite unreliable, indeed often grossly misleading, as measurements of a company's actual performance.

Most experienced executives have also learned that there is no one magic formula for measuring business performance. Just as an automobile needs a number of dials on the dashboard and also needs to have its tyre pressures checked once in a while, a business needs a number of 'dials' to have control. But the number is small; five such 'gauges' will tell how a business is doing and whether it is moving in the right direction.

The first true measurement of a company is its standing in its markets. Is market standing going up or going down? And is the improvement in the right markets? A pharmaceutical company, for instance, may need to know how its products are doing overall, but also how they are doing in both the human-health and the animal-health markets; how human-health products are doing with younger doctors, that is, with tomorrow's main customers; how they are doing in hospitals as well as with physicians and with specific groups, e.g. urologists. It also might need to know its market standing in specific competitive arenas such as anti-inflammatory drugs.

But a company also needs to know how its products or services are doing in respect to market share compared with alternatives of customer satisfaction. How does the structural steel our company produces stack up against pre-stressed concrete and on-site stressed concrete, the alternative materials in commercial and office construction?

Early Warning

The second 'dial' on a company's 'instrument board' measures innovative performance. Is the company's achievement as a successful innovator in its markets equal to its market standing? Or does it lag behind it? There is altogether no more reliable early warning of a company's imminent decline than a sharp and persistent drop in its standing as a successful innovator. And equally dangerous is a deterioration in innovative lead time, that is, in the time between the inception of an innovation and its introduction as a successful product or service in the market.

And does the ratio of successful innovations to false starts improve or deteriorate? Again the dial should show innovative action by major segments, and especially in the segments where future growth is likely to occur. Digital Equipment Corp. has done so much better these past few years than most other computer companies (including IBM) not primarily because it produced more successful innovations but because it concentrated its innovations on the growth markets in data processing.

The third set of measurements on the executive control panel measures productivity. It relates the input of all major factors of production – money, materials, people – to the 'value added' they produce, that is, to the (inflation-adjusted) value of total output of goods or services minus whatever is spent on buying supplies, parts, or services from the outside. Each factor has to be measured separately. Indeed, in the large organization – whether a business, a hospital, or a university – the productivity of different segments within each factor needs to be measured, e.g., blue-collar labour, clerical labour, managers, and service staffs.

Ideally, the productivity of each factor should increase steadily.

At the very least, however, increased productivity of one factor, e.g., people, should not be achieved at the expense of the productivity of another factor, e.g., capital – something that American industry has been guilty of far too often. Such a 'tradeoff' usually damages the company's break-even point of operations. Increased productivity in good times is then paid for by decreased productivity when a company needs productivity the most – in poor or depressed times.

No one needs to be told that productivity is in trouble in the U.S. But it also is in trouble worldwide. Since 1973, the rate of productivity increase has been falling steadily in all industrially developed countries, including Japan and West Germany. Whatever the causes – and no single one has yet been convincingly identified – this represents a tremendous opportunity for the individual business. The company that systematically concentrates on its productivity is almost bound to gain competitive advantage, and pretty fast.

The fourth 'dial' shows liquidity and cash flows. It is old wisdom that a business can run without profits for long years provided it has adequate cash flow. The opposite is not true, however. There are far too many businesses around – and by no means only small ones – that have to abandon the most profitable developments because they run out of cash. And increased profits, e.g., through rapid expansion of sales volume, which weakens rather than strengthens liquidity and cash position, is always a danger signal. It commonly means the company 'buys' rather than 'earns' its additional sales – through overly generous financing of its customers, for instance. And 'bought' markets don't last. But also an expected need for additional cash usually can be filled, and at a reasonable cost.

If a company waits till it needs the cash – for instance to finance the development of an unusually promising new product line – it may, in the end, have to sell the new product line to a competitor at a fire-sale price. Indeed, a liquidity crunch is usually more damaging than a profit crunch. In a profit crunch a company typically sells off or cuts out its least and most nearly obsolete businesses or products. In a liquidity crunch it typically sells its most profitable or most promising units, since these bring in the most cash soonest.

Yet liquidity is easy to measure and highly predictable. An ordinary cash-flow projection is usually all that is needed to identify future cash flows and cash needs.

The final 'dial' should measure a business's profitability – which is both more and less than conventional profit. Profitability measures show the capacity of a company's resources to produce a profit. They thus exclude profits or losses from nonrecurring transactions such as the sale or abandonment of a division, a plant, a product line. They also do not include overhead-cost allocations. But they also do not try to measure the profit in any given time period, focusing instead on the profitability of the going concern.

The easiest way to do this is probably to show operating profits on a 36 months' rolling basis – adjusted, if needed, for inflation or for fluctuations in foreign-exchange rates. When December 1986 is added, December 1983 is dropped, and so on. And the profitability trend is then projected three ways to test its adequacy: (a) cost of capital; (b) new ventures, new products, and new services (is profitability going up at these margins, or is it declining?); and (c) the need for profitability to be tested in respect to its composition.

No Precise Readings

Total profit is profit margin multiplied by turnover of capital. And usually profitability can be raised far more easily by increasing the turnover of capital – either by reducing the capital needed to produce, market and service a given unit of output, or by making the same capital serve a broader volume of output or a wider range of markets – than by increasing profit margins. But ideally both should improve simultaneously. And if one of the two profitability factors improves at the expense of a deterioration in the other one – e.g., if higher profit margins are being obtained by more liberal financing of the company's customers and distributors – the quality of profitability is deteriorating even though absolute profit may remain the same and may even be going up.

What exactly the best measurement is in each of these areas is hotly debated by economists, accountants, and management scientists. For the practitioner, however, it makes little, perhaps even no difference which of the measurements he adopts. None of them is perfect; and practically all are adequate. And no matter which specific measurement a company chooses, it will not give precise readings; all of them have built in a substantial margin of error, if only because accurate information does not exist in any of the areas.

But again this is not crucially important for the practitioner.

What matters to him is not the absolute magnitude in any area but the trend – what mathematicians call the 'slope of the curve' – that the measurements will give him no matter how crude and approximate the individual readings are by themselves. Without such information a business does not really know how it performs and whether it is headed in the right direction; it may not wake up early enough to the need to take corrective action. These measurements of performance give control. They should be on the desk of every CEO or on the walls of his chart room the second Monday of every third month.

[1986]

34

R & D: The Best Is Business-Driven

Only a few years ago, security analysts routinely ranked stocks by the percentage of sales a company spent on research and development. But R&D spending no longer correlates with business results.

Hoffmann-La Roche, the Swiss pharmaceutical giant, has a research budget second to none in the industry. It hasn't had a significant new product since the '60s. Siemens, the German electrical giant, though renowned for both its research quality and its research budget, has not come up with new products for years. America's best-known research centre, AT&T's Bell Laboratories, continues to give birth to one scientific 'spectacular' after the other – in acoustics and optics, in computers and in mathematics. But unlike the Bell Labs discoveries of the past, these new scientific breakthroughs have so far not generated great commercial successes. Bell Labs' Tokyo counterpart, the lab of NEC, similarly has not been able to turn its huge investment in telecommunications research into saleable products.

But other companies – often spending much less – show signal R&D results. Merck in the U.S. and some British firms, such as Glaxo and Wellcome, are bringing out one successful new drug

after another. The smallest of the old-line electrical manufacturers, Sweden's ASEA, has so successfully innovated as to
become a world leader in three highly competitive fields: electrical
locomotives, direct-current transmission, and industrial robots.
To blame 'outside factors', such as 'excessive government regulation', for what ails R&D simply will not do.

Prescription for Failure

For a hundred years it has been axiomatic that R&D has to be a
separate function, doing its own scientific and technical work by
itself. But the successful innovations in both pharmaceuticals and
computers – and in other fields – are now being turned out by
cross-functional teams with people from marketing, manufacturing and finance participating in research work from the very
beginning.

Most companies still believe that the better an innovation –
whether a product or a service – fits what the customer already is
doing, the more successful it will be in the market. The need for the
customer to buy costly new equipment, they think, should be kept
to a minimum. But this approach is becoming a prescription for
failure.

Federal Express, a couple of years back, correctly foresaw the
boom in facsimile transmission. It came out with a new service that
offered most of the benefits of facsimile without the customer's
having to spend a nickel on expensive new equipment. The service
was a resounding flop – but the same customers are now lining up
to buy their own fax machines. NEC's failure to become a major
factor in the world's telephone markets was caused in large
measure by its embodying the new technology in a hybrid: its
switchboards were only half electronic, thus enabling potential
customers to keep on using their existing electromechanical
equipment. The customers instead are buying fully electronic
switchboards from NEC's competitors.

Since the industrial research lab was created some 90 years ago
– by the chemical industry in Germany and by GE's Charles
Steinmetz in the U.S. – successful R&D has been 'technology-
driven'. Mr Steinmetz, for instance, began his pioneering work on
the fractional horsepower motor by spelling out the technical
specs: power inputs and outputs, running speeds, friction,
temperatures, durability, and reliability. This then enabled him to

define what new scientific knowledge and new engineering competence would have to be produced to obtain the desired end-product. This method gave us the major technical achievements of this century up to and including NASA's putting a man on the moon. But except in very young technologies such as biogenetics, the technology-driven approach is becoming unproductive. We increasingly need a 'business-driven' R&D strategy.

R&D in the American semiconductor firm is still largely technology-driven. The Japanese have overtaken us in large measure because they went into semiconductors with the question: What is the right business strategy? They concluded that research and manufacturing have to be integrated with a large user – i.e., a computer manufacturer – that provides a substantial captive market and thus a shield against the violent price fluctuations that are inherent in the industry's economics. Though the Americans pioneered in robotics they are way behind today; they based their strategy on the potential of technology. ASEA based its R&D on business strategy – which led it to develop very different tools for very different markets.

The best example of a business-driven R&D strategy is still the earliest one, and it is American: the way David Sarnoff, the builder and long-time chief executive of RCA, created colour television. In the mid-'40s, when black-and-white TV was just starting commercially, Mr Sarnoff foresaw the colour-TV-set market, thought through what the product would have to be to satisfy customers – in price, colour fidelity, channel capacity, appearance, and size – and then worked out the science and technology required to produce such a set.

The resulting requirements were almost the exact opposite of what were then considered the promising technological directions, and most of RCA's technical people considered them absurd. But Mr Sarnoff persisted, put to work extremely small teams of highly competent people, and had colour TV in 12 years.

The Japanese, quite consciously copying Mr Sarnoff, later used the same strategy to develop the videocassette recorder; they started out with a business goal and a business strategy and then put very small teams of highly competent people to work on the new science and technology needed. The Americans who had first put pictures on tape were technology-driven; they ended up with industrial applications for small, not-very-profitable niche markets. The Japanese now own a multibillion-dollar VCR consumer business worldwide.

Serious though these developments are, they may be only symptoms. The very concept of the company lab is becoming questionable. It assumes that one material, product, or service is uniquely right for a given market.

Steelmakers, for instance, still assume that their product has natural markets that it is destined to dominate. There may be substitutes, but they are second-rate – what the Germans contemptuously call *Ersatz*. But increasingly there are competitive products offering better – or at least, different – performance in practically every single 'natural' steel market – plastics, for instance, for the automobile.

Forty years ago, manual typewriters were being replaced by electric ones. But they were still typewriters, only with motors added, and produced by the traditional makers. Today word-processors are taking over. They come out of computer technology and are being made by computer companies.

Sixty years ago, the Supreme Court decided that the telegraph was the 'natural' way to transmit writing and the telephone the 'natural' way to transmit the spoken word – and it divided the electronic universe accordingly. Today telephone, videotex (growing like wildfire in Europe), telex, facsimile, and electronic mail compete in offering electronic transmission. Each represents a different technology with a different industrial base.

In practically all businesses today, the R&D lab primarily is concerned with what goes on in its traditional technology, be it steel, paper, or typewriters. What increasingly is needed is awareness of, and concern with, science, and technology outside of one's own lab, outside of one's own field, outside of one's own industry.

Does the traditional lab still make much sense? It assumes that all the technology needed by the company can be produced by its own lab, and, conversely, that most everything its lab produces can be put to profitable use by the company. This is simply no longer true – to the point where one of the country's leading research administrators, William Miller, the head of Stanford Research Institute, now says that 'a first-rate lab is too productive to belong to any one company.'

A Free-Standing Business

Bell Labs was founded to produce all the technology the telephone would require – and did so for many years. Conversely, its parent company, AT&T, was expected to be able to use whatever new technology the lab would come up with. It did so for many years. But since World War II, many of the technological breakthroughs to come out of Bell Labs – e.g., the transistor – have found their main applications outside of telephony. And more and more of the new telephone technology is coming from outside the tele-communications industry and its labs.

Siemen's one truly successful new product – the body scanner – was created not in its lab, but by a British producer of phonograph records.

The technological streams no longer run parallel. They increasingly cross each other, with frequent spillovers from one to the other.

Increasingly, therefore, the research lab may become a free-standing business, doing research work on contract for a multitude of industrial clients. Each client would then need a 'technology manager' rather than a 'research director' – someone who can develop business objectives based on the potential of technology and technology strategies based on business and market objectives, and who then defines and buys the technical work needed to produce business results. But no one today – and surely neither the engineering or business schools – knows how to teach technology management nor, indeed, even where to start.

[1988]

35

Sell the Mailroom: Unbundling in the '90s

More and more people working in and for organizations will actually be on the payroll of an independent outside contractor. Businesses, hospitals, schools, governments, labour unions – all kind of organizations, large and small – are increasingly 'unbundling' clerical, maintenance, and support work.

Of course, the trend is not altogether new. A great many American hospitals – and European and Japanese hospitals as well – now farm out maintenance and patient feeding; 40 years ago none did. 'Temporary help' firms go back more than 30 years; but while in the beginning they handled file clerks and typists, they now provide computer programmers, accountants, engineers, nurses, and even plant managers. Cities farm out 'waste management' (once known as street cleaning and garbage disposal); even prisons are being run by private contractors.

Farm Out Clerical Work

The trend is accelerating sharply in all developed countries. In another 10 or 15 years it may well be the rule, especially in large organizations, to farm out all activities that do not offer the people working in them opportunities for advancement into senior management. This may indeed be the only way to attain productivity in clerical, maintenance, and support work. And increased productivity in such work will increasingly become a central challenge in developed countries, where such work now employs as many people as manufacturing does.

Support work is rapidly becoming capital-intensive. In many manufacturing companies, the investment in information technology for each office employee now equals the investment in machinery for each production worker. Yet the productivity of clerical, maintenance, and support work is dismally low, and is improving only at snail's pace, if at all. Unbundling will not by itself make this work more productive. But without it the productivity of clerical, maintenance, and support work is unlikely to be tackled seriously.

In-house service and support activities are *de facto* monopolies. They have little incentive to improve their productivity. There is, after all, no competition. In fact, they have considerable disincentive to improve their productivity. In the typical organization, business, or government, the standard and prestige of an activity is judged by its size and budget – particularly in the case of activities that, like clerical, maintenance, and support work, do not make a direct and measurable contribution to the bottom line. To improve the productivity of such an activity is thus hardly the way to advancement and success.

When in-house support staff are criticized for doing a poor job, their managers are likely to respond by hiring more people. An outside contractor knows that he will be tossed out and replaced by a better-performing competitor unless he improves quality and cuts costs.

The people running in-house support services are also unlikely to do the hard, innovative, and often costly work that is required to make service work productive. Systematic innovation in service work is as desperately needed as it was in machine work in the 50 years between Frederick Winslow Taylor in the 1870s and Henry Ford in the 1920s. Each task, each job, has to be analysed and then reconfigured. Practically every tool has to be redesigned.

When Ray Kroc, the founder of McDonald's, set out to make hamburger shops more productive, he redesigned every single implement, including spoons, napkin holders, and skillets. To improve productivity, hospital-maintenance companies have had to redesign brooms, dustpans, wastepaper baskets, and even sheets and blankets. In building Federal Express, Fred Smith studied every single step in the collecting, transporting, and delivering packages, and in billing for the work. And then people have to be trained and trained and trained. This requires single-minded, almost obsessive dedication to one narrow objective – making hamburgers, making hospital beds, delivering packages – to the exclusion of everything else. But such single-minded dedication is far more characteristic of an independent outside entrepreneur than of a department head within an organization who is expected to be a team player.

The most important reason for unbundling the organization, however, is one that economists and engineers are likely to dismiss as 'intangible': the productivity of support work is not likely to go up until it is possible to be promoted into senior management for doing a good job at it. And that will happen in support work only when such work is done by separate, free-standing enterprises. Until then, ambitious and able people will not go into support work; and if they find themselves in it, will soon get out of it.

It is hardly coincidental that the productivity decline in American factories set in as soon as finance and marketing were taking over from manufacturing in the early '60s as the main avenues of advancement into senior management. Nor is it coincidence that stockbrokers have been plagued by recurrent 'back office' crises despite steadily increasing employment and increasing investment in clerical and support work. Until very recently even the head of the back office (though responsible for half the firm's expenses) was at best a 'titular' partner. Promotions, bonuses, but equally the time available on the part of top management were reserved by and large for traders, analysts and sales people.

They are 'we': the back office is 'they'. And one explanation why non-instructional costs in colleges and universities have risen twice as fast as instructional ones since World War II – to the point where they now account for almost two-fifths of the total bill – is surely that the people who run the dorms or the business office don't have Ph.D.s and are therefore nonpersons in the value system of academia.

Forty years ago, service and support costs accounted for no more than 10 percent or 15 percent of total costs. So long as they were so marginal, their low productivity did not matter. Now that they are more likely to take 40 cents out of every dollar they can no longer be brushed aside. But value systems are unlikely to change. The business of the college, after all, is not to feed kids; it is teaching and research.

However, if clerical, maintenance, and support work is done by an outside independent contractor it can offer opportunities, respect, and visibility. As employees of a college, managers of student dining will never be anything but subordinates. In an independent catering company they can rise to be vice president in charge of feeding the students in a dozen schools; they might even become CEOs of their firms. If they have a problem there is a knowledgeable person in their own firm to get help from. If they discover how to do the job better or how to improve the equipment they are welcomed and listened to. The same is true in the independent firm that takes over customer accounting in the mutual-fund company.

Pushing Vacuum Cleaners

In one large hospital-maintenance company, some of the women who started 12 or 15 years ago pushing vacuum cleaners are now division heads or vice presidents and own substantial blocks of company stock. As hospital employees, most of them would still be pushing vacuum cleaners.

Of course there is a price for unbundling. If large numbers of people cease to be employees of the organization for which they actually work, there are bound to be substantial social repercussions. And yet there is so far no other option in sight for giving us a chance to tackle what is fast becoming a central productivity problem of developed societies.

[1989]

36

The 10 Rules of Effective Research

Some businesses – not very many – get a fiftyfold, or even a hundredfold, return on the research dollar. Many more get little or nothing. The key to success is not knowledge, intelligence, or hard work – and least of all, luck. It is following the 10 Rules of Effective Research.

1. Every new product, processor, or service begins to become obsolete on the day it first breaks even.

2. Thus, your being the one who makes your product, process, or service obsolete is the only way to prevent your competitor from doing so.

One major American company that has long understood and accepted this is Du Pont Co. When nylon came out 50 years ago, Du Pont immediately put chemists to work to invent new synthetic fibres to compete with nylon. It also began to cut nylon's price – thus making it less attractive for would-be competitors to find a way around Du Pont's patents. This explains both why Du Pont is still the world's leading synthetic-fibre maker, and why Du Pont's nylon is still in the market, and profitably so.

A Meaningless Distinction

3. If research is to have results, the nineteenth-century distinction between 'pure' and 'applied' research is better forgotten. It may still work in the university, but in industry it is meaningless, if not an impediment. A minor change in machining a small part, for example, may require pure research into the structure of matter. Yet creating a totally new product or process may involve only careful rereading of a standard handbook. Nor is pure research necessarily more difficult than redefining a problem so that well-known concepts can be applied to its solution.

4. In effective research, physics, chemistry, biology, mathematics, economics, and so on are not 'disciplines'. They are tools. This does not mean, of course, that effective research requires universal geniuses. The most brilliant physicist or chemist today knows only a small corner of his own discipline. But effective research demands that the project leader or research director know when and how to call on what specialist. The best example may be the way in which Jim Webb, President Kennedy's head of NASA in the 1960s, mobilized a dozen different disciplines to put a man on the moon. Mr Webb was not a scientist but a lawyer-accountant.

5. Research is not one effort – it is three: improvement, managed evolution, and innovation. They are complementary but quite different.

- Improvement aims at making the already successful better still. It is a never-ending activity that requires specific quantitative goals, such as annual improvements of 3 percent or 5 percent in cost, quality, and customer satisfaction. Improvement starts with feedback from the front line: people who actually make the product or deliver the service; sales people; and, vitally important, the users. Then the company's own scientists, engineers, or product designers must convert the front line's suggestions and queries into changes in product, process, or service.

The best-known practitioners of continuing improvement today are the Japanese. Its inventor and most consistent practitioner however was an American company, the Western Electric subsidiary of the old Bell Telephone System.

- Managed evolution is the use of a new product, process, or service to spawn an even newer product, process or service. Its motto is 'each successful new product is the stepping stone to the next one'.

The best-known practitioner is probably Sony, which has systematically evolved a dozen new products – the Walkman, for instance – out of the original tape recorder. But the most successful practitioner is probably a 'no-tech' American business, ServiceMaster Co. of suburban Chicago, a multibillion-dollar multinational doing business successfully in the U.S., Japan, and Western Europe. ServiceMaster started with the systematic application of industrial engineering to hospital maintenance and the training of low-skill people. It then evolved this, step by step, into office maintenance and the care of elderly shut-ins. Managed evolution is always market driven; it often requires, however, new, or at least newly developed, technology and tools.

• Innovation, finally, is the systematic use as opportunity of changes in society and the economy, in demographics, and in technology.

The key to effective research is to pursue improvement, managed evolution, and innovation simultaneously though separately. The classic example is again Du Pont's strategy in synthetic fibres. As I mentioned earlier, the company immediately began work on inventing competing fibres. But it also immediately started to improve nylon and to pursue managed evolution. Nylon was developed for women's stockings. But soon it was modified to serve as automotive tyre cord – probably the most profitable application for many years.

The first five rules are about what to do. The last five lay down how to do it.

6. Aim high! Trivial corrections usually are as hard to make and as staunchly resisted as fundamental changes. Successful research asks: If we succeed, will it make a real difference in the customer's life or business? The Japanese control the market in videotape recorders and fax machines, both American inventions, because they set higher research goals than any American company thought attainable – in terms of product size, performance, and price.

7. Yet, effective research requires both long-range and short-range results. The efforts needed are too great to be satisfied with

the short term alone. A short-term result must also be a step in a continuing long-term process. The needed balance is difficult to design. But it usually can be attained by retrospective analysis.

Researchers have long known that they should go back and read their own lab notes. Did anything happen that was pushed aside because it was unexpected or because it did not seem to lead toward the desired research objective? If so, was it actually an indication of an opportunity? Above all, was it an indication of a usable and useful short-term result? The best-known example is how Alexander Fleming came to realize that he had stumbled upon penicillin but had thrown it away as spoiling his bacterial cultures.

In improvement, where results by definition are short-term, one looks for the long-term implications. One analyses the work of the past two or three years with this question: Did successful improvements cluster around one particular application, one particular market, one design, one process, one product? This often indicates an opportunity for fundamental, long-term innovation or change.

One large company that seems to have mastered this balancing act is Merck, one of the world's largest pharmaceutical companies. Another is the medical-electronics business of G.E. While working on such radical innovations as body scanning and nuclear magnetic resonance imaging, it has systematically fed back from these major long-term innovations to make constant, immediate improvements in its conventional X-ray apparatus.

8. Research is separate work, but it is not a separate function. Development – the translation of research results into products, processes, and services that can be manufactured, sold, delivered, and serviced – must go hand in hand with research. And manufacturing, marketing, and service all affect research from the beginning, just as much as the results of research in turn affect them. In the university, research may be the search for new knowledge as an end in itself. In industry, in government, and in medicine, research is the search for new utility.

9. Effective research requires organized abandonment – not only of products, processes and services, but also of research projects. Every product, process, service, and research project needs to be put on trial for its life every few years, with this question: Would we now start this product, process, service, or research project, knowing what we know now?

Three good clues to when to abandon:

First, when there are no more significant improvements.

Second, when new products, processes, markets or applications no longer come out of managed evolution. Third, when long years of research produce only 'interesting' results.

Reviewing Innovations

10. Research has to be measured like everything else. For improvements, it is fairly easy to set specific goals and to measure them. In managed evolution, too, goals can be set – e.g., one new significant product, market, or application every year. Innovation, however, requires appraisal. Every three years or so a company needs to review its innovative results. What did we innovate that made a difference in the wealth-producing capacity of this company? Were these innovations commensurate in numbers, quality, and impact with our market standing and our leadership position in our industry? What will our innovation results have to be in the next few years – again, in numbers, quality and impact – to give us the market standing and industry leadership we need?

Research expenditures in American business – flat or even declining the past few years – are starting to climb again. But spending money does not by itself guarantee results. Applying the 10 Rules of Effective Research does.

[1989]

37

The Trend Toward
Alliances for Progress

While mergers and takeovers, imports and exports grab headlines, business alliances rarely do. Nor do they generally show up in statistics. Yet for small and medium-sized businesses they are increasingly becoming the way to go international, and for big business, they are the way to become multitechnological.

Alliances of all kinds are becoming increasingly common, especially in international business: joint ventures; minority holdings (particularly cross-holdings, in which each partner owns the same percentage of the other); research and marketing compacts; cross-licensing and exchange-of-knowledge agreements; syndicates, and so on. The trend is likely to accelerate. Marketing, technology and people needs all push it.

The Only Way

In Japan as early as the '60s and '70s a foreign business could gain access to the domestic market only with a joint venture with a local company. Increasingly, such joint ventures are needed in Europe and the U.S. as well.

A few years ago AT&T entered an alliance with the Italian

telephone monopoly to reach a European market dominated by government monopolies. Even more often an alliance is the only way to obtain new, distinct, and foreign technology. Large computer makers buy into small software houses; large electronics manufacturers buy into small designers of speciality chips; large pharmaceutical companies buy into genetics start-ups; large commercial banks buy into bond traders or underwriters.

More and more, such alliances are also the way to get access to people with the know-how. The many research pacts between American universities and large European, Japanese, (and American) businesses are good examples.

And then there are the international alliances within industries. Two years ago, two medium-sized manufacturers of speciality machinery – one Japanese, one American – sealed their agreement to exchange research results and to sell and service each other's products in their respective home markets by swapping 16 percent of each other's stock. All three big U.S. auto makers have substantial minority holdings in independent Japanese and Korean car makers and sell on the U.S. market, under their own name plates, cars made by these Asian 'friends'.

These are all dangerous liaisons. While their failure rate in the early years is no higher than that of new ventures or acquisitions, they tend to get into serious – sometimes fatal – trouble when they succeed.

Often when an alliance does well, it becomes apparent that the goals and objectives of the partners are not compatible. Each partner may want the 'child' to behave differently now that it is 'growing up'. Each partner may have a different idea of what kind of people should run the successful enterprise, where they should come from and to whom they owe allegiances. What makes it worse is that there usually is no mechanism to resolve these disagreements. By that time it is usually too late to restore the joint enterprise to health.

But the problems can be anticipated and largely prevented:

Before the alliance is completed, all parties must think through their objectives and the objectives of the 'child'. Do they want the joint enterprise eventually to grow into a separate, autonomous venture? Do they agree from the start that it will be allowed, perhaps even encouraged, to compete with one or all parents? If so, in what products, services, markets?

Failure to think this through was the main reason, for instance, that one highly successful investment company, formed to find and develop promising industries in Southeast Asia, ultimately was liquidated by its parents. It had grown to the point where it had to do some commercial banking for its industrial clients. But while the three of its four parents that were European banks were not active in Asia, they still felt that their child going into commercial banking made it an ungrateful brat – and they killed it off in short order.

A similar failure to anticipate that success would – and should – make a joint venture a potential competitor explains the failure of a highly promising Spanish partnership between a German and an American chemical company. When the venture became competitive in a product line that, while minor in Northern Europe, was likely to be quite big in Spain and Portugal, the European parent withdrew its support and slowly throttled the child to death. (The objectives must be revised every three to five years for each parent and for the joint enterprise, and more often if the joint enterprise does really well.)

Equally important is advance agreement on how the joint enterprise should be run. Should profits, for instance, be ploughed back? Or should they be remitted to the parents as fast as possible? Should the joint enterprise develop its own research? Or should it contract for its research exclusively with one or both parents? In whose name will research results be patented – in that of the university that furnishes research scientists and lab, or that of the company that pays the bill?

Does the American company that markets the speciality products of its Japanese minority partner in the U.S. have the right to specify product designs and prices that fit the U.S. market? Or does it act solely as distributor for whatever the Japanese produce? This was the issue over which the partnership between the speciality-machinery makers broke up only a few months ago – after the Americans had gained a 26 percent share of the U.S. market for their Japanese partner's products.

Next, there has to be careful thinking about who will manage the alliance. Regardless of what specific form it takes, the joint enterprise has to be managed separately. And the people in charge have to have the incentives to make it successful.

Nummi, the joint venture of Toyota and GM, makes the same car for each parent in the same plant (in Fremont, California) with the same workers. The car is a success under the Toyota name in the U.S. but a near-failure as a Chevrolet. For the Toyota people, this car is their main U.S. product; their careers at Toyota depend on its success. But no one at Chevrolet is going to make a great career selling the Nummi car. For a good many people at Chevrolet the car, despite its Chevrolet plate, is probably a competitor to '*our* cars'. For the same reason, the other cars made for American manufacturers by their Asian partners are also doing poorly in the U.S. market. They are orphans.

The alliance, whatever its legal form, has to be managed by *one* of the partners. It cannot be managed by committee. And it has to be clear from the beginning that the people who manage the joint enterprise are measured solely by its performance. Their individual responsibility has to be to the joint enterprise, not to one of the parents. The one thing that must never be said about an executive working for a joint enterprise is: 'John doesn't do too well in the assignment; but he sure looks after our interests in any disagreement with our partners.'

Each partner needs to make provisions in its own structure for the relationship to the joint enterprise and the other partners. Even if the joint enterprise is quite subordinate for one of the partners – a small underwriting venture in Luxembourg, for instance, in which a major commercial bank holds a one-sixth interest – its management people must have access to someone in the parent organization who can say 'yes' or 'no' without having to go through channels.

The best way, especially in a large organization, is to entrust all such 'dangerous liaisons' to one senior executive.

An Arbitrator

Finally, there has to be prior agreement on how to resolve disagreements. Orders from the top do not work in an alliance. The best way is to agree, in advance of any disputes, on an arbitrator whom all sides know and respect and whose verdict will be accepted as final by all of them. He should be empowered to go beyond the specific issue in dispute. He should be able to decide for instance, that each party is entitled to buy out the other according to a pre-arranged formula. He should also be able to recommend that the joint enterprise be liquidated or that it become a separate business independent of its parents.

These are radical measures. But for this reason arbitration will be seen as a last resort. Such provisions make each party realize how much it has to gain by subordinating its individual interest, opinion, and pride to the perpetuation of the successful alliance.

[1989]

38

A Crisis of Capitalism: Who's in Charge

'Corporate capitalism' was the buzzword of the 1960s. 'The American Challenge', a worldwide best-seller by a prominent French intellectual, Jean-Jacques Servan-Schreiber, predicted that by 1980 the world's manufacturing would be in the hands of a dozen or so giant American multinationals.

Under corporate capitalism, these economic superpowers were run by autonomous managements. With share-ownership dispersed among millions of individual investors, corporate management had the power to appoint itself, was accountable only to itself, and enjoyed unchallengeable security except in the event of a huge scandal or the firm's bankruptcy. However, these managements promised to be 'enlightened despots' and to manage their companies in the best balanced interest of shareholders, employees, consumers, suppliers, plant-cities, and the economy and society as a whole – as any number of annual reports in those years asserted.

Even Jean-Jacques Servan-Schreiber would agree 20 years later that his prophecy was far off the mark. The multinational manufacturing giants are trying desperately to cope with changes in technology and demographics that threaten to make them obsolete if not to drive them out of business. Top managements in publicly owned U.S. companies, almost irrespective of size or performance, cower under golden parachutes and in deadly fear of the corporate raider and of his ultimate weapon, the junk bond.

Hostile takeovers and their raiders – such as T. Boone Pickens and Carl Icahn – get the headlines. But the hostile takeover is an effect rather than a cause, and perhaps only a symptom. What finished off corporate capitalism was the emergence of the 'institutional investor' – primarily the pension fund – as the controlling shareholder in the U.S. publicly owned corporation. With $1.5 trillion – and soon to each $2 trillion – in assets, pension funds now own a third of the equity of all publicly traded companies in the U.S. and 50 percent or more of the equity of the big ones. There are thousands of corporate pension funds, of course. But a few very large ones lead the pack, with most of the others following faithfully.

Vicious Circle

Stock ownership has thus become more concentrated than probably ever before in U.S. history. Therefore any business that needs money – every business sooner or later – has to be managed to live up to the expectations of the pension-fund managers. And a pension-fund manager has little choice but to focus on the very shortest term; his own job depends on showing immediate gains, with his performance in most cases judged quarter by quarter. This is because the earnings of his boss, the company whose pension fund is being managed, depend in large measure on the short-term performance of the pension fund. If it shows substantial short-term gains, the company's liability for its pension-fund contribution goes down that year and its reported profits go up.

Conversely, if the pension fund in a given year under-performs, the company's liability for pension-fund contribution goes up and its earnings go down. Company management thus put relentless pressure on their pension-fund people to produce immediate gains; the pension-fund people, in turn, pressure the managements of the companies in which they invest to produce short-term gains. These, in turn, pressure their pension-fund managers to produce short-term gains, and so on in a vicious circle.

But pension funds are also trustees for the beneficiaries, the company's employees, rather than owners themselves. If a raider offers a little more for a stock than its current market price, fund managers are legally obligated to say 'yes'. If they don't and the stock, a few months later, sells for less than the raider offered, they may face a suit for damages and for a breach of fiduciary duty.

Corporate capitalism promised that large corporations would be run in the interests of a number of 'stakeholders'. Instead, corporate managements are being pushed into subordinating everything (even such long-range considerations as a company's market standing, its technology, indeed its basic wealth-producing capacity) to immediate earnings and next week's stock price. A Marxist might well say that corporate capitalism has turned into 'speculator's capitalism'.

Corporate capitalism was a delusion from the beginning, and an arrogant one to boot. Management in the large corporation has – and must have – considerable power. And power, to be legitimate, has to be accountable. Enlightened despotism has always ended up impotent and repudiated. When attacked, no one supports it – as U.S. managements found out as soon as the raiders appeared. And most U.S. top managements spurned the constitutional safeguard that might have provided genuine accountability: a strong, independent board able and willing to set performance standards and to remove any management not living up to them.

But speculator's capitalism is the wrong remedy. Its side effects threaten to kill the patient.

Speculator's capitalism is probably not even very good for the shareholder. At least that seems to be the conclusion of America's major shareholders, the pension funds. They are forced to sell their holdings to the raider in the hostile takeover. But in most cases they then refuse to stay interested in the company that has been taken over. They either demand cash or they immediately sell whatever securities they get from the raider. They know why; many – perhaps most – businesses are doing less well a year or two later than they did before they succumbed to the hostile bid. And the shareholders in West Germany and Japan, where companies are still primarily being managed for the long term rather than for short-term gains, have, on the whole, done better – and certainly no worse – than American shareholders in comparable businesses.

But the evidence is also mounting that the short-term focus is bad even for the pension funds. Despite the armies of well-paid security analysts employed by stockbrokers, investment advisers, and pension funds, most pension funds have done rather poorly, and at best no better than the stock market. Their performance amply proves the old saw: 'Thinking short term makes traders rich and investors poor.' Indeed, there are growing complaints – for example, by Sen. William Cohen (R., Maine) – that their short-term focus forces pension funds to underperform and thus puts them into an irreconcilable conflict with the interests of the ultimate beneficiaries, the future pension recipients.

Finally, there is little doubt that the short-term focus that speculator's capitalism imposes on managements is deleterious to both U.S. business and the U.S. economy. In some cases it has been the main – perhaps the sole – cause of the loss of competitive position in an important industry or market. One example is video-cassette recorders, invented and developed in America. No U.S. company now produces VCRs, they all abandoned the field to the Japanese. The only reason was that the recorders would not have yielded immediate gains but would have required a few years of investment.

In other industries and markets the short-term focus has been a major contributing factor to the bad performance and decline of a U.S. company or industry; it explains in large measure why General Motors failed to respond in time to Japanese competition. Everyone who has worked with American managements can testify that the need to satisfy the pension-fund manager's quest for higher earnings next quarter, together with the panicky fear of the raider, constantly pushes top managements toward decisions they know to be costly, if not suicidal, mistakes. The damage is greatest where we can least afford it: in the fast-growing, middle-sized high-tech or high-engineering firm that needs to put every available penny into tomorrow-research, product development, market development, people development, service – lest it lose leadership for itself and for the U.S. economy.

Mr Pickens would argue – and so would Wall Street and even the SEC – that all this is irrelevant. The shareholders are the owners, and the company is theirs with which to do whatever *they* deem to be in their own immediate interest. But are the institutional investors really owners? They have no interest whatever in the business: all they care for is making a quick buck. More important: an owner is supposed to have the freedom to decide whether to buy, to sell, or to hold on. But the pension funds can decide freely only on buying. When it comes to selling, they cannot say 'no' even if they would rather hold on. They do not really have the owner's freedom either economically or even in law. This is a new and totally unprecedented situation for which we have no rules. But to call it 'ownership' may be more legal fiction than reality.

Or so the Japanese think. Their law is exactly like ours. But in practice they treat the public shareholder not as an owner but as a claimant whose interests (save in the event of liquidation) are subordinated to the maintenance of the business as a wealth-producing, goods-producing, jobs-producing entity. And we in the U.S. are slowly moving in the same direction.

We are beginning to limit the voting power for the institutional investor by splitting the shares of the publicly held company into two (or more) groups – one, for the 'insiders', having full voting rights; the other, for the 'outsiders', having sharply reduced voting power or none at all. Both General Motors and Ford are already travelling down this road. Both the institutional investors and Wall Street are protesting – and there is much to be said for the old principle of 'one share, one vote'. But while the institutional investors protest, they quite happily buy the low-vote or no-vote shares if they like a company's prospects.

Moreover, as Senator Cohen notes, it would take only one major scandal to make us change our laws so as to forbid a company to treat gains in its pension plan as earnings of its own – which would go a long way toward easing the pressure for short-term performance. Within the pension-fund fraternity there is also growing concern. Robert A. G. Monks – President Reagan's chairman of the Pension Benefit Guaranty Corporation – has founded Institutional Shareholders Services Inc. to infuse 'social responsibility' into pension-fund management. Speculator's capitalism may thus be nearing its peak.

But the real issues will still be with us. They are political and moral rather than financial or economic. Can a modern democratic society tolerate the subordination of all other goals and priorities in a major institution, such as the publicly owned corporation, to short-term gain? And can it subordinate all other stakeholders to one constituency – the shareholder – even to a 'socially responsible' one?

The Short and Long of It

Corporate capitalism failed primarily because under it management was accountable to no one and for nothing. In this the raiders are absolutely right. The first performance requirement in a business is economic performance. Indeed, the first social responsibility for a business is to produce a profit adequate to cover the costs of capital and with them the minimum costs of staying in business. Adequate profitability alone can provide for the risks, growth needs, and jobs of tomorrow. These needs are all, however, long-term rather than short-term. Indeed, the one thing we know about commitments to the future – which production and services require and trading does not – is that long-term profits are not being achieved by putting up short-term gains. Short-term earnings are promises rather than results in themselves.

But equally important: Should economic results, even long-term and lasting ones, be the one and only goal in the large publicly owned enterprise, the goal to which all other considerations are to be subordinated and sacrificed? Or are even optimum economic goals achieved only by balancing competing claims? All conservative thinkers have held since Aristotle that to subordinate a major institution to a single value is a grievous mistake that will ultimately deprive the institution of the ability to produce *any* results. We may indeed be best advised to strive for the balance that corporate capitalism proclaimed. This may be what 'free enterprise' really means – it clearly was meant to be more than a euphemism for capitalism let alone for speculation. But how can we build accountability for such balance into the management structure? And to whom and in what form is this accountability to be exercised?

The proponents of corporate capitalism 20 years ago thought that they had the right answers. Speculator's capitalism has proved them wrong. But they may well have asked the right questions. Now that speculator's capitalism is in turn proving inadequate, and indeed a threat to America's long-term economic future, we have to tackle these questions again. On our answers to them the future of free enterprise – and perhaps even whether it has much of a future – may well depend.

[1986]

39

The Emerging Theory of Manufacturing

We cannot build it yet. But already we can specify the 'post-modern' factory of 1999. Its essence will not be mechanical, though there will be plenty of machines. Its essence will be conceptual – the product of four principles and practices that together constitute a new approach to manufacturing.

Each of these concepts is being developed separately, by different people with different starting points and different agendas. Each concept has its own objectives and its own kinds of impact. Statistical Quality Control is changing the social organization of the factory. The new manufacturing accounting lets us make production decisions as business decisions. The 'flotilla', or module, organization of the manufacturing process promises to combine the advantages of standardization and flexibility. Finally, the systems approach embeds the physical process of making things, that is, manufacturing, in the economic process of business, that is, the business of creating value.

As these four concepts develop, they are transforming how we think about manufacturing and how we manage it. Most manufacturing people in the United States now know that we need a new theory of manufacturing. They know that patching up old theories has not worked and that further patching will only push us further behind. Together these concepts give us the foundation for the new theory we so badly need.

The most widely publicized of these concepts, Statistical Quality Control (SQC), is actually not new at all. It rests on statistical theory formulated 70 years ago by Sir Ronald Fisher. Walter Shewhart, a Bell Laboratories physicist, designed the original version of SQC in the 1930s for the zero-defects mass production of complex telephone exchanges and telephone sets. During World War II, W. Edwards Deming and Joseph Juran, both former members of Shewhart's circle, separately developed the versions used today.

The Japanese owe their leadership in manufacturing quality largely to their embrace of Deming's precepts in the 1950s and 1960s. Juran too had great impact in Japan. But U.S. industry ignored their contributions for 40 years and is only now converting to SQC, with companies such as Ford, General Motors, and Xerox among the new disciples. Western Europe also has largely ignored the concept. More important, even SQC's most successful practitioners do not thoroughly understand what it really does. Generally it is considered a production tool. Actually, its greatest impact is on the factory's social organization.

By now, everyone with an interest in manufacturing knows that SQC is a rigorous, scientific method of identifying the quality and productivity that can be expected from a given production process in its current form so that control of both attributes can be built into the process itself. In addition, SQC can instantly spot malfunctions and show where they occur – a worn tool, a dirty spray gun, an overheating furnace. And because it can do this with a small sample, malfunctions are reported almost immediately, allowing machine operators to correct problems in real time. Further, SQC quickly identifies the impact of any change on the performance of the entire process. (Indeed, in some applications developed by Deming's Japanese disciples, computers can simulate the effects of a proposed change in advance.) Finally, SQC identifies where, and often how, the quality and productivity of the entire process can be continuously improved. This used to be called the 'Shewhart Cycle' and then the 'Deming Cycle'; now it is *kaizen*, the Japanese term for continuous improvement.

But these engineering characteristics explain only a fraction of

SQC's results. Above all, they do not explain the productivity gap between Japanese and U.S. factories. Even after adjusting for their far greater reliance on outside suppliers, Toyota, Honda, and Nissan turn out two or three times more cars per worker than comparable U.S. or European plants do. Building quality into the process accounts for no more than one-third of this difference. Japan's major productivity gains are the result of social changes brought about by SQC.

The Japanese employ proportionately more machine operators in direct production work than Ford or GM. In fact, the introduction of SQC almost always increases the number of machine operators. But this increase is offset many times over by the sharp drop in the number of nonoperators: inspectors, above all, but also the people who do not *do* but *fix*, like repair crews and 'fire fighters' of all kinds.

In U.S. factories, especially mass-production plants, such nonoperating, blue-collar employees substantially outnumber operators. In some plants, the ratio is two to one. Few of these workers are needed under SQC. Moreover, first-line supervisors also are gradually eliminated, with only a handful of trainers taking their place. In other words, not only does SQC make it possible for machine operators to be in control of their work, it makes such control almost mandatory. No one else has the hands-on knowledge needed to act effectively on the information that SQC constantly feeds back.

By aligning information with accountability, SQC resolves a heretofore irresolvable conflict. For more than a century, two basic approaches to manufacturing have prevailed, especially in the United States. One is the engineering approach pioneered by Frederick Winslow Taylor's 'scientific management'. The other is the 'human relations' (or 'human resources') approach developed before World War I by Andrew Carnegie, Julius Rosenwald of Sears Roebuck, and Hugo Münsterberg, a Harvard psychologist. The two approaches have always been considered antitheses, indeed, mutually exclusive. In SQC, they come together.

Taylor and his disciples were just as determined as Deming to build quality and productivity into the manufacturing process. Taylor asserted that his 'one right way' guaranteed zero-defects quality; he was as vehemently opposed to inspectors as Deming is today. So was Henry Ford, who claimed that his assembly line built quality and productivity into the process (though he was otherwise untouched by Taylor's scientific management and probably did not even know about it). But without SQC's rigorous methodology, neither scientific management nor the assembly line could actually deliver built-in process control. With all their successes, both scientific management and the assembly line had to fall back on massive inspection, to fix problems rather than eliminate them.

The human-relations approach sees the knowledge and pride of line workers as the greatest resource for controlling and improving quality and productivity. It too has had important successes. But without the kind of information SQC provides, you cannot readily distinguish productive activity from busyness. It is also hard to tell whether a proposed modification will truly improve the process or simply make things look better in one corner, only to make them worse overall.

Quality circles, which were actually invented and widely used in U.S. industry during World War II, have been successful in Japan because they came in after SQC had been established. As a result, both the quality circle and management have objective information about the effects of workers' suggestions. In contrast, most U.S. quality circles of the last 20 years have failed despite great enthusiasm, especially on the part of the workers. The reason? They were established without SQC, that is, without rigorous and reliable feedback.

A good many U.S. manufacturers have built quality and productivity into their manufacturing processes without SQC and yet with a minimum of inspection and fixing. Johnson & Johnson is one such example. Other companies have successfully put machine operators in control of the manufacturing process without instituting SQC. IBM long ago replaced all first-line supervisors with a handful of 'managers' whose main task is to train, while Herman Miller achieves zero-defects quality and high productivity through continuous training and productivity-sharing incentives.

But these are exceptions. In the main, the United States has lacked the methodology to build quality and productivity into the manufacturing process. Similarly, we have lacked the methodology to move responsibility for the process and control of it to the machine operator, to put into practice what the mathematician Norbert Wiener called the 'human use of human beings'.

SQC makes it possible to attain both traditional aspirations: high quality and productivity on the one hand, work worthy of human beings on the other. By fulfilling the aims of the traditional factory, it provides the capstone for the edifice of twentieth-century manufacturing that Frederick Taylor and Henry Ford designed.

Bean counters do not enjoy a good press these days. They are blamed for all the ills that afflict U.S. manufacturing. But the bean counters will have the last laugh. In the factory of 1999, manufacturing accounting will play as big a role as it ever did and probably even a bigger one. But the beans will be counted differently. The new manufacturing accounting, which might more accurately be called 'manufacturing economics', differs radically from traditional cost accounting in its basic concepts. Its aim is to integrate manufacturing with business strategy.

Manufacturing cost accounting (cost accounting's rarely used full name) is the third leg of the stool – the other legs being scientific management and the assembly line – on which modern manufacturing industry rests. Without cost accounting, these two could never have become fully effective. It too is American in origin. Developed in the 1920s by General Motors, General Electric, and Western Electric (AT&T's manufacturing arm), the new cost accounting, not technology, gave GM and GE the competitive edge that made them worldwide industry leaders. Following World War II, cost accounting became a major U.S. export.

But by that time, cost accounting's limitations also were becoming apparent. Four are particularly important. First, cost accounting is based on the realities of the 1920s, when direct, blue-collar labour accounted for 80 percent of all manufacturing costs other than raw materials. Consequently, cost accounting equates 'cost' with direct labour costs. Everything else is 'miscellaneous', lumped together as overhead.

These days, however, a plant in which direct labour costs run as high as 25 percent is a rare exception. Even in automobiles, the most labour intensive of the major industries, direct labour costs in up-to-date plants (such as those the Japanese are building in the United States and some of the new Ford plants) are down to 18 percent. And 8 percent to 12 percent is fast becoming the industrial norm. One large manufacturing company with a labour-intensive process, Beckman Instruments, now considers labour costs 'miscellaneous'. But typically, cost accounting systems are still based on direct labour costs that are carefully, indeed minutely, accounted for. The remaining costs – and that can mean 80 percent to 90 percent – are allocated by ratios that everyone knows are purely arbitrary and totally misleading: in direct proportion to a product's labour costs, for example, or to its dollar volume.

Second, the benefits of a change in process or in method are primarily defined in terms of labour cost savings. If other savings are considered at all, it is usually on the basis of the same arbitrary allocation by which costs other than direct labour are accounted for.

Even more serious is the third limitation, one built into the traditional cost accounting system. Like a sundial, which shows the hours when the sun shines but gives no information on a cloudy day or at night, traditional cost accounting measures only the costs of producing. It ignores the costs of nonproducing, whether they result from machine downtime or from quality defects that require scrapping or reworking a product or part.

Standard cost accounting assumes that the manufacturing process turns out good products 80 percent of the time. But we now know that even with the best SQC, nonproducing time consumes far more than 20 percent of total production time. In some plants, it accounts for 50 percent. And nonproducing time costs as much as producing time does – in wages, heat, lighting, interest, salaries, even raw materials. Yet the traditional system measures none of this.

Finally, manufacturing cost accounting assumes the factory is an isolated entity. Cost savings in the factory are 'real'. The rest is 'speculation' – for example, the impact of a manufacturing process change on a product's acceptance in the market or on service quality. GM's plight since the 1970s illustrates the problem with this assumption. Marketing people were unhappy with top management's decision to build all car models, from Chevrolet to Cadillac, from the same small number of bodies, frames, and engines. But the cost accounting model showed that such commonality would produce substantial labour cost savings. And so marketing's argument that GM cars would lose customer appeal as they looked more and more alike was brushed aside as speculation. In effect, traditional cost accounting can hardly justify a product *improvement*, let alone a product or process *innovation*. Automation, for instance, shows up as a cost but almost never as a benefit.

All this we have known for close to 40 years. And for 30 years,

accounting scholars, government accountants, industry accountants, and accounting firms have worked hard to reform the system.
They have made substantial improvements. But since the reform
attempts tried to build on the traditional system, the original
limitations remain.

What triggered the change to the new manufacturing accounting
was the frustration of factory-automation equipment makers. The
potential users, the people in the plants, badly wanted the new
equipment. But top management could not be persuaded to spend
the money on numerically controlled machine tools or robots that
could rapidly change tools, fixtures, and moulds. The benefits of
automated equipment, we now know, lie primarily in the reduction of nonproducing time by improving quality (that is, getting it
right the first time) and by sharply curtailing machine downtime in
changing over from one model or product to another. But these
gains cost accounting does not document.

Out of this frustration came Computer-Aided Manufacturing-
International, or CAM-I, a cooperative effort by automation
producers, multinational manufacturers, and accountants to
develop a new cost accounting system. Started in 1986, CAM-I is
just beginning to influence manufacturing practice. But already it
has unleashed an intellectual revolution. The most exciting and
innovative work in management today is found in accounting
theory, with new concepts, new approaches, new methodology –
even what might be called new economic philosophy – rapidly
taking shape. And while there is enormous controversy over
specifics, the lineaments of the new manufacturing accounting are
becoming clearer every day.

As soon as CAM-I began its work, it became apparent that the
traditional accounting system could not be reformed. It had to be
replaced. Labour costs are clearly the wrong unit of measurement
in manufacturing. But – and this is a new insight – so are all the
other elements of production. The new measurement unit has to
be time. The costs for a given period of time must be assumed to be
fixed; there are no 'variable' costs. Even material costs are more
fixed than variable, since defective output uses as much material as
good output does. The only thing that is both variable and
controllable is how much time a given process takes. And 'benefit'
is whatever reduces that time. In one fell swoop, this insight
eliminates the first three of cost accounting's four traditional
limitations.

But the new cost concepts go even further by redefining what costs and benefits really are. For example, in the traditional cost accounting system, finished-goods inventory costs nothing because it does not absorb any direct labour. It is treated as an 'asset'. In the new manufacturing accounting, however, inventory of finished goods is a 'sunk cost' (an economist's, not an accountant's, term). Stuff that sits in inventory does not earn anything. In fact, it ties down expensive money and absorbs time. As a result, its time costs are high. The new accounting measures these time costs against the benefits of finished-goods inventory (quicker customer service, for instance).

Yet manufacturing accounting still faces the challenge of eliminating the fourth limitation of traditional cost accounting: its inability to bring into the measurement of factory performance the impact of manufacturing changes on the total business – the return in the marketplace of an investment in automation, for instance, or the risk in not making an investment that would speed up production changeovers. The inplant costs and benefits of such decisions can now be worked out with considerable accuracy. But the business consequences are indeed speculative. One can only say, 'Surely, this should help us get more sales,' or 'If we don't do this, we risk falling behind in customer service.' But how do you quantify such opinions?

Cost accounting's strength has always been that it confines itself to the measurable and thus gives objective answers. But if intangibles are brought into its equations, cost accounting will only raise more questions. How to proceed is thus hotly debated, and with good reason. Still, everyone agreed that these business impacts have to be integrated into the measurement of factory performance, that is, into manufacturing accounting. One way or another, the new accounting will force managers, both inside and outside the plant, to make manufacturing decisions as *business* decisions.

Henry Ford's epigram, 'The customer can have any colour as long as it's black,' has entered American folklore. But few people realize what Ford meant: flexibility costs time and money, and the customer won't pay for it. Even fewer people realize that in the mid-1920s, the 'new' cost accounting made it possible for GM to beat Ford by giving customers both colours and annual model changes at no additional cost.

By now, most manufacturers can do what GM learned to do roughly 70 years ago. Indeed, many go quite a bit further in combining standardization with flexibility. They can, for example, build a variety of end products from a fairly small number of standardized parts. Still, manufacturing people tend to think like Henry Ford: you can have either standardization at low cost or flexibility at high cost, but not both.

The factory of 1999, however, will be based on the premise that you not only *can* have both but also *must* have both – and at low cost. But to achieve this, the factory will have to be structured quite differently.

Today's factory is a battleship. The plant of 1999 will be a 'flotilla', consisting of modules centred either around a stage in the production process or around a number of closely related operations. Though overall command and control will still exist, each module will have its own command and control. And each, like the ships in a flotilla, will be manoeuvrable, both in terms of its position in the entire process and its relationship to other modules. This organization will give each module the benefits of standardization and, at the same time, give the whole process greater flexibility. Thus it will allow rapid changes in design and product, rapid response to market demands, and low-cost production of 'options' or 'specials' in fairly small batches.

No such plant exists today. No one can yet build it. But many manufacturers, large and small, are moving toward the flotilla structure: among them are some of Westinghouse's U.S. plants, Asea Brown Boveri's robotics plant in Sweden, and several large printing plants, especially in Japan.

The biggest impetus for this development probably came from GM's failure to get a return on its massive (at least $30 billion and perhaps $40 billion) investment in automation. GM, it seems, used the new machines to improve its existing process, that is, to make the assembly line more efficient. But the process instead became less flexible and less able to accomplish rapid change.

Meanwhile, Japanese automakers and Ford were spending less and attaining more flexibility. In these plants, the line still exists, but it is discontinuous rather than tightly tied together. The new equipment is being used to speed changes, for example, automating changeovers of jigs, tools, and fixtures. So the line has acquired a good bit of the flexibility of traditional batch production without losing its standardization. Standardization and flexibility are thus no longer an either-or proposition. They are – as indeed they must be – melded together.

This means a different balance between standardization and flexibility, however, for different parts of the manufacturing process. An 'average' balance across the plant will do nothing very well. If imposed throughout the line, it will simply result in high rigidity and big costs for the entire process, which is apparently what happened at GM. What is required is a reorganization of the process into modules, each with its own optimal balance.

Moreover, the relationships between these modules may have to change whenever the product, process, or distribution changes. Switching from selling heavy equipment to leasing it, for instance, may drastically change the ratio between finished-product output and spare-parts output. Or a fairly minor model change may alter the sequence in which major parts are assembled into the finished product. There is nothing very new in this, of course. But under the traditional line structure, such changes are ignored, or they take forever to accomplish. With competition intensifying and product life cycles shortening all the time, such changes cannot be ignored, and they have to be done fast. Hence the flotilla's modular organization.

But this organization requires more than a fairly drastic change in the factory's physical structure. It requires, above all, different communication and information. In the traditional plant, each sector and department reports separately upstairs. And it reports what upstairs has asked for. In the factory of 1999, sectors and departments will have to think through what information they owe to whom and what information they need from whom. A good deal of this information will flow sideways and across department lines, not upstairs. The factory of 1999 will be an information network.

Consequently, all the managers in a plant will have to know and understand the entire process, just as the destroyer commander has to know and understand the tactical plan of the entire flotilla. In the factory of 1999, managers will have to think and act as team members, mindful of the performance of the whole. Above all, they will have to ask: What do the people running the other modules need to know about the characteristics, the capacity, the plans, and the performance of *my* unit? And what, in turn, do we in my module need to know about theirs?

The last of the new concepts transforming manufacturing is

systems design, in which the whole of manufacturing is seen as an integrated process that converts materials into goods, that is, into economic satisfactions.

Marks & Spencer, the British retail chain, designed the first such system in the 1930s. Marks & Spencer designs and tests the goods (whether textiles or foods) it has decided to sell. It designates one manufacturer to make each product under contract. It works with the manufacturer to produce the right merchandise with the right quality at the right price. Finally, it organizes just-in-time delivery of the finished products to its stores. The entire process is governed by a meticulous forecast as to when the goods will move off store shelves and into customers' shopping bags. In the last ten years or so, such systems management has become common in retailing.

Though systems organization is still rare in manufacturing, it was actually first attempted there. In the early 1920s, when the Model T was in its full glory, Henry Ford decided to control the entire process of making and moving all the supplies and parts needed by his new plant, the gigantic River Rouge. He built his own steel mill and glass plant. He founded plantations in Brazil to grow rubber for tyres. He bought the railroad that brought supplies to River Rouge and carried away the finished cars. He even toyed with the idea of building his own service centres nationwide and staffing them with mechanics trained in Ford-owned schools. But Ford conceived of all this as a financial edifice held together by ownership. Instead of building a system, he built a conglomerate, an unwieldy monster that was expensive, unmanageable, and horrendously unprofitable.

In contrast, the new manufacturing system is not 'controlled' at all. Most of its parts are independent – independent suppliers at one end, customers at the other. Nor is it plant centred, as Ford's organization was. The new system sees the plant as little more than a wide place in the manufacturing stream. Planning and scheduling start with shipment to the final customer, just as they do at Marks & Spencer. Delays, halts, and redundancies have to be designed into the system – a warehouse here, an extra supply of parts and tools there, a stock of old products that are no longer being made but are still occasionally demanded by the market. These are necessary imperfections in a continuous flow that is governed and directed by information.

What has pushed American manufacturers into such systems

design is the trouble they encountered when they copied Japan's just-in-time methods for supplying plants with materials and parts. The trouble could have been predicted, for the Japanese scheme is founded in social and logical conditions unique to that country and unknown in the United States. Yet the shift seemed to American manufacturers a matter of procedure, indeed, almost trivial. Company after company found, however, that just-in-time delivery of supplies and parts created turbulence throughout their plants. And while no one could figure out what the problem was, the one thing that became clear was that with just-in-time delivery, the plant no longer functions as a step-by-step process that begins at the receiving dock and ends when finished goods move into the shipping room. Instead, the plant must be redesigned from the end backwards and managed as an integrated flow.

Manufacturing experts, executives, and professors have urged such an approach for two or three decades now. And some industries, such as petroleum refining and large-scale construction, do practise it. But by and large, American and European manufacturing plants are neither systems designed nor systems managed. In fact, few companies have enough knowledge about what goes on in their plants to run them as systems. Just-in-time delivery, however, forces managers to ask systems questions: Where in the plant do we need redundancy? Where should we place the burden of adjustments? What costs should we incur in one place to minimize delay, risk, and vulnerability in another?

A few companies are even beginning to extend the systems concept of manufacturing beyond the plant and into the marketplace. Caterpillar, for instance, organizes its manufacturing to supply any replacement part anywhere in the world within 48 hours. But companies like this are still exceptions; they must become the rule. As soon as we define manufacturing as the process that converts things into economic satisfactions, it becomes clear that producing does not stop when the product leaves the factory. Physical distribution and product service are still part of the production process and should be integrated with it, coordinated with it, managed together with it. It is already widely recognized that servicing the product must be a major consideration during its design and production. By 1999, systems manufacturing will have an increasing influence on how we design and remodel plants and on how we manage manufacturing businesses.

Traditionally, manufacturing businesses have been organized

'in series', with functions such as engineering, manufacturing, and marketing as successive steps. These days, that system is often complemented by a parallel team organization (Proctor & Gamble's product management teams are a well-known example), which brings various functions together from the inception of a new product or process project. If manufacturing is a system, however, every decision in a manufacturing business becomes a manufacturing decision. Every decision should meet manufacturing's requirements and needs and in turn should exploit the strengths and capabilities of a company's particular manufacturing system.

When Honda decided six or seven years ago to make a new, upscale car for the U.S. market, the most heated strategic debate was not about design, performance, or price. It was about whether to distribute the Acura through Honda's well-established dealer network or to create a new market segment by building separate Acura dealerships at high cost and risk. This was a marketing issue, of course. But the decision was made by a team of design, engineering, manufacturing, and marketing people. And what tilted the balance toward the separate dealer network was a manufacturing consideration: the design for which independent distribution and service made most sense was the design that best utilized Honda's manufacturing capabilities.

Full realization of the systems concept in manufacturing is years away. It may not require a new Henry Ford. But it will certainly require very different management and very different managers. Every manager in tomorrow's manufacturing business will have to know and understand the manufacturing system. We might well adopt the Japanese custom of starting all new management people in the plant and in manufacturing jobs for the first few years of their careers. Indeed, we might go even further and require managers throughout the company to rotate into factory assignments throughout their careers – just as army officers return regularly to troop duty.

In the new manufacturing business, manufacturing is the integrator that ties everything together. It creates the economic value that pays for everything and everybody. Thus the greatest impact of the manufacturing systems concept will not be on the production process. As with SQC, its greatest impact will be on social and human concerns – on career ladders, for instance, or more important, on the transformation of *functional* managers into *business* managers, each with a specific role, but all members of the same production and the same cast. And surely, the manufacturing businesses of tomorrow will not be run by financial executives, marketers, or lawyers inexperienced in manufacturing, as so many U.S. companies are today.

There are important differences among these four concepts. Consider, for instance, what each means by 'the factory'. In SQC, the factory is a place where people work. In management accounting and the flotilla concept of flexible manufacturing, it is a place where work is being done – it makes no difference whether by people, by white mice, or by robots. In the systems concept, the factory is not a place at all; it is a stage in a process that adds economic value to materials. In theory, at least, the factory cannot and certainly should not be designed, let alone built, until the entire process of 'making' – all the way to the final customer – is understood. Thus defining the factory is much more than a theoretical or semantic exercise. It has immediate practical consequences on plant design, location, and size; on what activities are to be brought together in one manufacturing complex; even on how much and in what to invest.

Similarly, each of these concepts reflects a particular mind-set. To apply SQC, you don't have to think, you have to do. Management accounting concentrates on technical analysis, while the flotilla concept focuses on organization design and work flow. In the systems concept, there is great temptation to keep on thinking and never get to the doing. Each concept has its own tools, its own language, and addresses different people.

Nevertheless, what these four concepts have in common is far more important than their differences. Nowhere is this more apparent than in their assumption that the manufacturing process is a configuration, a whole that is greater than the sum of its parts. Traditional approaches all see the factory as a collection of individual machines and individual operations. The nineteenth-century factory was an assemblage of machines. Taylor's scientific management broke up each job into individual operations and then put those operations together into new and different jobs. 'Modern' twentieth-century concepts – the assembly line and cost accounting – define performance as the sum of lowest cost operations. But none of the new concepts is much concerned with performance of the parts. Indeed, the parts as such can only underperform. The process produces results.

Management also will reflect this new perspective. SQC is the most nearly conventional in its implications for managers, since it does not so much change their job as shift much of it to the work force. But even managers with no business responsibility (and under SQC, plant people have none) will have to manage with an awareness of business considerations well beyond the plant. And every manufacturing manager will be responsible for integrating people, materials, machines, and time. Thus every manufacturing manager ten years hence will have to learn and practise a discipline that integrates engineering, management of people, and business economics into the manufacturing process. Quite a few manufacturing people are doing this already, of course – though usually unaware that they are doing something new and different. Yet such a discipline has not been systematized and is still not taught in engineering schools or business schools.

These four concepts are synergistic in the best sense of this much-abused term. Together – but only together – they tackle the conflicts that have most troubled traditional, twentieth century mass-production plants: the conflicts between people and machines, time and money, standardization and flexibility, and functions and systems. The key is that every one of these concepts defines performance as productivity and conceives of manufacturing as the physical process that adds economic value to materials. Each tries to provide economic value in a different way. But they share the same theory of manufacturing.

[1990]

Afterword: The 1990s and Beyond

The Changing World Economy

I begin with the remark that 1992 is after all not a terribly important date. Many things will be decided between now and then, but the important event has already happened, and it has nothing to do with governments. Governments are, alas, no longer performance centres, as they were in the nineteenth century. The main event is that the businessmen of Europe have already decided that there is a European economy. Has there ever been a precedent to guide us? Yes; and not so long ago, either.

When I first went to the U.S.A. as correspondent for five British newspapers in the mid 1930s, it was just becoming a national market. It had been a political unit for 150 years, but there were very few national U.S. businesses: none of the big banks, none of the big insurance companies, only 3 of the then 10–12 automobile companies and a few of the steel companies (and then only because the U.S. navy required it) had national scale or coverage. All the rest were local or regional. Most of them were unfamiliar with other parts of the country – after all, it took six uncomfortable days in the train, without air conditioning, to reach Los Angeles from

New York or Washington. Few people went there from the east except film stars.

Then, suddenly, in the mid-1930s every business had to learn to think national. Very few actually acted national. Contrary to what most foreigners think, the U.S.A. still has a tiny minority of companies that are fully national. The majority remain regionally based on the East Coast, West Coast, or in the Midwest to this day. Nevertheless, U.S. companies had to learn quickly to think and act in contemplation of the national market. This is what is happening in Europe.

Looking at this example will not, however, tell any business what to do in its own particular circumstances. Beware of prescriptions. A company must make up its own mind by examining its own business, its own market, its own competition and deciding where the new competition may arise – even though the CEO may never have been to Spain except on holiday, any more than many Americans had visited the West Coast. In any case, it must rethink strategy in contemplation of a fundamental change: location of markets, the need for expansion, alignment, and structure. This has to happen anyhow. Once it has been done, 1992 ceases to be a major event.

But New International Dynamics Do Matter

The European single market is, however, symptomatic of a capital change in the way the world economy functions. Whether you like it or not (and I for one do not), the world is very rapidly changing its form of economic integration. We are moving toward a world economy that is integrated not by free trade or protectionism, as in the past, but increasingly through a hybrid of the two which we can call reciprocity. What do I mean by reciprocity? International trade has evolved from a complementary exchange of goods and services to an adversarial exchange. In an adversarial trade relationship, if an attacking country excludes foreign competition and imports, as the Japanese did, in effect the defender is unable to counterattack. It cannot win; so what can it do?'

One answer is to form an economic bloc or region, such as the EC planned for 1992. This gives smaller economies the larger market they need for competitive scale. At the same time, regionalism creates an entity that can deploy an effective trade policy transcending both protectionism and free trade. Thus reciprocity – in which, in principle, each bloc's businesses would have the same degree of access to the other blocs' markets – is rapidly emerging as the new guiding principle for the world economy. It may be the only way of preventing it from slipping into extreme protectionism.

We do not yet know exactly what reciprocity will entail in practice. Does it mean that European banks can do business in the U.S.A. on the same terms as U.S. banks, or on the same terms as those on which they do business in Europe? That is still up in the air. Questions such as these will be decided *ad hoc*, with endless friction and compromise, and in every case the answer will be slightly different. What is certain is that the EC will adopt it as its main trade policy – and that is already having an effect elsewhere.

For example, the prospect of the European single market was the direct cause of the free trade agreement between the U.S.A. and Canada. In Europe it is impossible to comprehend the unlikeliness of this venture without the threat of the single market. It flies in the face of everything that Canada has ever felt important. Even now, Canadians are not enthusiastic; they simply had no choice but to throw in their economic lot with their dominating neighbour. After Canada, there is now an even bigger question: Does Mexico in its turn have any choice? There is no deeper cultural dividing line in the world than this unmarked border between two totally different civilizations and value systems. For 150 years the lodestar of Mexico's policy was to keep as far away as possible from the huge and dangerous monster next door. Yet suddenly, despite tremendous politico-cultural tensions, the possibility of Mexico being forced to integrate itself into the North American economy is better than 50 percent. It is no longer absurd to contemplate it.

In the East Too

There are other emerging regions. In China, the pressure of enormous unemployment on one hand and the disparity between the energy of the coast and the lethargy of the interior on the other is beginning to split the country into rival economic warlordships once again. If, as is distinctly possible, a coastal belt containing all the commercial energy develops along a stretch from Tientsin to Canton, then very soon we shall see a new Far Eastern bloc organized around Japan. The Chinese cities are already in their economic orientation (although not yet politically or socially) pointing toward their new superstar and centre, despite the tremendous Chinese fear and distrust of the foreigner, particularly the Asiatic foreigner. A Japan-centred Pacific Rim region is probably in the process of being formed.

A New International Economic Order Is Emerging

In the newly emerging world economic order – transnational, regionally integrated, and information intensive – two changes already stand out. First, tomorrow's transnationals are unlikely to be manufacturing companies. The service economy is going transnational. All 256 public hospitals in Japan are today maintained and managed by a Chicago-based maintenance company. Virtually every big office building in Manhattan is maintained and managed by a maintenance company based in Aarhus, Denmark. Since Japan lacks business and engineering teachers, it is bringing the students to the faculty; and, inconceivable just a few years ago, the three leading nongovernmental universities in Tokyo are building campuses on the West Coast of the U.S.A. for Japanese students. Banking and finance are more advanced still in transnational development. In large part because governmental politics are still focused on the concerns of the blue-collar factory worker, the service economy is going transnational much faster than manufacturing.

Second, in the new world economy investment is growing much faster than trade. Classic economic theory says that investment follows trade. In the nineteenth century that was true. In the twentieth century it is the other way around. To take a topical case, look at the Japanese automobile companies and their suppliers in the U.K. No sooner does Honda, Nissan, or Toyota establish a factory in the U.K. than it imports its own suppliers as well to provide it with components. This is in part because the Japanese do not find it natural to buy from an independent supplier. In Japan a company is either a master or a servant, and the supplier which sells to more than one master is not to be trusted. But consider a less obvious example of the same phenomenon. Why did U.S. exports not collapse in the years of the overvalued dollar in the mid-1980s? For a similar reason: in spite of the price penalty, Japanese subsidiaries of U.S. companies kept on buying machinery, spare parts, and materials from their tried and trusted suppliers back in the U.S.A.

Yet in an investment-led world economy, a strategy based on exports is out of date. One of the factors that lost the U.K. its economic leadership in the nineteenth century was, ironically, its mastery of exporting. This meant that in every port in the world, the main importer was a Scot, and a Scot who bought almost exclusively from Manchester and Glasgow. Since they could not penetrate their key markets by the traditional route of exports, U.S. and West German companies were obliged to establish factories there instead. They had to invest before they could trade. In this kind of world, proximity to and feel for markets have become decisive, and these require market presence and market standing. So now, one of the accepted facts that economic history (rather than the economic textbook) teaches is that a company cannot hold a leadership position in a key market unless it manufactures there. The Japanese have taken 20 percent of the U.S. automobile market, compared with the 30 percent captured by foreign manufacturers in all. Yet only half of the Japanese share has been taken from the U.S. Big Four. The rest has been stolen from the Europeans, notably Volkswagen, which had no less than 12 percent of the market in 1969. Alas, the unions barred Volkswagen from manufacturing in the U.S.A. the first time round. In 1973, when the oil shock struck, VW was not in the market as a manufacturer, and it misread the signs. When it did try to come back and manufacture, it was too late.

Once again, investment is the economic driver. The real economy of goods and services no longer dominates the transnational economy. The London interbank market daily turns over 10–15 times the amount of eurodollars, euromarks, or euroyen which are needed to finance world trade in goods and services. No figures exist for the foreign exchange markets, but they are certainly bigger still; far greater than needed for commercial trading purposes. These flows finance capital movements and investments. If the corporation does not maintain its investments in its key markets, it will have no sales.

In the transition, of course, these arrangements hold some difficulties for the wealth-creating sectors of national markets. We still hold the nineteenth-century assumption that there is a shortage of liquid funds. The reality today is that there is a surplus. One reason is that the economies of the developed world are becoming steadily more knowledge intensive and less capital and labour intensive. Another is the enormous amounts of money accumulated in small savings accounts and large pension funds. So instead of rationing, their traditional function, now the large investors are looking for places to put their money. The results are not necessarily always economically optimal, except in the very short run.

Look at junk bonds. In effect, junk bonds are simply another form of equity financing, the main purpose of which is to give industry and the takeover specialists very cheap money (because it is debt and the interest is tax-free) at a high yield to the lender. Not surprisingly, the banks have rushed to participate in a miraculous market that gives them 15 percent at a cost to the borrower of 6 or 7 percent. It is doubtful whether this is in the interests of the economy. Where there is excess liquidity there is a risk of making investments guided by short-term speculation, whether it is lending money to Zaire or to the latest takeover artist.

Finance, a Model for the Future: Adapt or Die

As this suggests, of all the changes so far, the fastest and most extensive are those which have transformed the world financial system. Money, like information, knows no fatherland, with the practical consequence that financial systems in countries at similar stages of economic development are strikingly similar irrespective of legislation or social habits. We can therefore look at what happens in one part of the developed world and see what it tells us about where the rest of the world is going. The U.S.A. has gone the furthest: partly because it was most severely regulated and partly because the markets, less dominated by a few very big units, were most flexible.

When the financial revolution began around 1960, we all predicted the imminent triumph of the financial supermarket: a money continuum, from total liquidity and minimum risk at one end, to minimum liquidity with very high risk at the other, all at a suitably graded price. We were wrong for two reasons. First, to most people money is not a commodity. U.S. retailer Sears Roebuck has always prided itself on being the buyer for the U.S. family. It looked at the investment demand on the part of the masses and bought a major brokerage house. It has been a total disaster. Very few of us are willing to buy our investments, even in government bonds, next to where we buy our children's underwear. It is not right. It is not becoming. Money is, if not sacred, at least different.

The second reason for the failure of the financial supermarket is that in every developed country there are two separate markets with entirely different characters: retail and institutional. Whether one institution can serve both of them is still unclear. The retail market is a strange beast. When I worked in the City of London 55 years ago, my very wise boss said to me: 'Mr Drucker, never forget that in the richest country in the world only one family out of every 20 can lay aside more money than is needed for the funeral of the head of the family.' Today probably at least half the families in all developed countries lay more aside than is required for a funeral. Not enormous sums: most people only spend less than they make once they are past the age of 50. Except in Japan, where compensation follows the life curve, income patterns are skewed so that rewards really begin to climb when the children are grown up and the spending needs begin to go down. At that stage people are too old to change. Suddenly they have a little money individually – and those small individual sums collectively add up to an almost unbelievable total.

Almost everyone has radically underestimated these amounts, as companies have found that dared to bring out new financial products. The U.S. saving rates are some of the lowest in the world, yet sales of unit trusts boomed in 1983–87, in two years actually exceeding the official total savings. And all this without affecting other forms of saving. Clearly, something is wrong with the figures. However, for companies the great challenge is how to service this formidable reservoir of money. For a start, do the big life insurance companies have the right distribution system? To be sure, there are several life insurance agents in every little town. They have their lists of customers, some of whom are the right age, 50+, which is where the money is. Yet most life insurance companies still stubbornly insist on selling the one product that is guaranteed not to survive this century, the whole life policy. In an affluent economy, whole life makes absolutely no sense. For anyone who is not poor, it is the worst buy on the financial market. Term insurance or group life provides more protection for one-sixth of the premium, but even that is a hopeless investment. If it can be unbundled, the same sum will provide twice as much life insurance and 50 percent more investment. And yet in Europe, at least, these terrible buys still flourish. But they will not survive even a mild bout of inflation. People are not that stupid. So far not one life insurance company has succeeded using agency channels. The agency system has not responded to the great challenge of serving the retail finance market.

Institutional Finance Must Change Too

On the other side of the financial markets are the enormous institutions of capital, the pension funds, which in every developed country will soon be the only true capitalists left. How will we organize them for constructive investment? Currently by their constitution the interests of the pension funds are purely financial. If they can make money by buying or selling, then they have no choice but to do it. The trouble is that, as any businessman knows, the short-term financial view is not enough to build a business. How therefore can we get the pension funds to be owners, and thus business builders, rather than investors? What tools shall we need? What instruments? These are crucial questions.

The final critical question about the financial system is whether the commercial banks can survive when they can no longer make a living out of interest differentials. The public has become too sophisticated, the costs of capital are much too high, and borrowers have so many different ways of raising money that the traditional commercial loan is the least attractive alternative. One bank, Citicorp, already makes 60 percent of its money in fees, compared with 20 percent at the most for the majority. Can banks switch from being paid for money to being paid for information? Assets in a bank are increasingly a liability. The bank of tomorrow will have no assets. It will be a market arbitrageur rather than an interest arbitrageur. This challenge is particularly acute for the small European banks that bestride the Netherlands, Belgium, Austria, and Spain like giants, but which are pygmies on the world scene. In terms of serving their countries, these have been the best banks of all, successfully building their domestic economies precisely because they were big enough to do everything and small enough to know what was required. Can they survive, and in what form?

These are some of the questions thrown up by the changing world economy. Nineteen ninety-two has caused them to be directly posed, but they were there all along. They will all be answered, by my best guess, before 1993, not by the process of thinking them through, but by acting on events.

The Knowledge Society

Information Matters

Just as modern money penetrated the whole world within less than a century and totally changed people's lives and aspirations, we can safely assume that information now penetrates everywhere. On my last and longest trip to China, I spent almost three weeks looking at factories and cotton plantations in the interior. The biggest cotton plantations are in the most remote province, near the Mongolian border in the extreme north. It was hard to get there, and the plantations were very poor and primitive: only the meeting halls had electric light, for example. At one site we held a meeting, and at 6 o'clock the 22 plantation managers got up, asked to be excused for a short period, and disappeared. After half an hour they came back, and we resumed the discussion. Why the interruption, I inquired, another meeting or a party of visitors? 'No,' they replied. 'It was *Dallas* on television.'

Information Means a New Type of Management

Thus information moves everywhere. And its effects are everywhere pervasive. In the case of the corporation, any business that has tried to organize itself around information has rapidly reduced its number of management levels by at least half, and usually by 60 percent. The first and most spectacular case was Massey Ferguson. Virtually bankrupt, the world's largest farm equipment and diesel manufacturer required radical surgery. It was a complex business in organizational terms, with headquarters in Canada, production primarily in Europe, and 60 percent of its markets in the U.S.A. Because it was managed by people who had previously worked at General Motors and Ford, it was organized like a U.S. automobile company, with 14 layers of management. Today it has 6 and the number is still coming down.

Massey Ferguson thought about the information it needed to run its business. The moment it did so, it discovered a great truth: many levels of management in fact manage nothing. They make no decisions. In reality they are only boosters, amplifying the very faint signals that come up and down through the organization. If a company can organize itself around its information needs, these layers become redundant.

There are good reasons why large organizations will have to

become information-based. Demographics is one. The knowledge workers who increasingly make up the work force are not amenable to the command-and-control methods of the past. Another reason is the need to systematize innovation and entrepreneurship, quintessentially knowledge work. And a third is the requirement to come to terms with information technology. Computers turn out data – vast amounts of it. But data is not information. Information is data endowed with relevance and purpose. A company must decide what information it needs to operate its affairs, otherwise it will drown in data.

To organize in this way requires a new structure. Although it is perhaps too early to draw an organization chart of the information-based organization, we can set out some broad considerations.

One hundred and twenty-five years ago, when large enterprises first came into being, the only organizational structure they had to model themselves on was the army: hierarchical, command-and-control, line and staff. Tomorrow's model is the symphony orchestra or the football team or the hospital. Mahler's symphonies require the presence of 385 instrumentalists on stage, never mind the singers. If it were to organize itself the way we organize our big companies today, a modern orchestra would have a chief executive officer plus a chairman conductor flanked by two nonexecutive conductors, six vice-chairman conductors, and countless vice-president conductors. Instead of which there is one conductor to whom every specialist instrumentalist plays directly, because everyone has the same score. In other words, there are no intermediaries between the specialists and the top manager, and they are organized as a gigantic task force. The organization is totally flat.

There is a famous 1920s joke about the then-new discipline of industrial engineering which takes on fresh meaning today. The story concerns a (needless-to-say) German engineer who attends a symphony concert on which he writes a report. He points out that most of the musicians sit around doing nothing most of the time: Would it not be more efficient if they played the Rossini, Beethoven, and Brahms simultaneously rather than in sequence, thus occupying the players all the time? Well, the orchestra still functions by playing one work at a time. Indeed, one of the lessons of organizing around information is the importance of concentration to prevent people from becoming fatally confused. The orchestra can perform precisely because all the players know they are playing Mozart, not Haydn. A medical team performing an operation also has a score, although an unwritten one. But the performance of a businesses or a government agency creates its own score, or many scores, as it goes along. An information-based organization must therefore structure itself around goals that clearly state expectations and objectives both for the enterprise and for each specialist. There must be strongly organized feedback so that every member can exercise self-control by comparing expectations with the actual outcome.

I believe, therefore, that we are moving toward more concentrated organizations and units of organizations, based on much clearer business and individual goals, on self-discipline and on systematic feedback. If this is truly the case, business will have to learn that they must build their communications system on information up rather than information down. Information becomes communication only if the recipient understands and accepts it. If information only moves down, that may not happen. The structure must be based on the upward communication of information that enables those at the top to know what goes on at the bottom, at the sharp end.

Changing Society: The Decline of the Servant . . .

Some of the greatest changes in social structure in the history of the human race have taken place this century. These changes have been nonviolent, which is perhaps why few people pay them any attention. Yet had any of the great economists or sociologists of the last century been apprised of them, they would have laughed in disbelief. Consider the cases of the domestic servant and the farmer. The first scientific census, the British census of 1910, famously defined lower middle class as the family that could not afford more than three servants. How many people have spotted even one servant lately, other than at Madame Tussaud's? Servants antedate history by millennia, and in 1913 they were the largest single employee group in any developed country. Thirty percent of all wage earners were domestic servants. They are all gone.

. . . The Farmer . . .

So, almost, are farmers. There is now no developed country in the world in which farmers form more than 8 percent of the population. The political power of the farmer has evaporated. In the 1988 U.S. election the farmer became a nonperson. Both candidates went to Iowa for two hours, but that was all. They could not care less how the 3 percent of the U.S. population who are still farmers cast their vote. Politicians have good antennae. They know that the farmers' power has become the smile on the face of the Cheshire cat. In Japan, there is one farm vote for seven city votes; but one-third of all the money for the war chest of the Japanese politicians comes from the Farmers' Cooperative Bank. This power is likely to be broken as a result off the Recruit scandal. Farmers' power will soon be over, even in Japan.

. . . and the Worker

The blue-collar industrial worker is going the same way. No century has seen anything like his rise and his decline. A very short time ago it seemed that this group was ineluctably controlling society, politics, and markets. To test market a new product in the U.S.A. in the 1950s, a company went to the solid blue-collar communities that would make or break it. Not today; not even in the U.K. By the end of the century in every developed country, blue-collar workers will be no more important or numerous than farmers. Their numbers have declined by a full third in the past 20 years.

It is not only the numbers that have fallen, however. There are now few manufacturing companies where blue-collar labour costs rise above 15 percent. A country such as Spain has 5–7 years during which its reservoir of highly trained, cheap labour will remain an asset. By the end of the century, if its manufacturing has not evolved to the point where labour costs are below 15 percent, that labour force will have become a liability. No Western country can compete with Shanghai, where $1 a day is an excellent wage, and only the top 10 percent of the work force makes even $1.

The answer for Western manufacturing is not necessarily automation. Information is not the same as automation, or even information technology, and no firm should start by buying a machine. Rather, the first step is to rationalize the process in order to identify what machines are necessary. A company that begins by buying robots or automating its existing process will almost certainly waste monstrous amounts of money and become less productive in the process. General Motors proves the point. GM spent the not inconsiderable sum $30 billion on robots, with the result that labour costs went up, not down. GM's blue-collar labour costs are now 28 percent compared with Ford's 15 percent and Toyota's 16 percent (in the U.S.A.). At the new Honda plant, built in a high-wage area, the figure will come down to 11.5 percent. Cars, remember, are a relatively ancient industry. In the new industries labour costs should be even lower.

Most people believe that the favourite child of capitalism was the owner of capital: the capitalist. A better candidate is the blue-collar industrial worker. In 1850 he was still a labourer hired by the hour, paid a few pennies, without social standing or political power. He was neglected and despised. By 1950 he belonged to the dominant social class. He enjoyed health insurance, pensions, job security and political power that would have seemed unthinkable only two generations before. He still has the benefits, of course. But the brief moment of dominance is suddenly over. And all this without real social convulsions.

The Learning Society Is Taking Over

In the place of the blue-collar world is a society in which access to good jobs no longer depends on the union card, but on the school certificate. Between, say, 1950 and 1980 it was economically irrational for a young American male to stay at school. In three months a 16-year-old school leaver with a job at a unionized steel plant could be taking home more money than his university-educated cost accountant brother would make in his life. Those days are over. From now on the key is knowledge. The world is becoming not labour intensive, not materials intensive, not energy intensive, but knowledge intensive.

Japan today produces two and a half times the quantity of manufactured goods it did 25 years ago with the same amount of energy and less raw material. In large part this is due to the shift to knowledge-intensive work. The representative product of the 1920s, the automobile, at the time had a raw material and energy content of 60 percent. The representative product of the 1980s is the semiconductor chip, which has a raw material and energy content of less than 2 percent. The 1990s equivalent will be biotechnology, also with a content of about 2 percent in materials and energy, but with a much higher knowledge content.

Assembling microchips is still fairly labour intensive (10 percent). Biotechnology will have practically no labour content at all. Moreover, fermentation plants generate energy rather than consume it. The world is becoming knowledge intensive not just in the labour force, but in process.

Knowledge is always specialized. The oboist in the London Philharmonic Orchestra has no ambition to become first violinist, or at least no realistic one. In the last 100 years only one instrumentalist, Toscanini, has become a conductor of the first rank. Specialists remain specialists, becoming ever more skilful at interpreting the score. Yet specialism carries dangers, too. Truly knowledgeable people tend by themselves to overspecialize, because there is always so much more to know. As part of the orchestra, that oboist alone does not make music. He or she makes noise. Only the score tells the players what to do; playing a joint score makes music. For both soloist and conductor, getting music from an orchestra means not only knowing the score, but learning how to manage knowledge. And knowledge carries with it powerful responsibility, too. In the past, the holders of knowledge have often used (abused) it to curb thinking and dissent, and to inculcate blind obedience to authority. Knowledge and knowledge people have to assume their responsibilities.

Most Education Does Not Deliver Knowledge . . .

The advent of the knowledge society has far-ranging implications for education. Schools will change more in the next 30 years than they have since the invention of the printed book. One reason is modern learning theory. We know how people learn, and that learning is not at all the same thing as teaching. We know, for instance, that no two human beings learn in the same way. The printed book set off the greatest explosion in learning and the love of learning the world had ever seen. But book learning was for adults. The printed book is basically adult-friendly. In contrast, the new learning tools are child-friendly, as anyone with a computer-using eight- or nine-year-old child will know. By the age of eleven most children except the freaks begin to be bored with the computer; for them it is just a tool. But up to that age, children treat computers as extensions of themselves. The advent of such powerful tools alone will force the schools to change.

... So Organizations Must Do It Themselves

But there is another consideration. For the first time in human history it really matters whether or not people learn. When the Prince Regent asked Marshal Blücher if he found it a great disadvantage not to be able to read and write, the man who won the battle of Waterloo for Wellington replied: 'Your Royal Highness, that is what I have a chaplain for.' Until 1914 most people could do perfectly well without such accomplishments. Now, however, learning matters. The knowledge society requires that all its members be literate, not just in reading, writing, and arithmetic, but also in (for example) basic computer skills and political, social, and historical systems. And because of the vastly expanding corpus of knowledge, it also requires that its members learn how to learn.

There will – and should – be serious discussion of the social purpose of school education in the context of the knowledge society. That will certainly help to change the schools. In the meantime, however, the most urgent learning and training must reach out to the adults. Thus, the focus of learning will shift from schools to employers. Every employing institution will have to become a teacher. Large numbers of Japanese employers and some European already recognize this. But what kind of learning? In the orchestra the score tellsthe employees what to do; and orchestra playing is team playing. In the information-based business, what is the equivalent of this reciprocal learning and teaching process? One way of educating people to a view of the whole, of course, is through work in cross-functional task forces. But to what extent do we rotate specialists out of their specialities and into new ones? And who will be the managers, particularly top managers, of the information-based organization? Brilliant oboists, or people who have been in enough positions to be able to understand the team, or even young conductors from smaller orchestras? We do not yet know. Above all, how do we make this terribly expensive knowledge, this new capital, productive?

The world's largest bank reports that it has deployed $1.5 billion in information and communications systems. Banks are now more capital intensive than ICI. So are hospitals. Only 50 years ago a hospital consisted of a bed and a sister. Today a fair-sized US hospital of 400 beds has several hundred attending physicians and a staff of up to 1,500 paramedics divided among some 60 specialities, with specialized equipment and labs to match. None, or very few, of these specialisms even existed 50 years ago. But we do not yet know how to get productivity out of them; we do not yet know in this context what productivity means. In knowledge-intensive areas we are pretty much where we were in manufacturing in the early nineteenth century. When Robert Owen built his cotton mills at New Lanark, he tried to measure their productivity. He never managed it. It took 50 more years until productivity as we understand it could be satisfactorily defined. We are currently at about the Robert Owen stage in relation to the new organizations. We are beginning to ask about productivity, output, and performance in relation to knowledge. We cannot measure it. We cannot yet even judge it, although we do have an idea of some of the things that are needed.

How, for instance, do famous conductors build a first-rate orchestra? They tell me that the first job is to get the clarinettist to keep on improving as a clarinettist. She or he must have pride in the instrument. The players must be craftsmen first. The second task is to create in the individuals a pride in their common enterprise, the orchestra: 'I play for Cleveland, or Chicago, or the London Philharmonic, and that is one of the best orchestras in the world.' Third, and this is what distinguishes a competent conductor from a great one, is to get the orchestra to hear and play that Haydn symphony in exactly the way the conductor hears it. In other words, there must be a clear vision at the top. This orchestrating focus is the model for the leader of any knowledge-based organization.

Innovation and Entrepreneurship

I turn now to crucial issues for managers in the knowledge society: innovation and entrepreneurship.

It is not a coincidence that these necessary concepts are back in fashion. For a long period they were neglected, to the point where for all intents and purposes they vanished from the list of corporate concerns. Only in the last 15–20 years have these two practices – for that is what they are, neither science nor art – come to the fore again.

On neither side of the Atlantic is the record of the new entrepreneurial companies exemplary. It is probably better than those of the nineteenth century, but it is still not nearly good enough. By now we know pretty much what is needed for those companies to survive and to prosper: the practice of entrepreneurship, like the practice of management, has its rules and knowledge base, and I shall not go into them in detail here. But to confine the focus of innovation and entrepreneurship to the new individual entrepreneur is too narrow. If start-ups and new businesses were the main or only locus of innovation, our societies could probably not survive.

Lessons from the Nineteenth Century's Innovative Climate

There is one great difference between the innovative climate of the last 20 years and the late nineteenth century. Our rate of innovation (social as well as technical, that is just as important) is equally rapid. But practically all the institutions, business or other, of the nineteenth century were new: they emerged in the 50 or so years between 1865 (the year of Perkin's first aniline dye, Siemens's first dynamo) and 1914, when the World War I paralysed the entrepreneurial energies of the West. During that period a new institution, a major invention or innovation emerged on average more often than once a year. Some of them led to the founding of new industries. But they did not displace existing institutions. They emerged, as it were, into a vacuum. Thus, the Home Office set up British local government in 1856 from scratch. In the same year the first modern U.S. university was founded; there existed no other institutions that deserved to be called universities. Today the task is different: we have to learn to make existing institutions capable of innovation. We know what is needed, and it is relatively uncomplicated, although that does not mean it is easy. But if existing institutions cannot learn to innovate, the social consequences will be almost unbearably severe.

Innovation Matters Because Ours Is a Knowledge-Based Society

Knowledge changes extremely fast. But that in itself is not new; knowledge has always changed fast. What is new is that knowledge matters. In a crafts society, which ours essentially was until late in the nineteenth century, major changes occurred perhaps every 80 years. In military technology, between the disappearance of the longbow in the reign of Elizabeth I and the launching of the *Dreadnought* in 1906, a significant innovation took place every 60 years. Today, courtesy of the Pentagon, it is probably every 60 days. We have learned to innovate because we cannot expect that the accumulated competence, skill, knowledge, product, services, and structure of the present will be adequate for very long. The change is not so much that the pace of accumulation is so much more rapid. It is rather that the centre of gravity of knowledge is constantly on the move.

I have talked about institutions rather than businesses. This is intentional. In a market economy, innovation comes easier to businesses. In fact it is equally important in every other field of endeavour. But although the principles of innovation and entrepreneurship apply just as well to government institutions or universities, the practice is different. There is nothing more reactionary that a liberal faculty in a university. It is the ultimate in reaction. It is the motto of the U.S. universities that when a subject becomes totally obsolete, then a course should be built round it. To survive and be useful, they must learn how to innovate.

Innovation Means Abandoning the Old

What do we know about innovation? First, it has very little to do with genius. It has very little or nothing to do with inspiration. It is hard, systematic work. The myth is that an owner-entrepreneur can depend on a flash of genius. I have been working with owner-entrepreneurs for 40 years: the ones who depend on the flash of genius also go out like one.

Innovation depends rather on what we might call 'organized abandonment'. When the French economist J. B. Say coined the word *entrepreneur* 200 years ago, he meant it as a manifesto and a declaration of intent: the entrepreneur in his scheme was someone who upsets and disorganizes. Later Joseph Schumpeter, the only modern economist to take entrepreneurship seriously, described the process as 'creative destruction'. To get at the new and better, you have to throw out the old, outworn, obsolete, no longer productive, as well as the mistakes, failure, and misdirections of effort of the past. To put it another way, think of the old medical saying: 'As long as the patient eliminates there is a chance. But once the bowels and the bladder stop, death does not take long.' If organizations cannot get rid of their waste products, they poison themselves. They must organize abandonment, a most difficult thing to do, because most organizations develop a strong emotional attachment to the products they make.

Take a typical case. He is the head of a company that makes writing instruments. When he was 25 years old, he had an idea for a mechanical pencil. Everybody ridiculed the notion, but he put his job on the line and fought for it, and it turned out to be a successful product. He is now the head of the company that makes it, and as a consequence he has seen much more of it than he saw of his wife and children and is deeply emotionally involved with this company and this object. And then some eager young whippersnapper comes along as he did 30 years ago with an idea which makes the old product obsolete. He has very little love for that young man and he will not encourage him to persist with his idea, unless he builds organized abandonment into the company.

Innovation is not genius, nor is it necessarily, or even primarily, technical. There was not much technology involved in moving a lorry body off its wheels and putting it on a ship. But containerization roughly quadrupled the productivity of the ocean-going freighter and made possible the colossal expansion of world trade over the last 40 years. Similarly, few technical innovations can compete for impact with the humble textbook, newspapers, or insurance. Instalment buying, invented by a U.S. maker of farm implements to enable poorly off farmers to buy his equipment, literally transforms economies. And so the list goes on. For all its visibility and glamour, science-based innovation is actually less reliable, less predictable, and probably less likely to lead to company profits than almost any other sort.

The Zero-Based Audit

So now we know what innovation is not. More positively, we also know what is needed to put it into action. The key to innovation is to sit down every three years and systematically put every aspect of the company on trial for its life: every product, service, technology, market, and distribution channel.

Here is a clue: nothing is changing quite so fast today as distributive channels. Very few economists or newspaper commentators seem to realize that the service economy, which is expanding so fast, does not operate in contradiction to, or grow at the expense of, the goods economy. It is a distibutive channel for the goods economy. And the fastest-growing segment of the channel is leisure. There is no developed country in which people now work more than half the hours they worked in 1910.

Economists may not consider leisure part of the economy, but it is responsible for a huge amount of goods distribution. The same sort of growth is visible in other service institutions such as hospitals and schools. Sixty years ago, health care took less than 1 percent of developed GNP or consumer spending. Now, health care, and especially hospitals, account for 7–11 percent of enormously expanded national products. To repeat: the service economy is a distribution channel for goods, economically speaking, and distribution channels change faster than goods or services themselves. So examine them closely.

The zero-budgeting exercise also demands that managers look at every process and procedure, not to mention every staff activity, inside the organization and ask, 'If we did not do this already, given what we now know, would we do it the same way?' If the answer is no, do not say, 'Let us call in a management consultant to make a study.' Say, 'What do we do?' Sometimes the right thing to do is to make minor changes, sometimes to reposition the company entirely. Sometimes the answer is to simplify. Where there are six product lines, perhaps they should be cut to one or two. Sometimes they should be abandoned altogether. But the important thing is to do something. At that point the organization is open to innovation. Dr Johnson said that nothing so concentrates a man's mind as the knowledge that he is to be hanged in a fortnight. Nothing quite so sharpens a manager's mind as the knowledge that his mechanical pencil will be taken away from him – then he starts to innovate.

Innovation Means Looking on Change as an Opportunity

Systematic innovation requires a willingness to look on change as an opportunity. Innovations do not create change. That is very rare. They may if successful make an enormous difference, but most of the innovations that aim at changing society, or market, or customer, fail. Innovations that succeed do so by exploiting change, not attempting to force it.

In *Innovation and Entrepreneurship* I wrote that 'systematic innovation . . . consists in the purposeful and organised search for changes, and in the systematic analysis of the opportunities such changes might offer for economic or social innovation.' I went on to identify seven sources to look out for as signs and sources of a chance to innovate. Four of these sources are within the enterprise (business or otherwise) or the industry in which they operate. They are basically symptoms of change. They are: the unexpected, the unexpected success or failure; the incongruity, the discrepancy between reality as it is and reality as it is assumed to be; innovation based on process need; and changes in industry or market structure that take people unawares. The other three sources involve changes outside the industry or enterprise, namely, demographics; changing tastes, perceptions, and meanings; and new knowledge, both scientific and non-scientific.

The most useful of the seven 'windows' of innovation (which is why I list it first) is always the unexpected, especially the unexpected success. It is the least risky and the least arduous. Yet it is almost totally neglected. What is even worse, managers often actively reject it.

Consider for a moment the prime product of modern accounting: the monthly or weekly report. This was a tremendous eye-opener. Nobody had ever had systematic figures before. Most people see the first page that shows them they are over budget, but how many receive the other page that shows where they are ahead of budget? They should order their accountants to produce it immediately. Without this information an organization becomes fixated on its problems. However, it is usually the case that the first indication of an opportunity is where a company is faring better than expected. Most of the figures and variations turn out be not significant, of course, and managers can explain them immediately. But 1 out of every 20 might mean something. It might be pointing to something we did not know.

A leading hospital supplier launched a new line of instruments for clinical tests. The new products did quite well. Then suddenly orders started appearing from a quite different spectrum of customers: university, industry, and government laboratories. No one noticed that the company had tripped over a new and better market. It did not even send a sales person to visit the new customers. The result: a competitor has not only recognized and captured the industrial laboratory market; exploiting the scale of the new segment, it has seized the hospital market, too. This is a very typical story. The first firm had failed to understand the significance of an unexpected success. It has now been bought by a pharmaceutical company.

Of the other sources of innovation, scientific and technical research is listed last because, although undeniably important, it is also the most difficult, has the longest lead time, and is the most risky. We know quite a bit about how to manage research. But, as with other change opportunities, the important part is systematically to look out of the windows and ask, is this an opportunity for the company? And if so, what kind of an opportunity? Most changes for most companies are not. Changes in population structure are very important for some businesses and totally unimportant for others. For a steel mill, except in so far as it affects the labour supply, there is almost no interest in demographics. On the other hand, changes in environmental awareness are of tremendous importance to a steel mill.

Innovation Is Work above All

Everyone knows the second law of thermodynamics: all work degenerates into heat and friction. Drucker's first law is that everything degenerates into work, and if it does not degenerate into work, nothing gets done. A lot of it then becomes heat and friction, but first it has to be work. How we organize for work on innovation is a matter for the individual company. Very big and bureaucratic firms can be as innovative as small and nonbureaucratic ones. I am not actively proposing bureaucracy; the point is that it is a matter of systematic organization, clear strategy, and (again) hard work.

Du Pont, a notably bureaucratic company, has an enviable record as a successful and rapid innovator. 3M is not bureaucratic, but it is a very large company which has institutionalized innovation to the extent of incorporating it into the company's goals: at any period, no less than 25 percent of its turnover must come from products invented in the last five years. It always meets this target. And the goals are internalized. At 3M nobody gets into upper middle management who has not innovated, and everyone knows it. Forty years ago we were not so sure how to do these things. Now there is no excuse. The common pretext of waiting for the genius with the flash of inspiration will no longer wash. Any enterprise, no matter what its function, can today organize itself to undertake systematic entrepreneurship and purposeful innovation.

Personal Effectiveness

We now come to the fourth and final part of our survey. In the light of the changing world economy, the advent of the information-based organization and the need to systematize innovation and entrepreneurship, what skills and abilities will an executive need to practise (not just keep in mind) to be effective in the next years? The old skills are, of course, required, but there are some new ones which are likely to become increasingly important. I can think of three.

Skill 1: Management By Going Outside

All managers are now *In Search of Excellence.* In that book Tom Peters preaches that managers should walk around. Walking around within the company is still to be recommended, but I believe that the emphasis has changed. The important thing now is to be enough on the outside of the company to be able to stand back and draw the right conclusions.

When everything around the company – markets, technologies, distributive channels, and values – is in a ferment of change, to wait in the office until the reports arrive on an executive's desk may be too long. One paramount piece of advice to senior managers; the next time a salesman goes on vacation, go out and take his or her place. Ignore the returning salesman's complaint that the customers are up in arms about the incompetent who took his place. The point of the exercise is that it forces you outside into the marketplace, where results are. Remember that there are no results inside the firm. Up to the point where the customer reorders, there are only costs.

The external perspective might, for example, profitably prod companies to look at those who are not their customers but ought to be. A firm with a 22 percent market share is the market leader in most industries. Yet the more significant figure is that 78 percent of potential customers buy elsewhere. Why? That is usually the first indication of opportunities.

For some years I have worked with the joint management and labour committees of our two largest automobile companies, General Motors and Ford. I cannot persuade either unions or management that what they mean by the word *quality* is not what customers mean. Ford and GM are very proud of the fact that when their cars come off the line they are 'better' in quality terms than the Japanese. The trouble is that management and union people alike define quality as what is in the car when they deliver it.

But it is the customer who defines quality, not the manufacturer. For example, I have a summer house in the Colorado Rockies, a 1,200-mile drive from my home in California. When something goes wrong with my car, I expect the local dealer in the next small town to have the part and fix the car. Yet GM and Ford have a compensation structure that rewards dealers for sales of new cars, not for service, and certainly not for keeping spare parts, so I have to wait a week for a spare part to arrive from a warehouse. Toyota, on the other hand, rewards service, so the dealer has the part in inventory and can replace it at once. Why can I not persuade Ford and GM that I am right? Because when I tell them to go outside, they simply talk to their own dealers.

So the first imperative is to learn to be outside, where the results of the business take place. And the only way to be on the outside is to work, not to visit. Nothing is more wasteful than a visit to the Barcelona subsidiary. But work for two days, standing behind the counter, and it is surprising how much the manager will learn about that company.

Skill 2: Find out the Information You Need to Do Your Job

Second, people must learn to take responsibility for their own information needs. Information responsibility to others is increasingly understood. But everyone in the information-based organization needs constantly to be thinking through what information he or she needs to make a valuable contribution in his or her own job. This may well be the most radical break with the present conventions of work. Even in the most highly computerized companies, perhaps especially in these companies, very few people have the latest information. What they actually have is data, in such quantities that it causes information overload or blackout.

Information responsibility addresses another key problem. Most managers still believe that they need an information specialist to tell them what information they should have. But information specialists are providers of tools. They can tell us to use a hammer to bash an upholstery nail into a chair. But they cannot tell us whether we should be upholstering a chair in the first place. It is the manager's job to figure out what information he needs to identify:

1. what he is doing now;
2. what he should be doing; and
3. how he can get from (1) to (2).

This is by no means an easy task. But only if it is carried out will information begin to be the servant and the tool, and MIS departments results centres rather than the cost centres which they are now.

Until very recently there was no such thing as information. There were only experience and anecdotes. Now, for the first time, there are data. To convert those data into information means asking what you need, from whom, when, and in what form, and making sure that those who can provide the information also know and understand their responsibilities. A manager must ask, too, what information others require from him or her.

In the information-based organization of tomorrow, people will very largely have to control themselves. This does not mean we shall all be working in free-form organizations. That is nonsense. A land animal on this earth cannot be more than six inches high without having a skeleton. Companies are the same. Above a very small size, every company needs the skeleton of a formal command structure. But an animal does not perform work or feel through the skeleton. It has a nervous system and a musculature for that. In the same way, information systems enable a person to organize and integrate his or her own work. They are also what someone takes control of and responsibility for. At that point the apparently insurmountable task of operating in a form that requires an *ad hoc* team looms much less large. The cross-functional team is the key. No one begins with pure research, applied research, engineering, development, manufacturing, or marketing any more. It takes much too long and results in wonderful products that nobody buys.

Focus for Effectiveness

In the same vein, managers should spend a little time thinking through what their company should hold them accountable for by way of contribution and results over the next 18 months. 'What is the one thing that I, and only I, can do that if done well will make a difference?' A clear priority is essential. Do not diversify, do not splinter, do not try to do too many things at once. Without priorities, managers will be pulled in 5,000 directions at the same time. This applies particularly to top managers. Textbooks dwell, quite rightly, on the need to delegate down. What they fail to mention is that the real delegation is always up. In the end, the problem always comes to rest on the boss's desk. The buck stops there. That is his job, or course. But he above all needs to have time to do his own work; and he above all needs to know what his one, or two at most, contributions are to be.

As managers, we are not effective enough because we try to do too many things. The other great bane of organizations is that we believe that what we are trying to achieve is so obvious that we do not need to tell the person next door. Modern psychology began when Bishop Berkeley stated that because no two bodies can occupy the same space, nobody else could see what was obvious to one person. The people on whom you depend must understand what it is you are trying to accomplish, and you must communicate your priorities to them.

Skill 3: Build Learning into the System

The third element of effectiveness is building learning into the system.

One of the great puzzles of history has always been the sixteenth century. By 1560 Europe was dominated by two institutions which 25 years earlier did not even exist: the north by the Calvinist church and the south by the Jesuit order. Both came into being in 1535, and by the seventh decade of the century they had become dominant institutions. Most of their members worked by themselves, in considerable danger and under great pressure. What was their secret? With the benefit of modern learning theory, we can begin to see what happened. Calvin and Loyola applied the most important principle in learning: that of feedback. In any key activity area, the first step is to set down what you expect will happen. Nine months later, the actual results are examined and compared with original expectations.

As Loyola and Calvin discovered, feedback is the primary key to learning. Crucially, since no one is productive by putting weaknesses to work, feedback identifies the strengths. Learners need to know their strengths in order to find out where to improve. What bad habits inhibit those strengths? In what areas has the Good Lord simply not provided any ability at all? Most schools and most education are problem-focused; they concentrate on correcting weakness. Up to a point, that is necessary. Every student needs the basic skills. But real world-beating performance, like learning, is built on strengths. When it is so organized, learning is astonishingly rapid, for the simple reason that it has focus.

Learning, moreover, must be continuous. We have to recognize the unwelcome fact that the knowledge of those who are five years out of school is by definition obsolescent. The U.S. authorities now require physicians to take refresher courses and sit requalifying exams every five years. This causes initial grumbles from the examinees, which almost without exception give way to wonderment at how much has changed and how much they have forgotten. The same principle should apply for engineers, and even more so for marketing. It should therefore be part of every manager's practice to go back to school every so often for a week at a time. Many big companies are currently building their own in-house education facilities. I advise caution here. The greatest danger to the big company is the belief that there is a right way, a wrong way, and our way. In-house training tends to emphasize and strengthen that view. Skills, yes; teach them in-house. But for purposes of broadening the horizon, questioning established beliefs, and for organized abandonment, it is better to be confronted with diversity and challenge. For these, managers should be exposed to people who work for different companies and do things in different ways.

Those are some of the key things for an individual to know and do about making and keeping himself or herself effective as an executive in a challenging world. There are enormous opportunities, because change *is* opportunity. But there is no predictability. Turbulence – for those who still remember a little mathematics – is characterized by having no predictability. It is certain that the unexpected will happen; but it is impossible to predict where, when, or how. We live in a very turbulent time, not because there is so much change, but because it moves in so many different directions. In this situation, the effective executive has to be able to recognize and run with opportunity, to learn, and constantly to refresh the knowledge base.

[1990]

Index